WRITINGS
ON THE
WALL

WRITINGS ON THE WALL

SEARCHING FOR A NEW EQUALITY BEYOND BLACK AND WHITE

KAREEM ABDUL-JABBAR

AND RAYMOND OBSTFELD

Copyright © 2016 by Kareem Abdul-Jabbar

Published by Liberty Street, an imprint of Time Inc. Books
225 Liberty Street
New York, NY 10281

LIBERTY STREET and Time Books are trademarks of Time Inc.

ISBN 10: 1-61893-171-7
ISBN 13: 978-1-61893-171-9
Library of Congress Control Number: 2016936260

First edition, 2016

1 QGF 16

10 9 8 7 6 5 4 3 2 1

We welcome your comments and suggestions
about Time Inc. Books. Please write to us at:
Time Inc. Books
Attention: Book Editors
P.O. Box 62310, Tampa, FL 33662-2310

timeincbooks.com

To my mother and father and all of the teachers and
mentors who have come into my life.
—*Kareem Abdul-Jabbar*

———————

To my reason for everything: Loretta, Max and Harper.
—*Raymond Obstfeld*

Very superstitious, writings on the wall,
Very superstitious, ladders 'bout to fall . . .

When you believe in things that you don't understand,
Then you suffer—
Superstition ain't the way.

—STEVIE WONDER, "SUPERSTITION"

TABLE OF CONTENTS

Introduction
BRIDGING TROUBLED WATERS

"Is a danger to be trusting one another
One will seldom want to do what other wishes
But unless someday somebody trust somebody
There'll be nothing left on earth excepting fishes."
—"A PUZZLEMENT," *THE KING AND I*

I'VE BEEN ASKED MANY TIMES OVER THE YEARS WHAT PROFES-
sion I would have chosen had I not become a basketball player.
My answer surprises many people: I probably would have become
a history teacher. Not just so I could amaze kids with cool historical trivia, like the fact that when Thomas Jefferson was president,
he had the bones of a prehistoric mastodon shipped to the White
House so he could assemble the skeleton in the East Room. Or that
Ben Franklin not only invented the rocking chair but in 1752 helped
found one of the Colonies' first insurance companies: the Philadelphia
Contributionship for the Insuring of Houses from Loss by Fire. Or
that George Washington bred hound dogs, which he treated like
family, giving them adorable names like True Love and Sweet Lips.

Although I do appreciate History McNuggets like those, my real
passion for history is in using it as a critical guide to our future, both

personal and cultural. History illuminates the safest path in front of us by revealing the pitfalls of the past. It is a secular bible of cautionary and inspiring stories that distills the wisdom of thousands of years of human endeavor into practical lessons about humanity's morals, politics and personal relationships. It is the ultimate self-help book. And right now, given the political and social turmoil in America, we need all the help we can get.

However, in the hands of the greedy, the power-hungry and the unscrupulous, history is also a powerful tool of mass manipulation. It can be used to herd the unaware into self-destructive choices. History is open to interpretation, of course, but why do so many people fail to recognize the basic patterns, like the fact that oppression leads to revolutions or that war almost always has unintended consequences? Lots of reasons: the negligence of educators failing to teach properly, the malice of politicians anxious to force-feed corrupted versions of the past, the ignorance of individuals too lazy or fearful to seek the truth. Whatever the cause, the result is the same: enslavement without awareness of it.

The consequences of this manipulation can be devastating. For example, before America's decision to engage in a second war with Iraq, many opponents warned that although such a war could be easily won in the short run, the aftermath would take a heavy toll on America in terms of lost lives, staggering financial costs and bad blood throughout the Middle East that would radicalize many Muslims. These were the costly lessons that could have been learned from our experience in Vietnam. Stanton S. Coerr, a Marine officer and a veteran of the war in Iraq who holds degrees from Duke, Harvard and the Naval War College, wrote on the website The Federalist in 2015, "We are losing the war in Iraq for the same reason we lost the war in Vietnam: we are fighting one war, while the insurgents fight another." He explained, "The Americans want to leave. The insurgent is staying until he dies or wins. This makes him unstoppable." The question is: How can we make the same mistake only a few decades after the previous one?

I think it's because we prefer to ignore our past mistakes rather than learn from them. That's why so many Americans rejected the comparison between the Vietnam and Iraq invasions and embraced a romanticized revenge-movie mentality in which ass-kicking somehow equals victory. This was a case of pride, politics and ignorance getting the better of reason. It's ignoring history that allows leaders to persuade us to keep repeating such colossal mistakes that our future generations must pay for. One of my favorite movies, *The History Boys* (2006), is about a group of high school history students in the early 1980s in England. One of their teachers, Mr. Irwin, takes them to a World Wars I and II memorial, a cenotaph, which is an empty monument honoring people whose remains are buried elsewhere. He tells them a startling truth about how war memorials exist not to honor the dead but to make us forget we are responsible for their unnecessary deaths:

> "The truth was, in 1914, Germany doesn't want war. Yeah, there's an arms race, but it's Britain who's leading it. So why does no one admit this? That's why. *[Nodding to war memorial.]* The dead. The body count. We still don't like to admit the war was even partly our fault 'cause so many of our people died. And all the mourning's veiled the truth. It's not 'lest we forget,' it's 'lest we remember.' You see, that's what all this is about—the memorials, the cenotaph, the two minutes' silence. Because there is no better way of forgetting something than by commemorating it."

The teacher's point is that we often settle for a glorified falsehood in order not to face the harsh truths and then *have to do something about them*. It's just easier to go with the flow, even if the flow is a current of lies. The unwanted lesson here: most people choose to feel good rather than do good.

What makes some people feel good during times of economic struggle, terrorism and political discord is to be told that their problems can be attributed to particular groups who want to take their jobs, rip them off or attack them. And that the world can be made better and safer by keeping those other people down or keeping them out or keeping closer watch on them. The problem with that kind of thinking is that America was built of waves of those other people struggling for their place in society. Buying into falsehoods and simplistic assumptions about people not like ourselves creates fractures in our society and weakens us. We have too many continental divides today: left versus right, wealthy versus working-class, black versus white, men versus women, young versus old, religion versus religion. With this book, my purpose is to show how many of these conflicts are the result of fear and misunderstanding, often propagated by those looking for political or financial gain. If there is one lesson of history that we would be wise to remember today, it's what Abe Lincoln said about a house divided against itself.

Despite Abe's warning, we have never been more divided. One reason for this is the insidious ways history is manipulated to marginalize people based on race, creed, gender or other differences, binding them to false versions of themselves and discouraging them from seeing any other possibilities for their future. When I was growing up, my school textbooks were mostly devoid of African Americans in any positive role. They were portrayed as society's pathetic victims or happy-go-lucky simpletons, grateful for whatever scraps they were given, with a smile that said, "I got plenty of nuthin', and nuthin's plenty for me." The news media weren't much kinder. Civil rights leaders were often characterized as well-meaning but misguided because they didn't understand how to be patient and wait their turn. Or, if they were more aggressive in demanding equal rights, they were portrayed as subversives or thugs.

My experiences as a youth growing up in that atmosphere, in which there were few role models deemed acceptable by the general white population, made me examine history much more closely. I wondered why we keep making the same mistakes over and over when we have plenty of voices from the past screaming warnings. That was my main motivation for writing history books that celebrated the achievements and influence of African Americans: *On the Shoulders of Giants: My Journey Through the Harlem Renaissance*, which details the influence that black artists, writers, musicians and political leaders had in reshaping American culture; *Brothers in Arms: The Epic Story of the 761st Tank Battalion, WWII's Forgotten Heroes*, which is a history of an all-black armored unit that served with distinction in Europe; and *What Color Is My World? The Lost History of African-American Inventors*, which introduces to children the many African-American inventors responsible for the devices they use on a daily basis. This last book was especially rewarding for me because I traveled around the country visiting elementary and middle schools to promote STEM education (science, technology, engineering and math), often meeting various children of color who said, "I never thought someone like me could become a scientist, but now I think I can." It doesn't matter whether they actually do—just that they know it's an option.

WHY ME?

In preparation for an interview show I was scheduled to do in early 2016, the George Mason University professor Tyler Cowen asked his Internet followers to post some questions they would like him to ask me. One of the first responses was "Who cares what the old, big guy has to say about anything?" I wasn't offended. Believe me, I've asked that same question a lot more than the general public has. And some of them have asked it with significant anger, resentment and colorful expletives. After all, to many folks I'm only a former basketball player, someone whose business attire consisted of jockstraps and sweat socks. Successful, sure, but still just a pituitary freak who jammed an orange ball through a red hoop.

Despite the fact that I've been writing about social issues longer than I played basketball, many of my critics on social media begin their comments with "Stick to basketball, Kareem." However, aside from having played basketball a couple of decades ago, I am also an American, a father, a businessman, an education advocate, a journalist, a charity organizer, a history buff, a filmmaker, a novelist, a former global Cultural Ambassador for the U.S., a political activist and a Muslim. I began my lifetime of writing back in high school when I was given a chance to participate in a press conference with Martin Luther King Jr. and have since written hundreds of articles, several history books, autobiographies, children's books and novels.

Yet some people can't think past the stereotype of the dumb jock who is too busy stuffing kids into lockers to know anything about the world around him. Nor are they aware that by dismissing someone's opinions based only on his profession, they are also scorning pretty much everyone else's opinions, including their own ("Stick to plumbing!" "Stick to real estate!" "Stick to proctology!").

Very few people's vocation or avocation makes them an expert on all social or political matters. Ben Franklin was a printer; Theodore Roosevelt studied birds; Ronald Reagan acted with a chimpanzee. It was passion and commitment that persuaded them to step out onto the political stage and suffer the slings and arrows of outrage with the hope that by doing so, as the song from *Norma Rae* very purely wishes, "maybe what's good gets a little bit better and maybe what's bad gets gone."

In my best moments, I like to think I contribute to making the good get better and the bad get gone. In my moments of doubt, I feel more like the King of Siam in *The King and I*: "There are times I almost think / I am not sure of what I absolutely know / Very often find confusion / In conclusion, I concluded long ago." While those conflicting moments may seem contradictory, I believe it is the combination of those two elements—hope and self-doubt—that motivates me to also step onto that political stage. Hope, because as a father, as an American, as a black man and as a Muslim, I am committed to at least trying to add my "old, big guy" voice to the public discourse. Self-doubt, because the world is constantly changing, and so damn quickly, with new information bombarding us 24/7, that I realize that it's best not to cling too tightly to conclusions we concluded long ago. We have to be mentally agile in adapting our opinions based on this new information and not arrogantly defend opinions only because they are part of a tradition that makes us comfortable.

It may surprise some people, especially those who have disagreed with my columns for TIME and the *Washington Post*, that I don't start with a knee-jerk opinion about major issues. I've always been an avid reader, even as a young boy. Riding the New York City subway, I had a book in front of my face. During all the flights to away games when I played college and pro basketball, I could always be found in my seat reading a book, mostly about history. One thing all that history has taught me is the dangers of the uninformed, quickly formed and ill-informed opinion. Passionate defense of bad logic is the main cause of most of the world's misery. So when I find myself starting to lean toward an opinion on an issue about which I'm not well informed, I assume my opinion to be faulty, based on some internal bias. Before I write a column, I read as much as I can from credible authorities on both sides in order to gather facts and statistics that illuminate the topic for me. It's only then that I'm ready to work my way toward an opinion that I am confident to hold and comfortable to share.

Facts, statistics and the opinions of authorities aren't enough to form solid opinions, though. One also has to filter that information through the insights gained from reflecting on personal experiences. Although this book has a much broader focus than just race, my experience as an African American and as a sports celebrity has given me access to a broadly diverse array of Americans and their assumptions about me. Being conspicuously different has helped forge a unique perspective. Whether I wanted it or not, being both black and famous thrust me into the uncomfortable position of role model in which all African Americans would be judged by my behavior. This started for me in high school when a coach chided me during halftime not to be lazy on the court by saying, "You're acting just like a nigger!" At first I was hurt and angry, but I also realized the great burden of how my actions reflected on others.

Since those days of my youth, we've had many admirable black role models in every walk of life: President Barack Obama, Serena and

Venus Williams, Misty Copeland, Neil deGrasse Tyson, Colin Powell, Spike Lee, Denzel Washington, Toni Morrison, Oprah Winfrey and many more. It's a testament to African-American achievement that there are too many wonderful role models to list here.

But being a black role model is a double-edged sword of inspiration and frustration.

Yes, you are an inspiration to children of color, living proof that even though you face a lot of closed doors, that doesn't mean they're all locked. As a black kid from Hawaii, Barack Obama faced a double dose of closed and locked doors: no black person had ever been president, and no one from Hawaii had ever been president. As a black girl from California, Misty Copeland also encountered double doors: she started ballet at 13, whereas most ballerinas start practically in utero, and was rejected from a ballet academy for having the wrong body type. Yet somehow the ballerina and the president both rolled the Sisyphean rock of being black to the top of the mountain and it stayed right where they planted it.

The frustration for the black role model is knowing that although you are proof it can be done, like a happy lottery winner waving a million-dollar ticket, the odds are so astronomically against others that it sometimes feels as if you're more the source of false hope and crushed dreams, a casino shill they let win so the suckers will keep playing the slots. At every opportunity, rousing million-to-one success stories are trotted out in history textbooks and popular media to bedazzle the American dream.

Unfortunately, the dream has lost a lot of luster in recent years. Rather than shining like a bright beacon of hope to optimists everywhere, it flickers like a winking flashlight on the verge of a complete battery drain in a horror movie. Only 64 percent of Americans surveyed in a 2014 *New York Times* poll agreed that they still believed in the American dream, the lowest result in nearly 20 years. Loss of faith is even more pronounced among America's youth. A 2015 Harvard Institute of Politics poll found that among millennials (which it defined as ages 18 through 29), 48 percent considered the American dream to be "dead." As Bruce Springsteen said, "I have spent my life judging the distance between American reality and the American dream."

For Americans of color, bridging that distance may seem a bridge too far. Having successful ethnic role models is great because it affirms the country's commitment to the principle of equal opportunity. But at the same time, we see so many messages to the contrary: police killing unarmed African Americans, voter ID laws keeping poor minorities from voting, the federal government slashing programs that offer critical food and medical care, assaults on affirmative action, and an inferior education for poorer children that will keep them from competing in higher education and for better-paying jobs. Doors not just closed and locked but boarded, nailed and cemented.

So when we hold up the wildly successful role model, we're telling those who can't overcome the towering obstacles blocking their progress that they are to blame for their failure. They didn't try hard enough, weren't clever enough, just didn't have the fortitude. That's like blaming rape victims for not running fast enough.

Role models of color face a unique form of judgment. If you're black and you fail, many will assume you failed because you're black and that proves blacks aren't up to the task. But if you're black and you succeed, they will then claim that you succeeded because you're black and were somehow given an advantage. You are not allowed to succeed or fail on your own merits. Yet if George W. Bush is judged to be a bad president, no one says, "Well, we tried a white guy and it didn't work, so no more white presidents." Or Southerners. Or Texans. Or painters of dogs.

The irony is that despite facing closed doors for generations, it is people of color who have the most faith in the American dream. In a 2015 CNN/Kaiser Family Foundation poll, 55 percent of blacks and 52 percent of Hispanics said they believed it was easier for them to attain the American dream than it was for their parents. Only 35 percent of whites believed that. This brazenly optimistic attitude, in the face of systemic racism, is in large part due to pioneering role models like Misty Copeland and President Obama.

In Stephen King's novel *11/22/63*, a man time-travels to the past to prevent the assassination of President Kennedy. But his attempts to change history are met with supernatural resistance because, as a character tells him, the past doesn't want to be changed, so "the past pushes back." That's how it is in American culture. We fear change so much that we fight it, even when the change makes the country more in line with our founding principles. The past pushes back.

We just have to push back too. Only harder.

That's what this book is about: pushing back against those who wish to corrupt the American dream, to make it harder to achieve, to make it exclusive to only certain people. And as a person who has had his share of being pushed and pushing back, I felt ready to write about it.

WHY THIS BOOK?

For me, there would be no point in writing a book like this unless I had some hope that it might help improve life for Americans. I don't imagine anything grand, just that some contentious issues might be clarified, that some people might hear a reasonable voice that isn't from the same background as others they listen to. Maybe they will become a little more understanding. Mostly, I hope to expand the discussion about what America is and what it means to be an American. Not with waving flags and sentimental speeches but with a return to exploring the document that defines who we are and what we stand for: the U.S. Constitution.

Americans need to recognize and cherish the Constitution for what it is: one of the most revolutionary political documents in the world and the articulation of our values as Americans. It is an unparalleled ideal of democratic principles, personal freedoms, heritage and ethnic inclusivity that has been a model for other democracies and an irritant to despotic regimes around the world. We stand as a symbol of hope for people in all oppressed countries. All because we strive to live up to the spirit of the Constitution.

Too often people who are all puffed up on their own ideals of patriotism propose actions that are contrary to what the country stands for in an effort to codify their personal beliefs as law. These are America's greatest threat, because they undermine our political, ethical and moral foundation—all while proclaiming their love for the country.

The importance of the Constitution is powerfully asserted in the 2015 movie *Bridge of Spies*, based on a real-life American hero, James Donovan, who negotiated the release of a spy-plane pilot from the Soviet Union in 1962. When the CIA asks Donovan to do something unethical and illegal in the name of national security, he refuses.

> **Agent Hoffman:** Don't go Boy Scout on me. We don't have a rule book here.
> **James Donovan:** You're Agent Hoffman, yeah?
> **Agent Hoffman:** Yeah.
> **James Donovan:** German extraction?
> **Agent Hoffman:** Yeah, so?
> **James Donovan:** My name's Donovan, Irish, both sides, mother and father. I'm Irish, you're German, but what makes us both Americans? Just one thing. One, one. The rule book. We call it the Constitution and we agree to the rules, and that's what makes us Americans and it's all that makes us Americans. So don't tell me there's no rule book . . .

The rule book for being an American is our Constitution, just as the rule book for being a Jew is the Torah, for being a Christian is the New Testament, for being a Muslim is the Quran. The genius of the document is that it was written by men who acknowledged their own frailties and biases. Some owned slaves; they marginalized women; they protected some immigrants but not others. In the first presidential election, only white men with property were able to vote. But realizing that they were creatures of their times and that history can be a harsh judge of that narrow thinking, the Founding Fathers made provisions for changing the document as the country became more enlightened. They promoted the spirit of the Constitution, and we have amended it to reflect that spirit as it manifests itself in subsequent generations. Abolishing slavery. Recognizing women's rights. Equal justice for rich and poor. These are changes we made to reflect our understanding of that spirit. And we've all been the better for it.

WHAT I HOPE TO GAIN

America was founded on the principles emanating from the Age of Reason, also known as the Age of Enlightenment. Founders such as Ben Franklin, Thomas Jefferson and Thomas Paine were enthusiastic converts to the Age of Reason, rejecting the stranglehold of superstition and the tyranny of tradition in favor of making decisions based on reason and the scientific method. The Age of Reason championed liberty, tolerance, democratic governance and the separation of church and state. It was also responsible for the giant leaps forward of humanity in terms of economics, technology and medicine. Politically, it inspired the movement to disband the rigid class system in order to provide education and career opportunities outside the circumstances of one's birth; it also paved the way for women's rights and the abolition of slavery. Many of these radical ideals from the Age of Reason were deliberately included in the Declaration of Independence and the U.S. Constitution.

Many Americans, as evidenced by the 2016 presidential campaign, abandoned these founding principles of reason to voice their fear, anger, frustration and rage. They openly and proudly expressed their racial bigotry, religious intolerance and misogyny as if the past 100 years of our history of incremental social progress had never happened. Without even knowing it, they have dragged the American flag through the mud by rejecting all the principles it represents. As cartoonist Walt Kelly said in *Pogo*: "We have met the enemy and he is us."

With this book, I hope to shine a flashlight on the path back to the Age of Reason and the ideals of the U.S. Constitution.

My qualifications to write about social and political issues in

America come from experiencing life from many different points of view. My lifetime of being black in America has given me a rich perspective on the disparity between the promise and the practice of a blended America. My athletic success has given me firsthand experience with celebrities and politicians around the world to better understand the way ambition and corruption can sometimes feed off each other. My advocacy for STEM education has sent me to schools across the country to witness the needs of our educational system. And being the father of five children (and now a grandfather) has made me especially vigilant about contributing to making a better world for them.

I recall reading a letter from a politician from ancient Athens to his son. The letter was written more than two millennia ago, yet he offered the same advice about being kind and humble yet cautious that I might have given my own son. His expression of love, fear, pride and loss for his child leaving home mirrored my own. That letter really drove home the universality of our deepest concerns that bridge time and geography. Which is why what's most daunting about writing about social and political issues is the awareness that everything I have to say has undoubtedly already been said over the past 5,000 years of written language. And said better. Probably by Shakespeare.

I take comfort in what Paul Simon sings in "The Boy in the Bubble": "Every generation throws a hero up the pop charts." Which means that although the ideas themselves may be drifting endlessly through space like light from distant stars already gone, to each generation who sees that long-gone star, it's a new light. Each generation has to confront these challenging ideas and find ways to incorporate them into their personal belief systems as they go about their daily lives.

You've probably already noticed that I integrate a lot of popular-culture references in illustrating my ideas. That's because I am a fan of the many artistic ways that our society chooses to communicate its darkest fears and brightest hopes. Pop culture vitalizes the public discourse in myriad ways: through music, movies, TV shows, poetry, comic books, literary novels, plays, YouTube, graffiti and new forms of expression that come along every day. It provides the embraceable melody of our cultural song—it doesn't matter how profound the words of the song are if no one wants to listen. Whether Tarantino or Truffaut, all points of view and creative presentations have a place. Popular culture is a language that bridges generations, economic statuses and ethnic backgrounds. It provides a common heritage-in-the-making that brings our diverse community closer.

What do I hope to gain with this book? I hope we'll all huddle closer around the campfire, share our blankets, pass the hot dogs (veggie and gluten-free ones too), cherish what we have in common and figure out ways to make everyone's lives happier.

Will it work? Again, I put my faith in Paul Simon's song: "These are the days of miracle and wonder / This is a long-distance call." I hope people choose to answer the call and together we bring about the miracle and wonder.

1

American Politics
THE BROOM OF THE SYSTEM

"Come senators, congressmen
Please heed the call
Don't stand in the doorway
Don't block up the hall
For he that gets hurt
Will be he who has stalled
There's a battle outside
And it is ragin'. "
—BOB DYLAN, "THE TIMES THEY ARE A-CHANGIN' "

B OB DYLAN WROTE THOSE LYRICS IN 1963 AS AN ANTHEM
to the tumultuous social revolution that was erupting at the
time. As the social revolution of women's liberation, civil rights and
antiwar protests on the street evolved into a political revolution at
the ballot box, the song came to embody the anger and frustration
that the '60s generation had with the clock blockers who wanted to
push back time to some 1950s fantasy of small-town virtue. A time
when women, blacks and young adults were seen and not heard. A
time when *Father Knows Best* wasn't just a TV show but a social and
political mantra.

Although a lot has improved in the 53 years since, the anger and frustration with our government's resistance to change has only gotten worse. In 1964, when Dylan's song was released, 77 percent of Americans in a poll said they trusted the government "always or most of the time." In a 2015 poll by the Pew Research Center, only 19 percent of citizens surveyed felt that way, suggesting an alarming turn by more than half the population. A 2013 poll showed Congress with a 9 percent favorability rating—worse than how people in the survey rated cockroaches, hemorrhoids and traffic jams.

The American political system is our No. 1 propaganda export when we're trying to convince the rest of the world how great democracy is. Yet as these figures show, we're losing faith in our own ability to sustain this greatness. It's not that Americans have lost faith in the political system, it's that they have lost faith in the politicians who have corrupted it.

When I was in college at UCLA, I became a history major because I wanted to better understand the context of how people in any particular historical era justified the cruelties that everyone seemed to accept as conventional wisdom and normal behavior. Every culture in every country in every era participated in some form of socially acceptable madness, and I was fascinated with why that was true. To me, the key to improving the world was understanding how so many people could rationalize that it was OK to enslave people, to treat women as property, to beat children in the name of parental discipline, to exploit workers and their families and to use religion to justify acts contrary to the teachings of that religion. History was like a series of mass hypnosis events in which society was basically a large cult, accepting beliefs without question—and willing to alienate, imprison or execute any who disagreed.

It's easy to see how this might happen in a totalitarian system dominated by a secular or religious dictator. People are either coerced or brainwashed to obey, usually a combination of both. Information is choked off from the populace, as it is in China and North Korea, where Internet access is censored. Or the pressure to adhere to religious authority is so great that any questioning is harshly punished, as it is by the Taliban and ISIS. But in America, with freedom of speech and freedom of the press, information is available for all people. So how is it that American politics has fallen so far from grace in the people's eyes?

Anyone who doesn't think there's a battle outside raging should look at the 2016 presidential race. If any burning-bush revelation emerged, it's that many Americans wanted Washington, D.C., to know that, like the deranged newscaster Howard Beale in *Network*, they are mad as hell and they aren't going to take this anymore. They were rejecting the self-serving lies, numbing incompetence and partisan greed that have put a stranglehold on government progress. To express their outrage, some Republicans rallied around so-called outsiders with no political experience, no detailed policies and wacky ideas subversive to the very Constitution that they would be required to swear to uphold. Electing any of them would be like asking the balloon clown at a children's birthday party to start juggling chain saws.

But electing these symbolic naïfs was never the point. The real point was letting Washington know that a lot of people were out of patience with the status quo.

When I was a child, I remember adults complaining that voting often came down to selecting the lesser of two evils. I still hear that today. But while it feels cathartic to blame elected officials and demonize them for their many failings, the sad truth is that we voters are the real villains in this story. Our profound laziness and unyielding arrogance as voters have allowed our system to become polluted by hucksters, egomaniacs, dimwits and mack-daddy pimps willing to rent out their stable of votes. Worse, we often ignore the evidence of such corruption. Well, the bad news is that Americans are going to have to rethink their criteria for electing our leaders if we want to have a realistic hope of turning the system around.

David Foster Wallace is said to have titled his first novel *The Broom of the System* after a saying of his great-grandmother's that if someone was feeling sick, they should eat an apple because an apple was "the broom of the system," cleansing the insides. If we really want

American politics to improve, then American voters will have to start the process by becoming more educated about the facts, more critical in our thinking and more demanding of our elected officials. We are going to have to become the brooms of the system, cleansing politics from the inside out.

THE BABOONS OF BABEL:
HOW POLITICIANS UNDERMINE DEMOCRACY

Not all politicians are Frank Underwood wannabes. A precious few take the principle of public service seriously and work tirelessly to improve the country, while the majority of other, less dedicated politicians throw banana peels and nails at their bare feet.

Sound too harsh? Like warmed-over stick-it-to-the-Man/power-to-the-people/give-peace-a-chance rhetoric? Actually, it's not nearly harsh enough. According to a Princeton University and Northwestern University study in 2014 that examined 21 years of data, the top 10 percent of Americans in terms of wealth have influence over what Congress does, while the bottom 90 percent have *little or no influence whatsoever.* The study claimed that any proposal that a small majority of the people support has a 30 percent chance of becoming law—and that any proposal that an overwhelming majority of the people support has just a 43 percent chance of becoming law. Whether Americans support or condemn an issue has no real impact on legislation. The researchers concluded, "The preferences of the average American appear to have only a miniscule, near-zero, statistically non-significant impact on public policy." That's an emphatic middle finger to our democratic ideal of the will of the people.

The Princeton-Northwestern study also found that in the previous five-year period, the top 200 politically active companies in the U.S. spent $5.8 billion on lobbying and campaign contributions. As a result, those companies received $4.4 trillion in subsidies and taxpayer support, which is 750 times what they spent. Typically, members of Congress spend 30 to 70 percent of their time in office on fund-raising, and because only 0.05 percent of Americans donate more than $10,000 in any election, politicians are more likely to do what a few generous donors want.

Here's how that works specifically. In July 2015, the *Guardian* reported that, based on internal correspondence, ExxonMobil Co.'s own researchers had confirmed the existence of climate change more than three decades ago, yet the company spent millions of dollars over the next 30 years to convince the public otherwise. One of the country's leading environmentalists, Bill McKibben, referred to this as "unparalleled evil" that has set the world back decades in combating the problem.

It's not that politicians didn't know about climate change. A recent survey of studies published in peer-reviewed scientific journals found that 97 percent of actively publishing climate scientists agree that global warming has been caused by human activity. At least 18 scientific organizations have endorsed these findings. But many politicians in Congress refuse to believe these experts. Why? Because they are paid to. According to journalist Bill Moyers's website:

> All told, 170 elected representatives in the 114th Congress have taken over $63.8 million from the fossil fuel industry that's driving the carbon emissions which cause climate change . . . And their constituents are paying the price, with Americans across the nation suffering 500 climate-related national disaster declarations since 2011.

Republican senator James Inhofe of Oklahoma, chairman of the Senate's Committee on Environment and Public Works, is one of those who disagreed with 97 percent of the world's experts. He attempted to convince the most powerful legislative body in the world that there is no global warming by telling them, "It's very, very cold out." Then he threw a snowball to the Senate president. Another energy-belt Republican, Lamar Smith of Texas, is investigating the National Oceanic and Atmospheric Administration scientists who wrote a study refuting a supposed global-warming slowdown that deniers had been touting, claiming the scientists rushed their conclusions, although lawmakers have offered no evidence to confirm that.

Americans don't want to believe that climate change is upon us and might result in environmental catastrophes like the recent severe drought in California. Politicians who deny global warming are often the same ones who exaggerate the threat of foreign terrorism in this country. The reason is that they are protecting big-money donors with one, while gaining votes by exploiting fear with the other. Global warming would require the average person to make personal concessions in terms of energy consumption and taxes; foreign terrorists require no daily inconvenience, just growing the military bigger for additional resources to fight them.

The worst-case scenario is that these politicians are deliberately manipulating the truth in order to mislead the voters to protect their wealthy political donors, which makes them corrupt. The best-case scenario is that they are too dumb to understand how to gather accurate information, which makes them unworthy to hold office. Either way, they're a danger to democracy because the process of getting truthful information to the people, which is key to making informed choices, is debased. It's like cooking from a recipe with ingredients deliberately left out.

What politicians don't acknowledge is that Americans are more afraid of politicians than they are of terrorists. In a 2015 Chapman University Survey of American Fears, "corruption of government officials" ranked highest at 58 percent, compared with fourth-place "terrorist attacks" at 44 percent. And we are right to be afraid. A 2015 State Integrity Investigation of state governments by the non-profit investigative reporting group the Center for Public Integrity concluded that only three states scored higher than a D+, with 11 states receiving an F. The highest grade went to Alaska, which received a C. These are the people in whose hands we put our future and the future of our children. Surely we're not willing to let this self-destruction of our country continue.

While most Americans will nod in agreement with the above assessment of politicians, few are willing to do what it takes to break the cycle. We get mad and vote out candidates, replacing them with the same lame product simply because they claimed to be new and improved. This is followed by bitter disappointment, more anger and the election of yet another ineffective clone. We're like the person who's had a long string of bad romantic relationships who complains that there are no "good ones" out there. Maybe it's time to look at the kind of person we choose to date in the first place. Every time we cast a vote for politicians who choose commerce over conscience or who use faux patriotism and whip up public fear, we are destroying who we are and what we stand for.

What makes democracy such a chaotic system is that its desire to be humane, inclusive and fair means there will be constant disagreements about what those terms mean and how to achieve them. In totalitarian governments, there is no conflict about these issues because people are told what to believe and are punished if they disagree. In 2015, Americans had a spirited dialogue about many such issues, including gay-marriage laws, racial discrimination by police officers and attempts to pass "religious freedom" laws that would allow some people to discriminate against others. But the issue that most exemplified political cynicism was that of the Syrian refugees, over which Washington politicians essentially declared war on American values. The assault included a mix of racism, immigration alarm, attacks on religious freedom and fearmongering over terrorism. Washington legislators lied, pandered and exploited America's anxieties as well as the needs of the desperate refugees. The saddest aspect: politicians did this not to protect America, but solely and cynically to get votes. To get these votes, they would have to lie to the public and debase the U.S. Constitution.

Some 1 million refugees from Syria had been flooding Europe because of the violent atrocities committed by Syrian forces and ISIS, as well as bombing by Russia and the U.S. On Nov. 13, 2015, the ISIS-led bombings and shootings in Paris that killed 130 created an ideological battle in the U.S. Many American politicians called for a halt to allowing Syrian refugees into the U.S. or for enforcing more stringent vetting. Some critics of this response reminded Americans of the shame of our past reactions to immigrants during Hitler's rule, when in 1939 the U.S. turned away a ship carrying more than 900 German Jews. Those who didn't find refuge in Great Britain were returned to countries later controlled by Nazis; 254 of the passengers died in the Holocaust because we didn't take them. At the same time, the U.S. rejected a proposal that would have permitted 20,000 Jewish children to come to the U.S. to avoid the death camps.

Instead of saving refugees at that time, we locked up 120,000 people of Japanese ancestry (many of them native-born U.S. citizens) for no good strategic reason, even while some of their sons were fighting in our armed forces. In 1980, a federal commission was appointed to investigate the internment. They concluded that there was little evidence that the Japanese Americans were disloyal or a threat and that the incarceration was due mainly to war hysteria and racism. Some historians believe that the principal reason the Japanese Americans were targeted, since most were on the West Coast, was so white farmers could take over their fertile farmlands, worth an estimated $72 million, which they never got back. In 1988, President Ronald Reagan signed the Civil Liberties Act, which not only apologized for the imprisonment but paid reparations of $20,000 per person.

Because of our past mistakes, today we entrust politicians to have a much better awareness of history and racism. Yet in response to the Syrian refugee crisis, the Democratic mayor of Roanoke, Va., David Bowers, announced that his city would not welcome Syrian refugees: "I'm reminded that President Franklin D. Roosevelt felt compelled to sequester Japanese foreign nationals after the bombing of Pearl Harbor, and it appears that the threat of harm to America from ISIS now is just as real and serious as that from our enemies then." If that's true, then they are absolutely no threat at all, as was confirmed by President Reagan when he said, "Yet we must recognize that the internment of Japanese Americans was just that: a mistake."

Still, the hit parade of mistakes by politicians continued. More than half of the governors in America requested that the U.S. stop accepting Syrian refugees, with most of the governors saying they wouldn't accept the refugees in their states. Since they didn't have the legal grounds to stop the immigrants, the whole show was just posturing for political gain. While President Obama announced the U.S. would be taking in 10,000 Syrian refugees over the next year, Canada announced it would be accepting more than 20,000 over *six weeks*, and France—the victim of a deadly terrorist attack—said it would be admitting 30,000. (To put these numbers in perspective, there are about 4.8 million U.N.-registered Syrian refugees.) Six months after Obama's announcement, the U.S. had admitted only 1,300 Syrian refugees.

The U.S. reacted to the other countries' humanitarianism by the House passing a bill to limit Syrian refugees until certain national-security agencies certify that they don't pose a threat. Seems reasonable on the surface, until one considers that the U.S. already has the toughest standards in the world for admitting such refugees. Security clearance, performed by several agencies including the FBI and Homeland Security, takes two years. The vetting is already so stringent that there are cases reported of Syrian refugees being denied admittance because they served food to a jihadist in their sandwich shop. Most of the legislators who passed the House bill refuse to pass one that would prevent people on the terrorism watch list from buying guns or explosives, which they are legally able to do now, because the legislators fear offending the powerful gun lobby. Yet which bill would actually keep us safer?

Nothing quite revealed the willingness of politicians to abandon the basic principles of the Constitution more than the suggestion by presidential candidates Jeb Bush and Senator Ted Cruz to focus only on Syrian refugees who are Christian. When Bush was asked by a reporter how the refugees would prove they were Christians, he shrugged and said vaguely, "I mean, you can prove you're a Christian." Candidate Donald Trump said he wouldn't rule out establishing a database that lists all people of Muslim faith in the U.S. Those with a rudimentary knowledge of history recalled Hitler doing something similar with the Jews before forcing them into concentration camps.

More to the point, the politicians calling for all this proactive activity should know very well that these measures are illegal, unconstitutional and impotent in defending us. Terrorists can come in very easily as students or tourists. The so-called mastermind of the French assault was Belgian. Worse, by refusing to take in the refugees, most of whom are women and children, we are confirming to the world that we put fear over conscience. In doing so, we become the bigoted monsters that ISIS and other terrorist organizations depict us as, helping them recruit more soldiers and suicide bombers.

TOO BIGOTED TO FAIL:
HOW THE PEOPLE UNDERMINE DEMOCRACY

We Americans are fond of saying, "It's a free country. I'm entitled to my opinion." But it's destructive arrogance to not want that opinion to be an informed one. Rather than do the reading and listening required to hone rational opinions, we take the easier path of just joining with other people who have the same opinion, and thereby our beliefs are never challenged. This perpetuates a fundamental flaw in the way many people see government: as a parent. Words like "fatherland," "motherland," even references to the Founding Fathers make us see ourselves as children of the country. As a result, we act like children when it comes to politics. We want government leaders to take care of us, but we still want to complain that they're the boss of us. We want to spite them by dating motorcycle-riding "outsider" candidates who have crazy ideas that our fussy Constitution wouldn't approve of.

But we aren't the children of America; we are the parents. We are raising this country to have the values laid out in the Constitution. We have to shoulder the responsibilities that come with raising children by setting the proper example of people who live by their expressed principles, even when times are tough and it's tempting to abandon them. We start this process by being more demanding of those we elect and by holding them responsible for every lie, misdirection and corruption. Sure, it's more work. But that's what's needed: eternal vigilance.

Vigilance means treating every bit of information fed to us, regardless of the source—respected news outlets, politicians, family, friends—with skepticism. Not just hipster-cynical skepticism or government-conspiracy skepticism, but the skepticism born of enough experience to take the advice of a Russian proverb that President Reagan often quoted: "Trust, but verify." The *verify* part is where we actually take action: look for sources, understand the arguments and explore dissenting opinions.

In 2015, presidential candidate Trump retweeted a list of so-called statistics from the "Crime Statistics Bureau—San Francisco" claiming that 81 percent of murdered white people are killed by blacks. In fact, the opposite is true: 82 percent of murdered white people are killed by whites. The source, which sounds official on the surface, was really just a white supremacist active on Twitter. Even when confronted with the facts, Trump refused to acknowledge culpability, saying, "Am I gonna check every statistic?" Well, yes, when you're running for political office, when you have the money to hire researchers and when the misinformation is racist and inflammatory. The real issue here is that many of the people who read the tweet will never read the news reports that discredit the information. Repeat this kind of episode dozens of times, and a fog of fiction descends. Then when voters reach opinions about how to cast their ballots, they will be doing so based on lies, which continues the cycle of electing bad politicians.

Americans take pride in the popular saying that democracy is the worst form of government—except all those other forms. While we may agree that it is better than others, that doesn't mean we can't improve it. We need to strive to live up to our Constitution's potential, not just get by saying, "Hey, at least we're not North Korea."

The most fitting symbol of how much contempt politicians have for voters is the typical campaign sign, stuck in grass medians along busy streets like crosses mourning a fatal accident. The signs usually announce only a last name and the office being sought, such as "McConnell for Senate." They are often red, white and blue to affirm that the candidate is a staunch patriot, but they are otherwise barren of relevant information. No policy ("Git Outta Gitmo!"), no political philosophy ("Working Hard for the Working Class!"), no social stance ("Sexism Isn't Sexy!"). Instead, they ask us to select our leaders based on how often we see or hear their names, as if name exposure alone somehow subconsciously translates into "I've heard good things about this person."

Sadly, there's a poll to back up this political strategy of "If less is more, than nothing is the most." In a 2015 *Des Moines Register/ Bloomberg Politics* poll of Iowa voters, 57 percent of Republicans admitted that they don't care about a candidate's specific policies and would simply trust the candidate to figure out what to do once elected. If that poll is reflective of the U.S. in general, then a significant number of voters have chosen to abandon trying to understand the complexities of important issues in favor of high-wattage charisma. This cult of personality occurs when people discard the responsibility of self-governing in order to bet their future on an idealized savior ("Help us, Obi-Wan Candidate. You're our only hope!"). This surrogate parent is expected to lead them to the promised land, though it is most often the land of broken promises.

In *The Matrix*, when Morpheus tells Neo, "You are the One, Neo," he is expressing this same mythical archetype: the lone redeemer who has the responsibility of saving humanity from destruction. From *Shane* to *Harry Potter* to *The Hunger Games*, one person—wielding a gun, a wand or a bow—defeats the corrupt overlords to free the people. Too many Americans interpret this to mean we should wait around for the savior to arise and lead us rather than be inspired by such stories to do the leading ourselves. This damsel-in-distress mentality allows us to place the blame on the heroes when they fail rather than on ourselves for lacking due diligence in vetting our saviors.

In the 2016 presidential election, many Republicans looked to be saved by the outraged outsider: candidates such as Donald Trump, Ben Carson and Carly Fiorina, who claimed purity because they hadn't been tainted by exposure to other politicians. "The bottom line is that you turn to outsiders when you lose faith in the insiders," says Samuel Popkin, a political-science professor at the University of California, San Diego. Films like *Mr. Smith Goes to Washington*, *Billy Jack Goes to Washington* and *Dave* perpetuate the folklore that an average Joe or Josephine could take off their stained uniform or put aside their inky pocket protector and, through the magical power of their innate decency, humility and common sense, put America back on track to greatness. Such fantasies are terrific at inspiring us to do better but are otherwise convincing only if the viewer knows nothing about the Constitution and the actual political process. Like the people in the biblical land of Shinar building the great Tower of Babel, when it comes to the specifics of what we want changed or how to make those changes, Americans don't all speak the same language.

We have to begin fixing the system by rejecting the notion that our political candidates are saviors. It's not the fault of typical politicians that the more they make insulting, vague and factually incorrect claims, the higher they poll. The fault is in our starry-eyed worship of style over substance, of entertaining personality over enlightened policy. They are, to quote Brenda Shaughnessy's poem "I'm Over the Moon," like "having a bad boyfriend in a good band."

America is not a pure democracy. Each citizen does not vote on every issue. We have a republic, which means that we elect officials to make those decisions for us. The issues that face America, both domestically and internationally, are often so complex that no single person can be expected to be an expert on everything. Instead, our politicians should display the ability to be strong critical thinkers, which means they gather all relevant information from reliable nonpartisan sources, weigh the pros and cons, and then make an informed decision free of personal bias, the pressures of lobbyists or even their own uninformed constituents. We need people who don't want to just lead in polls but lead in integrity as well. As leaders, they should be willing to do the right thing, even if it goes against what might be momentarily popular to those who don't have all the facts or who can't see past their own prejudice.

Unfortunately, many American voters prefer to elect opportunists who don't care about or understand the issues, who only repeat whatever will get the most campaign contributions and the most votes in order to hold on to their jobs. The truth is that by not demanding substance and truth, we are allowing ourselves to become enslaved by politicians who give us glossy patriotic zealotry and person-of-the-people rhetoric. We are abused spouses expecting behavior to change because they smile and promise it will. When you don't recognize you're enslaved, you perpetuate the idea that you deserve to be enslaved. And there are plenty of politicians lining up to take advantage of that.

NOTHING UP MY SLEEVE: THE SLEIGHT OF HAND IN ATTACKING POLITICAL CORRECTNESS

According to many politicians, America has a life-threatening illness that is more deadly than the Zika and Ebola viruses combined. Its name: political correctness. Since the early 1990s, "politically correct" has been the go-to phrase to whip up support from people who think social tolerance has become threatening, excessive or frivolous. The 2016 presidential election was especially virulent about the issue.

"Political correctness is killing our country," Donald Trump tweeted. Ben Carson, when he was briefly the leading Republican candidate, told Fox's Bill O'Reilly that political correctness was "destroying our nation." Ted Cruz criticized President Obama's policies toward ISIS by claiming that "political correctness is killing people." Carly Fiorina said, "Political correctness is now choking candid conversation." Marco Rubio complained that the reason he didn't discuss his faith in public was that "I had been conditioned by political correctness." Jeb Bush joined the hallelujah choir with "The political correctness of our country needs to be shattered."

A majority of Americans agreed with them. In a 2015 Rasmussen

Reports poll, 71 percent of Americans said political correctness is a problem in our country. Those worried that we've gone too far in our pursuit of political correctness fall pretty solidly along party lines: twice as many Republicans as Democrats think it's a problem. Only 18 percent think we aren't politically correct enough.

This apocalyptic backlash against what seems like a relatively benign combination of good old-fashioned manners and simple sensitivity toward others stems from several factors, including a growing rage, fear and frustration among many Americans as the country continues to evolve into something different from what they are used to. Just as it did for their parents and grandparents. New technology can make us feel foolish, rapidly changing trends make us feel marginalized, and the eroding of our familiar and comforting traditions leaves us uncertain and uncomfortable. Every generation must deal with mourning the loss of its good ol' days. It's hard for many Americans to reconcile their romanticized fantasy of Main Street, USA, with today's reality. The truth is that only 46 percent of children 18 and under live in a home with two heterosexual parents who are in their first marriage. In 1960, 73 percent did. That Mayberry world isn't coming back again, but many Americans are feverishly piling sandbags to keep the tide from washing in.

Right now, this understandable but misplaced angst is directed at incidences of political correctness that seem to go to new extremes to avoid insulting, offending or marginalizing anyone. We all get that. It seems as if every day there's another report of some public officials overreacting to a perceived insensitivity. A survey at Yale University had 63 percent of students wanting professors to issue "trigger warnings" before saying anything that someone might find offensive or cause painful emotions. Many critics have described this new avoidance of microaggression as coddling students, who should expect their opinions to be challenged in college to better prepare them for the real world outside. That "coddled" assessment seemed confirmed when 25 students at UCLA staged a sit-in because a professor corrected the spelling and grammar errors on graduate-level essays. They accused him of creating a "hostile campus climate" for students of color. Students at the University of New Hampshire were issued a list of resources to help them avoid offensive language such as *American* (because it suggests the U.S. is the only country in the Americas), *homosexual* (PC version: "same-gender-loving"), *elderly* ("people of advanced age") and *healthy* ("nondisabled"). Comedians Jerry Seinfeld and Chris Rock have said that the climate of political correctness is so restrictive that they have stopped performing on college campuses. Comedian Bill Maher has complained of "political-correctness Nazis" who "hound me to censor every joke and apologize for every single slight."

For many Americans, the abuses of political correctness extend to beloved social traditions. Saying "Happy holidays" instead of "Merry Christmas" seems to some a sinister attempt to restrict religious expression rather than a way to include non-Christians in the holiday spirit. A school in Connecticut attempted to ban Halloween costumes out of concern that some children might feel "excluded from activities due to religion, cultural beliefs, etc." Angry parents quickly forced a reversal of that policy.

Here's the problem with using these examples to attack the validity of political correctness: every political and social policy or tradition has examples of excess. We don't define the value of a policy based on incidences that might seem extreme. We can point at absurd behavior of zealots around all our most cherished values. We poke fun at "helicopter" parents being fiercely overprotective of their children, but that doesn't mean we want to erase safety laws and policies that protect our children.

We can look rationally at the original problem that political correctness was supposed to address and ask if it's had a significant effect on making things better. The success rate of political correctness is difficult to judge because there are so many other factors that can influence an outcome, including not knowing how many generations have to commit to political correctness in order to scrub out the centuries-old biases of America's collective unconscious. For now, it's a declaration to the world, not unlike our Declaration of Independence, that America stands for certain inalienable rights.

There is some evidence that it works. Research at Cornell University concluded that political correctness may aid the creativity of mixed-gender work teams. "[Political correctness] facilitates idea expression by reducing the uncertainty that people tend to experience while interacting with the opposite sex," said Jack Goncalo, an associate professor of organizational behavior. "[E]stablishing a clear guideline for how to behave appropriately in mixed-sex groups made both men and women more comfortable sharing their creative ideas." Even on a purely anecdotal level, we can look around and see younger generations growing up to be more aware of instances of discrimination based on gender, race, religion or gender identity and not accepting it as the status quo. Armed with this awareness, they are less likely to accept bullying or exploitation simply because it's endorsed by a code of permission in our society. They will be more self-reliant, stronger and more tolerant of others. Better Americans.

Yet opponents are using extreme examples to do exactly what we were doing before political correctness pointed out the racism, misogyny and homophobia embedded in the cultural foundation of America. Which is to do nothing. Deriding political correctness gives people permission not to fix a problem, because we can claim instead that it doesn't exist. The real problem, they want to tell us, is the cure. As do vaccination deniers and climate-change skeptics. Or all those hard-core smokers back in the 1960s and 1970s who laughed at the warning labels about the damage cigarette smoking could do. They accused the government of being too much of a scolding parent. Rallying that ol' "we'll show you government intruders who's boss" spirit, smokers boosted cigarette sales by more than 7.8 billion in 1966, the year the labels first appeared on cigarette packs. To prove the government's point, about half of all those who smoke regularly will die prematurely. This doesn't include the damage to nonsmokers who are harmed by secondhand smoke or by their mothers smoking while pregnant. Arrogantly clutching onto wrongheaded traditions is damaging to the country.

At a February 2016 rally, Donald Trump repeated with mock shock what a woman in the audience had just shouted about Ted Cruz: "She said—I never expect to hear that from you again! She said: 'He's a pussy.' That's terrible." Of course, the audience shouted their approval, even as Trump pretended to be offended.

Sure, we could all laugh at his frat-boy humor and call him a straight-talking regular Joe. But there are serious consequences to insulting someone by calling him or her a vagina. (Don't bother pretending the reference was to a cat.) It furthers the association of women with weakness. Every time we laugh at this context, we're endorsing the continuing narrative of women as less than men. Every time a male coach berates his players by referring to them as "ladies" or tells them to "hike their skirts" while playing, we're perpetuating an atmosphere that women are not men's equals.

The anti-PC rhetoric is a clever tool by politicians who wish to distract voters from the real issues by tapping into their darkest fears about people who are different from them and, at the same time, allowing the politicians not to have to fix the problem. It's the magician's trick of misdirecting the audience's attention to the left hand while the right hand does the work. It's genius—as long as voters are zombified to the point of not thinking for themselves.

Which is exactly what politicians want. They want you to feel and behave like children while they pretend to be the all-knowing benevolent father. While they rile you up about how immigrants are stealing your jobs, they distract you from enlightening facts, including the assessment of some experts that the influx of Latino immigrant workers of the past 25 years has had less effect on employment patterns than factories that moved abroad, the decline of labor unions and the recurring recessions. So while we're told to focus on building a massive wall to keep out immigrants, the real causes of job loss and economic instability continue unabated.

We're better off taking back the reins of our future by following the suggestion of 1 Corinthians 13:11: "When I was a child, I talked like a child, I thought like a child, I reasoned like a child. When I became a man, I put the ways of childhood behind me."

Of course, to be PC, it should read, "When I became an adult."

"WHAT ELSE YA GOT?": HOW AMERICANS CAN RECLAIM THE POLITICAL PROCESS

The mistake we've been making is trying to fix the situation by hoping the next candidate will be the one who's true and good and righteous. Though a few are, most aren't, because the voters who elect them can't see past their own biases to elect the best leaders. These biases are amplified by the echo-chamber effect, in which people perpetuate their beliefs by exposing themselves only to media sources that already agree with them. Conservatives tune in to Fox News—for more about its problems with accuracy, see the chapter on media—and liberals visit MSNBC. This closed system often includes social interaction (hanging out with people who agree with you) and social media (following only those who agree with you). Because of this limited view of the world, these people often think that their beliefs are much more universally agreed upon than they really are. Which means they will rarely change their minds. They are like the ouroboros, the ancient symbol of the snake eating its own tail, an endless loop of self-destruction and rebirth.

Never before in history has it been easier to manipulate voters, because never before have we been so hardwired with intractable political bias. In a poll in 1960, 5 percent of Republicans and 4 percent of Democrats admitted that they would be upset if their child married someone who was of the opposite political party. In a similar poll in 2010, almost 50 percent of Republicans and about 30 percent of Democrats said they would be upset. The latter study shows that the level of political bigotry today surpasses racial bigotry. The study suggests that the level of bias is so strong that it influences every aspect of private life, from where we live to whom we choose as friends. Worst of all, we refuse to fairly consider any other viewpoints beyond those we already agree with, and we instantly reject any evidence that contradicts our opinions. That makes us incapable of reaching rational decisions about the most important aspects of our lives.

In the 2009 *Star Trek* movie, a black hole is swallowing the U.S.S. *Enterprise*. As the ship starts to crack apart, Captain Kirk asks chief engineer Scotty to use more power to pull the ship free. "I'm giving her all she's got, captain!" Scotty replies helplessly. To which Kirk replies, "All she's got isn't good enough! What else ya got?" That's pretty much the state of American politics right now. We're being pulled apart, and all we've got isn't good enough. So we have to figure out what else we've got.

Three steps that we haven't tried that will boost our political engines are: (1) Institute a federal education program that emphasizes critical thinking and logical fallacies in every grade of public school. (2) Make voting easily available to every citizen, but stop diluting the power of informed voters by encouraging people to vote who don't want to. (3) Broadcast a nonpartisan fact-check and logical analysis as often as possible when a politician speaks publicly.

1. Teach the children well.

In 1964, during the free-speech movement at the University of California, Berkeley, a young activist named Jack Weinberg coined the phrase "Don't trust anyone over 30." He's in his 70s now and has probably rethought that pronouncement. However, the theory behind it might be pretty sound after all. As we get older, we become more and more set in our ways and beliefs until suddenly we're yelling at kids, "Get off my lawn—I'm keeping your damn football." Or, as psychologist William James wrote in 1890, "In most of us, by the age of thirty, the character has set like plaster, and will never soften again." Since then, a lot of research has confirmed his assessment.

Embracing reason is an uphill battle for humans. Almost 400 years ago, philosopher Francis Bacon said, "The human understanding when it has once adopted an opinion . . . draws all things else to support and agree with it. And though there be a greater number and weight of instances to be found on the other side, yet these it either neglects and despises, or else by some distinction sets aside and rejects . . ." Recent studies explain why nothing much has changed since that diagnosis. During the 2004 presidential campaign, Emory University psychology professor Drew Westen and his colleagues did brain scans on 15 George W. Bush supporters and 15 John Kerry supporters. What they discovered was that when the subjects rejected evidence contrary to their belief, their brains lit up like addicts getting a fix. Westen said, "Essentially, it appears as if partisans twirl the cognitive kaleidoscope until they get the conclusions they want, and then they get massively reinforced for it." It's both stimulating and addicting to reject, without examining, any information contrary to our beliefs.

We seem to be built to discard such evidence. We have the Internet, the single most powerful information source and educational tool ever invented, but many of us use it only to confirm conclusions we've already reached. We go to sites that agree with our position in order to arm ourselves with snippets that we can use as ammunition to snipe at those who disagree with us.

The bad news is that in terms of fixing our political process, it's too late for most adults to be part of the solution. Not because they are incapable of changing, but because we have failed to teach them as children how to be critical thinkers. At best, we send them mixed messages: be critical thinkers on the job, but be emotional in personal behavior. We teach children to use the scientific method of gathering facts before reaching a conclusion, but we also encourage them to "go with your gut." The author Nick Hornby summarizes this problem nicely in his novel *High Fidelity*: "I've been thinking with my guts since I was fourteen years old, and frankly speaking, between you and me, I have come to the conclusion that my guts have shit for brains."

The reasons for these conflicting messages are clear: we want to raise children who are smart, innovative and good at their jobs so they can be successful, but we also want to raise children who will embrace our moral values and political beliefs without challenging them. On one hand, we teach them to challenge a hypothesis; on the other, we tell them to blindly accept a hypothesis. Most choose to do both in order to avoid conflict within the family and to fit in better with others in the community. This can include joining their parents' religion and political party as well as following their beliefs on social issues. This is how we have raised people who are geniuses at solving scientific problems or making fortunes in business but who are completely clueless when it comes to looking at social and political issues. Success in one area does not grant insights into all areas.

However, just because a son or daughter has the same beliefs as a parent, that doesn't make those beliefs wrong. What's wrong is adopting them without submitting them to the same rigorous thinking we'd use in buying a computer or selecting a cellphone carrier. If we are ever going to be able to break out of the echo chamber and fix our political system, children will have to learn the methods of critical thinking from elementary school and practice it throughout their education in every class possible. They must be taught to question every premise, no matter who offers it. This teaches students not just the individual subject matter but also how to continue to learn once they are out of school, rather than harden their mind like plaster.

Renowned Harvard University psychologist Steven Pinker describes the best educational focus for raising children who can be successful in their careers as well as be informed and responsible citizens:

> [A] liberal education should make certain habits of rationality second nature. Educated people should be able to express complex ideas in clear writing and speech. They should appreciate that objective knowledge is a precious commodity, and know how to distinguish vetted fact from superstition, rumor, and unexamined conventional wisdom. They should know how to reason logically and statistically, avoiding the fallacies and biases to which the untutored human mind is vulnerable. They should think causally rather than magically, and know what it takes

to distinguish causation from correlation and coincidence. They should be acutely aware of human fallibility, most notably their own, and appreciate that people who disagree with them are not stupid or evil. Accordingly, they should appreciate the value of trying to change minds by persuasion rather than intimidation or demagoguery . . .[T]he more deeply a society cultivates this knowledge and mindset, the more it will flourish.

This is not an issue of Mr. Spock's cold logic versus Dr. McCoy's gooey sentiment. Logical thinking does not preclude reaching the same conclusions one would make by pure emotional reaction. We aren't all suddenly going to stand around like the pod people in *Invasion of the Body Snatchers*, indifferent to human suffering. Instead, we will use our intelligence to solve the problems that cause human suffering without the impediments of all those who "block up the halls."

Emotion is our initial reaction to an event; logic is how we choose an action to take to address the event. If someone insults us in front of a crowd, do we punch the person or just walk away? (Trump's rallies in 2016 were kind of a laboratory of this phenomenon.) We are torn because most of our movie heroes throw the punch. But logic tells us the punch is a foolish reaction that demeans us because it reveals just how easily manipulated we are.

This is the kind of emotion-over-logic thinking that met Ben Franklin's invention of the lightning rod. Church elders referred to it as a "heretical rod" that would bring down the wrath of God for trying to "control the artillery of heaven." The more common church practices of warding off lightning strikes, which burned hundreds of buildings and as many people, were attaching an angel figure at the summit, using bells consecrated to repel devils and witches in the air (in fact, the metal bells rung to ward off lightning actually attracted it), having holy relics within the church or even conducting exorcisms. Although Saint Mark's Basilica in Venice did all these things, it was frequently struck by lightning. Since it attached a lightning rod in 1766, it has never been struck by lightning.

One can understand the resistance to a curriculum that emphasizes critical thinking. Parents don't want to have their personal beliefs challenged by their children. No one wants to ask their kids, "What did you learn in school today?" only to hear "Everything you believe is wrong." Yet our goal should be to raise independent thinkers, not clones. At the same time, politicians who were put into office because of those parental beliefs don't want the next generation of voters changing those beliefs and voting them out of office. Their policy seems to be "Keep 'em dumb, and they'll keep voting for us." Or, as Donald Trump famously said of a segment of his supporters, "I love the poorly educated."

That's why some local and state governments fight so vigorously against certain federal standards for education. They want to keep the children politically and socially misinformed in order to alleviate the fears of parents and maintain political biases that ensure party loyalty. When the Common Core State Standards Initiative released its guidelines for mathematics and English-language arts, 42 states and the District of Columbia were members. The states that rejected the program (Oklahoma, Texas, Virginia, Alaska, Nebraska, Indiana and South Carolina; Minnesota adopted only the English standards) contended that they didn't want the federal government establishing educational standards. The libertarian Cato Institute warned, "[I]t is not the least bit paranoid" to say the federal government wants a national curriculum.

This provincial conspiracy against educational standards is revealed through the manipulation of school textbooks. Texas, one of the states rejecting Common Core and which ranks 39th in the nation in education, adopted public-school textbooks that opponents said deliberately teach misinformation, including exaggerating the influence of biblical figures on the founders of our country, undermining the constitutional ideal of separation of church and state, negatively portraying Islam, providing inaccurate accounts of religions other than Christianity, downplaying the role of conquest in the spread of Christianity and giving undue credence to Confederate beliefs about states' rights and slavery.

Texas did not fare any better in its proposed science textbooks, which included passages denying climate change as the result of human activity. (Publishers removed the passages.) As we know, 97 percent of scientists who specialize in this area agree that it is caused mostly by human activity. One textbook said that the warming trend will eventually "even out." In response to this assertion, the National Center for Science Education stated that its scientists were unaware "of any currently publishing climatologists who are predicting a cooling trend where 'things will even out.' " In response to criticism, the textbook publisher, McGraw-Hill Publishing, defended itself by saying, "We develop products that are designed to meet the education standards of that specific state or region." In other words, to make the sale, it is willing to customize "facts."

This isn't just a problem for Texas youth, who are being deliberately misled. Because Texas is such a large state, with 5 million children in public schooling, its schools buy a lot of textbooks, so publishers who don't meet their standards risk losing an important customer base. The problem is that publishers are pandering to a state school board not intellectually equipped to make decisions that affect the rest of the country's education. A few years ago, the Texas State Board of Education chairman, Don McLeroy (who had once said that "evolution is hooey"), explained his process: "The way I evaluate history textbooks is, first I see how they cover Christianity and Israel. Then I see how they treat Ronald Reagan—he needs to get credit for saving the world from communism and for the good economy over the last 20 years because he lowered taxes." A candidate for the Texas State Board of Education seat, Mary Lou Bruner, has campaigned on her intent to "promote conservative curriculum standards aligned with Texas values," which she believes include that the theory of evolution is atheist propaganda, climate change is not real, slavery was not a major cause of the Civil War, and Islam is to be distrusted. Reports also indicate that she believes President Obama worked as a gay prostitute and that the Democrats killed Kennedy.

And so massive ignorance trickles down to corrupt the education of our youth, perpetuating politicians who are basically carny barkers. One such barker during the 2015 presidential campaign was Senator Marco Rubio, who, while supporting more vocational training, commented, "Welders make more money than philosophers. We need more welders and less philosophers." Rubio's attempt to appeal to the working-class voter by ridiculing a stereotype of a frivolous education actually backfires when closely examined. First, he gives inaccurate information. According to *Forbes*, postsecondary teachers of philosophy and religion make 78 percent more money than the average welder. Second, he offers the logical fallacy of a false dilemma (which any philosophy student could have told him), in which he gives only two options. But there's a third option, which is "Let's have more of both" (and a fourth option, that we need fewer of both). Third, his contempt for philosophers suggests ignorance about the importance they played in the formation of this country. The writing of the U.S. Constitution was directly influenced by the philosophers Plato, Aristotle, Machiavelli, Hobbes, Locke, Montesquieu and Rousseau. Without them, we wouldn't have the country that politicians are so eager to dumb down. Fourth, studies in England showed that children who were taught philosophy (in the form of discussions about truth, justice, friendship and knowledge) as early as the fourth and fifth grade improved their math and literacy skills, with disadvantaged students showing the most significant gains.

Philosopher George Santayana warned, "Those who cannot remember the past are condemned to repeat it." Yet the way society justifies its past mistakes is by conveniently forgetting them or rewriting history, as in the dystopian society of *1984*. That's why there has been such an effort by politicians and others to distort truth in favor of myth or sanitized history.

Federally mandated educational standards are exactly what is necessary to elevate the democratic process from insipid name-calling and knee-jerk issues to a real and meaningful discourse among well-meaning citizens. This way, all our youth will have the same advantages and will not be held back by certain states that prefer their children to be less informed and less independent-minded.

The root of all evil in this world is not the love of money but the addiction to illogical thinking. Because with emotion-based decision-making comes the perpetuation of ignorance. The person believes he or she already knows all that is needed to know through what he or she would call "common sense" or "spiritual guidance." That conveniently removes any responsibility for learning facts or applying logic. Violence justified by religious beliefs is one such example. The suicidal terrorist who blows up a busload of children in the name of his or her god is a product of irrational thinking. So are the violent attacks on Sikhs in the U.S. committed because they wear turbans and the anti-Islamic attackers don't realize that most Muslims don't wear turbans. Or the desecration of a 35-year-old Denver store called Isis Books and Gifts after the ISIS-sponsored Paris terrorist attacks in 2015 because the vandals didn't realize that Isis is also an ancient Egyptian goddess who represents the ideal mother and wife, as well as a patron of slaves and the downtrodden.

Training our youth in critical thinking provides them with a defense against brainwashing, whether it be domestic or foreign, whether in the form of schoolroom teachers unprofessionally foisting their personal political opinions on students, religious radicals seducing the alienated kids who transform their virtual reality into violence or politicians shouting half-truths like an Old West rabble-rouser in a saloon trying to fire up a lynch mob.

2. Stop encouraging people who don't want to vote to vote.
"The people who tend not to vote are young, they're lower-income, they're skewed more heavily toward immigrant groups and minority groups," President Obama said in 2015. "There's a reason why some folks try to keep them away from the polls."

He's right. Because these groups tend to vote for Democratic candidates, Republican politicians have developed a campaign to keep these groups from the polls by using tactics that range from passing laws requiring voter IDs to radical gerrymandering. (Democrats also use gerrymandering to dilute Republican votes.) In an effort to combat this, Obama suggested the possibility of the U.S. adopting mandatory voting, as some two dozen countries have done, including Australia and Belgium.

Bad idea.

America has one of the lowest rates of voting among developed countries. In the 2014 midterm elections, less than 37 percent of eligible voters showed up, which left 144 million voters taking a pass on democracy. But that's not necessarily a bad thing. If voters are denied access through political maneuvering, then that needs to be fixed. But voters who don't want to cast a ballot because they're too lazy or uninformed should stay home.

We shouldn't have to persuade people to vote. They should see it as their joyful right and sacred responsibility. When we pressure people to vote, we're diluting the democratic process by bringing out those who are easily manipulated because they lack any sense of social commitment.

A large part of the lack of desire to vote is the feeling of being disenfranchised by society. The poor, minorities and the young may feel overwhelmed and impotent in the face of the political machine that seems indifferent to them, except to make promises at election time. Voting for any of the candidates might seem like visiting your mugger's home to give him a Christmas present. But that perception doesn't have to be the reality. A federal school program to emphasize critical thinking would address some of this. But we also need nonpartisan grassroots organizations to help educate the disenfranchised about the political process and their power in it. The goal would be the same as the civil-rights-era drive to register black voters: to empower them to make choices that could improve their lives. Teach, don't persuade.

3. Fact-check politicians as often as possible when they speak publicly.

What really distinguished the 2016 presidential campaign was how often politicians openly lied to the public and were not held accountable by the voters. Part of the reason is that many people hear only what the politician says, not the responses that come a day later that reveal the factual evidence. The first Republican debate drew an audience of 24 million, but how many of those viewers saw the websites or news shows that disputed the many factual errors candidates threw out? The lying has gotten so bad that when politicians are caught, they simply do what bluffing gamblers do: they double down, betting on voters' ignorance and indifference. The politicians ignore the evidence and indignantly repeat the lie. One example was Trump's insistence that he saw on TV "thousands and thousands" of Muslims in New Jersey cheering when the Twin Towers were destroyed, which was disputed by every reliable news source; no such footage was ever found. But Trump simply said they were all wrong because he has one of the world's greatest memories. Other politicians have employed this same strategy, often to great success.

There are several excellent nonpartisan fact-checking sites that evaluate statements by candidates for truthfulness, including FactCheck.org, PolitiFact, Sunlight Foundation, Poynter and Snopes. Any voter wishing to stay informed should consult these sites. However, we can do better in informing the public. For example, during all political debates, a team of fact-checkers should be posting onscreen corrections to misinformation uttered by candidates. Moderators asking questions should then ask the candidates about such misinformation. No politician should be allowed to make a public claim without being challenged. This should discourage politicians from lying and force them to support their positions with real evidence.

To encourage critical thinking, we should have professional nonpartisan logicians analyze politicians' arguments as they assert them. The analysis could be scrolled on the bottom of the screen, describing each logical fallacy. For example, following the horrific mass murders in San Bernardino, Calif., in December 2015, there was the usual outcry for stricter gun control, particularly a failed attempt in the Senate to pass a law that would make it illegal to sell guns to suspected terrorists on the no-fly list. Senator Ted Cruz and Senator Marco Rubio, who opposed the gun-sales restriction, explained their stance by saying that it could violate the rights of law-abiding citizens. This is another example of the logical fallacy of the false dilemma, which suggests that there are only two choices to solving a problem when there are actually more possible choices. It's like someone saying, "Either we visit my aunt in Iceland for Christmas or you don't love me." Clearly, those aren't the only two possibilities. In this case, Rubio and Cruz use the buzzword of terrorism to whip up public fear that would override desire for gun safety legislation. They want to suggest that doing one means being more vulnerable to the other. But the unmentioned third option is that it's about *both* gun control *and* terrorism and that both issues could be addressed simultaneously to make the situation better. This use of logical fallacy to confuse the public makes sense when we realize that the 50 senators who voted against expanding background checks following the San Bernardino shootings were the recipients in 2014 of $27,205,245 in donations to their campaign committees from the National Rifle Association, according to the Center for Responsive Politics. Money talks; truth does the walk of shame.

WHAT IS THIS ROUGH BEAST, SLOUCHING TOWARDS WASHINGTON TO BE BORN?

My proposals ask us to rethink the status quo of our educational system and how the media present certain news. Right now we are all frustrated with the corruption, inefficiency and ineffectiveness of the government, which hinders social improvements in all parts of our country, from economic opportunity to a fair judicial system. Yet we keep doing the same things that have failed, thus allowing this broken system to continue to limp along.

In a speech to the Massachusetts Anti-Slavery Society in 1852, abolitionist Wendell Phillips said, "Eternal vigilance is the price of liberty—power is ever stealing from the many to the few . . . Only by continual oversight can the democrat [meaning a supporter of democracy, not the political party] in office be prevented from hardening into a despot; only by unintermitted Agitation can a people be sufficiently awake to principle not to let liberty be smothered by material prosperity." The idea that we must be eternally vigilant is sometimes interpreted to mean we need to build vast armies to protect against foreign enemies who wish to destroy our way of life. But what Phillips meant was that the biggest threat to democracy comes from within.

Being a member of a democracy takes work—that's what eternal vigilance means. Democracy is a machine that needs constant maintenance or the parts will rust and grind to a halt. It's so much easier for us to continue this hero-will-rise myth, hoping to eventually elect someone who will fix it all for us. But that song is sung out. Patriotism sometimes means fighting on a foreign battlefield, but it also means fighting on the domestic battlefield, arming ourselves with information, basic-training ourselves to think logically for what best serves the ideals of the Constitution—and not just for putting money in our pockets or advancing a biased agenda.

2

Racism
MAKE ME WANNA HOLLER

*"The most dangerous creation of any society
is that man who has nothing to lose."*
—JAMES BALDWIN

THE STRUGGLE FOR RACIAL PARITY IN AMERICA CAN BE summed up in two exquisite lines from Robert Browning's poem "Andrea del Sarto": "A man's reach should exceed his grasp / Or what's a heaven for?" It's appropriate that these lines have been quoted so often in movies and TV shows, from *The Prestige* to *The Starter Wife* to *Star Trek*, because they reflect America's wishin'-and-hopin' approach to combating racism. Though the quote encourages us to, like the intrepid Don Quixote, reach for the unreachable star, it also advises us to get real and settle for an imagined place of equality called Someday, where we shall finally overcome.

That's just not good enough anymore.

When it comes to securing equal opportunity to thrive, African Americans must grasp in the here and now—or what's a Constitution for?

The problem is that the longer we continue to deny the problem exists, the longer it takes to solve it. It's like ignoring that Texas-shaped mole on your cheek that keeps getting darker and more tender. You could just give it a cute name and ignore it, hoping it magically goes away on its own. Or you could seek aggressive treatment that would probably save your face and even your life.

Most of the rest of the world sees our unpleasant mole of racial disparity and uses it as a propaganda tool to damage our international reputation. Enemies use it as a recruiting tool to enlist soldiers and terrorists. In 2014, the United Nations Human Rights Council questioned U.S. delegates about what they claimed was continuing racial discrimination against African Americans and other minorities in jobs, housing, education, health care and the criminal justice system. One of the council members noted that "segregation [in the U.S.] was nowadays much worse than it was in the 1970s" and that "some 39 million African Americans [are] particularly affected by structural racial discrimination in the United States." It's only here in the U.S. that there is such a high degree of denial.

Part of the problem is what I call the Obama Effect. When Barack Obama was elected America's first black president, much of the country celebrated that a major obstacle to racial equality had been destroyed. The joyful symbolism was similar to the tearing down of the Berlin Wall, another oppressive barrier to democracy. King's dream was rekindled in the imagination of every American who felt hopeful that the holy grail of fair treatment promised by the Constitution was finally within reach. Few deluded themselves that one man's presidency would mark the end of deeply embedded institutional racism, but certainly it would mark the beginning of actively eliminating racial disparity. Americans, black and white, would become like bomb-locating dogs, sniffing out archaic, lunkheaded racism and barking at it until it was dismantled and made harmless.

Though the country gave itself a well-earned pat on the back for electing a black man to the presidency, the systemic racism in the country seemed to get worse. It was as if some people figured, "We just proved we're not racist by electing Obama; now we're free to continue to deny equal education, job opportunities, voter access and whatever else is on our agenda." The police shootings of unarmed black men and women escalated; protests ensued. In a *New York Times*/CBS News poll in 2015, 68 percent of blacks said race relations in the U.S. were bad, more than double the percentage who felt that way immediately after Obama was elected. It was as if President Obama had become that one black friend from work that some white people always claim to have as proof they aren't racist.

The danger of the Obama Effect is that people might think that every time we reach a milestone, the journey is over. We relax, kick up our feet and take a well-deserved rest. And that's when the backlash hits us like a flash flood, sweeping away most of the gains that have just been made. The war for racial equality has a thousand fronts, and victory on one front should not mean being less vigilant on all the others.

Why is the existence of racism such a big deal? Because it subverts the American ideal of a level playing field on which every person has equal access to the opportunities to succeed. No one should expect to be handed success, but no one should be denied the chance at achieving success based on color, ethnicity or religious beliefs. Success is competitive, like a foot race, and winning generally goes to the diligent, disciplined and hardworking individuals with a burning vision and an unshakable work ethic. Historically ingrained social racism has shackled heavy weights to the legs of many minorities at the starting line that make them less competitive and therefore less likely to have a real shot at success. All people of color are saying is that we should help remove those weights and make the race fair, the way the Constitution intends it to be. In 1971 Marvin Gaye released "Inner City Blues," singing, "Make me wanna holler / The way they do my life / This ain't livin'." The fact that the grim lyrics of anger and frustration are just as true and poignant more than four decades later tells us how glacial the movement of overcoming racism is.

When entire societies cling to a state of denial, rejecting overwhelming historical evidence that something is wrong, stress builds up. Sustained denial breeds violence; the riots, protests and revolutions of the past are evidence of this. Today, the shooting deaths of nine innocent churchgoers in Charleston, S.C., as well as the Ferguson and Baltimore riots that followed the deaths of unarmed black men at the hands of the police, prove that the price of denial is the blood of innocents. And as long as America keeps denying, the cost in lives unfulfilled, destroyed and lost will keep climbing.

DENIERS GONNA DENY

The existence of racism in America isn't an opinion. It's a quantifiable fact. Like the Earth circles the sun, water is wet, and cosmologist Neil deGrasse Tyson's mustache is the most awesome facial hair in the universe. Indisputable facts.

But as is usual when someone points out a flaw, we are quick to deny the problem exists ("I am *not* too obnoxious at parties. That's just my personality!"). Especially when that flaw is contrary to what the country and most religions stand for. A claim of racism isn't just an accusation of awkward social behavior, like burping during dinner; it's calling into question the person's patriotism and code of morality. Few people would accept such an attack on their character without rigorously defending themselves.

Acting as spokespeople for this mentality of "Ain't no racism here, folks" are conservative bastions of the popular media. In 2015, the *Wall Street Journal* announced, "Today the system and philosophy of institutionalized racism identified by Dr. King no longer exists." (That was quite a relief to the black voters in North Carolina, Texas and other states where restrictions are being instituted to make voting a hardship for many minorities, since they tend to vote for Democrats.) Fox commentator Bill O'Reilly said the previous year, "We are not a racist nation. . . . Fair-minded Americans should be deeply offended, deeply offended that their country is being smeared with the bigotry brush." Fox News's Eric Bolling agreed as well: "Is there racism? I don't believe there's racism." A Republican National Committee tweet on the 58th anniversary of Rosa Parks's arrest confirmed that the corpse of racism had finally been buried: "Today we remember Rosa Parks' bold stand and her role in ending racism."

Perhaps the most puzzling comment was from hedge-fund manager and Fox News contributor Jonathan Hoenig on a Fox panel discussing the protests in Ferguson: "You know who talks about race? Racists!" Putting aside the fact that he had just been talking about race, I'm surprised this phrase hasn't become a popular Internet meme by swapping words: "You know who talks about crime? Criminals!" "You know who talks about rape? Rapists!"

There's plenty of proof that the Obi-Wan Kenobi mind trick ("We are not the racists you are looking for") is working. A 2015 Gallup poll showed a new 15-year low in Americans' satisfaction with the way blacks are treated. While only 33 percent of black respondents were satisfied with how blacks are treated in society, 53 percent of whites were satisfied with black treatment. That 20 percent difference reveals the gap between the perception of bias and actually living with it. After the 2015 rioting in Baltimore following the death of Freddie Gray, a *Wall Street Journal*/NBC poll found that 58 percent of whites believed the rioting was just an excuse to loot, while 60 percent of blacks believed it was a reaction to police behavior. In an AP poll preceding the 2012 national elections, 56 percent of Americans expressed explicit and implicit antiblack attitudes (up from 48 percent four years earlier). The figures are nearly the same for anti-Latino attitudes. Clearly, those who don't have to live in skin colors other than white don't see a problem. Perhaps that's why polls show that more Americans believe in guardian angels than believe racism exists.

The public debate over the use of the Confederate flag illustrates this disparity of attitudes between whites and blacks. According to a 2015 CNN/ORC poll, 75 percent of Southern whites felt the flag was more a symbol of Southern pride than a symbol of racism. But 75 percent of Southern blacks agreed that it was mostly a symbol of racism. Removing the flag, as South Carolina did (along with many businesses), is an acknowledgment that maybe the new Southern pride would be inclusive of *all* Southerners by not taking pride in a history of enslaving, raping, lynching and denying basic civil rights. Instead, all Southerners could take pride in doing what Americans have done since our founding: admitting mistakes, redressing griev-ances and coming together as Americans. These qualities are the cor-nerstone beliefs of patriotism and Christianity, which are so prevalent in the South. To deny them would be to desecrate Southern pride.

And yet, not content to deny racism exists, some whites argue that they are the real victims of racism. A 2011 study from researchers at Tufts University's School of Arts and Sciences and Harvard Business School found that many white Americans believe reverse racism has left them more discriminated against than blacks. Researchers found this particularly interesting because, they wrote, "by nearly any met-ric—from employment to police treatment, loan rates to education—statistics continue to indicate drastically poorer outcomes for Black than White Americans." Clearly, racism is a matter of perception for some whites, while it's a matter of statistical fact for most blacks.

It's understandable why so many white people believe there is no racism. The most important reason is that most are not personally rac-ist. They harbor no ill will toward people of color, they probably have some close friends who are of a different ethnic background, and they undoubtedly would go out of their way to help a minority person in trouble. To them, saying racism is rampant in America, or lumping them in with haters, is not only inaccurate but also personally insulting.

The second reason they deny racism's existence is that it has never been directed at them. They don't experience the humiliation and frustration; therefore, they don't see it how prevalent it is. Like most African Americans, I experienced racism from the time I was a little boy and am sadly aware that I will undoubtedly continue to expe-rience it until I die. I was called a nigger in high school and I was called a nigger when I played at UCLA and I was called a nigger last week by someone who didn't like an article I wrote. Celebrity has not shielded me; in fact, it has made me a more recognizable and accessible target. My Facebook page is a super-magnet for racial slurs. And that's how it feels when your skin is a different color from what is more acceptable: you feel like a living, walking target and every day is hunting season. (And being 7'2", I'm an even more prominent target.)

As a minority population, we have to constantly walk into rooms in which we are the only black face or one of only a few. When whites turn to look at us, the first word that pops into their head is "black." Nothing wrong with that, because every human does an instant evaluation: tall, short, fat, skinny, attractive, ugly. This is natural and doesn't indicate any malice. Most people take in that information, store it, and then treat the person with an open and friendly attitude. But enough people never get past the "black" part that we are forced to be hyperaware of everyone whose bias might be triggered by that mere fact. Everyone is a possible threat. The cop on the street is profiling us. The judicial system is punishing us. Businesses are exploiting us. Because most whites have never experienced that relentless social scrutiny, they can't imagine it to be true.

Since they aren't overtly racist, they are offended by the constant war cry of "racism!" that they hear directed at white society and, by extension, America. Who can blame them? Just by describing our country as racist, we might seem to be implying that all whites are sharpening pitchforks and watching YouTube videos on how to tie lynching nooses. This interpretation is inherently unfair to them. It also goes against how we want to see ourselves as a country: The world's melting pot. A place where anybody from anywhere can rise to the top, like Obama, Diddy, Jay Z, Tyler Perry and Oprah. But, as Sportin' Life says in *Porgy and Bess*, "it ain't necessarily so." Those few blacks who do climb the mountain are mostly in entertainment, including sports. What about all the other careers, in science, law, business and politics? Those mountains are like the Alps—almost all white at the top.

Racism deniers are masters of misdirection. While discussing a racial issue, they bring up a topic that is irrelevant or misleading, the way an illusionist uses an attractive assistant to misdirect the audience from what's really going on. And the audience, wanting to be fooled, never pays close attention. The current card trick of politicians and pundits is black-on-black crime, which they use to show that the real problem isn't white racism but blacks attacking each other. The not-so-subtle suggestion is that black problems are black society's own fault because they can't control their own people.

Black-on-black crime actually makes the opposite point, because it's a by-product of centuries of interning blacks in economic gulags. It's like the Uruguayan rugby players who ate their dead friends after their plane crashed in the Andes. This wasn't a meat-on-meat crime; it was the inevitable act of people with no other options. No one in the black community excuses this criminal behavior simply because we know the causes. But neither do we accept that its existence is proof of anything other than growing up in an atmosphere of fear for safety, a lack of real jobs, substandard education and pervasive hopelessness. This public outcry that blacks take more responsibility is the most outrageous racism of all because it comes from people making pronouncements from inside their gated communities who were afforded every opportunity to succeed.

Nor do we want to constantly hear about those few blacks who, despite the direst of circumstances, clawed and scratched their way into some Ivy League school and went on to fabulous wealth and success. The people who do that, regardless of race, are certainly to be admired, but in general it promotes the Good Negro myth, a throwback to the early days of the civil rights movement, when whites would point at the black man in a suit and tie as a role model to other blacks that all you needed to succeed was a dream and a whole lotta gumption. Rags-to-riches stories are the rare exception and suggest a Darwinian class bias that says it's OK to punish those less ambitious, skilled or academically capable because they don't deserve happiness. We don't berate a child because he can't run as fast as the track-and-field star at his school: "Come on, slacker. If Jimmy can run that fast, so can you!" We don't disparage white kids who have no desire to attend Harvard or live white-collar lives. We devise programs for them to pursue other professions.

For those denying the presence of racism in America, ask yourselves a simple question: How many experts—sociologists, anthropologists and political scientists—believe there is significant racism in the U.S., and how many don't? The vast majority believe it does exist. If the same number of medical experts told a patient to drink this medicine or he would die, he'd gulp it down in an instant.

The bottom line is this: A certain number of people will deny that racism exists no matter how much evidence is presented. We have to ignore those people, because they are incapable of rational thinking. Instead, we must focus on a dialogue with people to whom evidence and expertise and personal experience matter. We must constantly show them where racism exists and how it devastates not just people of color but our whole society, and we must promote ways to eliminate it. Those are the people who would want racism to end—if they just realized it existed.

WHAT WE TALK ABOUT WHEN WE TALK ABOUT RACE

To best understand the current state of racism in America, we have to be aware that, according to many scientists, there is no such thing as race. In 1950, an international group of anthropologists, geneticists, sociologists and psychologists issued a report through the United Nations Educational, Scientific and Cultural Organization (UNESCO) concluding that the notion of "race" was a biological myth and that all humans belonged to the same species. Since that report, the American Anthropological Association and the American Association of Physical Anthropologists have reached the same conclusion. Not all scientists agree with this finding, but most believe that the commonly held notion of "race" is a false distinction.

What does it say about us that we insist on using the term "race" when it's not even a scientifically agreed-upon label? It's like a holdover from the Dark Ages, when barbers would bleed people to make them feel better and alchemists would try to turn lead into gold. To keep using the term legitimizes the proclamations of racists who seek to justify their bigotry with voodoo science. This is what Leonardo DiCaprio's racist plantation owner Calvin Candie does in *Django Unchained* when explaining the science behind why black slaves don't just rise up and kill the numerically inferior whites: "The science of phrenology is crucial to understanding the separation of our two species." He proceeds to show "evidence" of black submissiveness through indentations in the skull.

The word "race" is ghettoizing language that perpetuates seeing people of color as a different species. The word encourages fear and distrust. Language is the fuel that feeds the great racist generator, so to dismantle racism, we'll need to start with selecting more accurate words. Eventually, "race" should become the new "nigger" and people refer to it in hushed tones as the R-word. But that day is not today. In the meantime, for the sake of sharing a common, though inaccurate, language in order to foster a solution, most of us, myself included, will continue to talk about race as if it actually existed—and racism because it does actually exist.

The general public uses the word "race" to designate a collection of cultural beliefs, social conventions, shared history and physical similarities. On a practical level, this is just another way to describe the internal reaction: *Stranger danger: proceed with caution!* Differences trigger our fight-or-flight reflex, which is a legitimate reaction to encountering anything strange in our daily lives. We feel safer with "our kind" than with those who look or act differently, because they may not share our values. The preservation of a group's values is directly related to the survival of the community. A motorcycle gang rides into a suburban community, and the residents immediately respond to the appearance of those people as a potential threat. A group of orange-robed Buddhist monks walking through the same community might not arouse as much fear, but it would certainly put residents on alert. Anything different, whether it's a group of people or a radical idea, is a possible threat. Some cultures use prisons and concentration camps for groups who look different, and they burn or ban books that express different ideas. It's all in the name of preservation of common values.

Banning books or information because they are contrary to accepted values is the cornerstone of racism, because it encourages people to reject what they don't know out of fear. Instead of seeking knowledge themselves to make an informed choice, they rely on others to tell them what to think. President Dwight Eisenhower expressed this contradictory idea when he said, "Don't join the book burners! . . . Don't be afraid to go to the library and read every book so long as that document does not offend our own ideas of decency— that should be the only censorship." It's weird that he couldn't see that's what *all* censorship is! He then supported allowing books about communism written by anticommunists to remain in U.S. military and diplomatic libraries abroad but the removal of books about communism written by communists. Apparently, American minds are too fragile to choose for themselves.

A book burning by a church in North Carolina included torching any Bible that was not the King James translation, because all others are "perversions" (despite the fact that many biblical scholars find the King James version, while very poetic, not to be the most accurate translation). *Harry Potter* novels are banned by various groups for promoting magic. Other banned books around the country include the Tarzan series by Edgar Rice Burroughs, the 1969 edition of the *American Heritage Dictionary*, Anne Frank's *The Diary of a Young Girl*, Dr. Seuss's *The Lorax* and dozens of other beloved books. This mindset of fearing unfamiliar people and ideas is what drives racism. To stop one, we must stop the other.

Choking off the free flow of information is like choking off oxygen to the brain of democracy. The oxygen-deprived brain sees everything through the distorted lens of paranoia, exaggerating all our instinctual prejudices: racism, sexism, homophobia, transgender-phobia, religious persecution and more. As responsible members of a democratic society, we need to gather evidence, weigh the facts and educate ourselves, not give in to the tempting familiarity of prejudices simply because that's how we were raised. If the colonists hadn't been able to shake off their assumptions, we'd all still be British citizens.

RAISE YOUR HAND IF YOU'RE NOT RACIST. THINK AGAIN!

Under the broad definition of race I gave earlier, everybody's superficially racist. That is, we instinctually prefer the familiar to the unfamiliar, and since we use the word "race" to identify the unfamiliar, we're practicing a form of racism. Imagine that two men of equal size, age and looks are about to be killed by a runaway car. One is black, the other white. You can push one to safety. Not knowing anything else about them—not their morality, relationships or personality—which do you save? Probably the one who looks more like you. What if the two men are white and you're white, but one wears a Christian cross around his neck and the other wears a Sikh turban? You're also a Christian. With only seconds to act, whom do you save? This instant chauvinism is the essence of allegiance to families, tribes, religions, countries and even sports teams. Rooting automatically for the hometown team makes very little logical sense, since most teams aren't championship-worthy and some are consistent losers. We do it anyway because it feels good to be part of a group identity. To express loyalty, whether deserved or not, makes us feel part of something greater than ourselves. Rooting for the home team is an unconscious show of support for your community's values. Supporting the home team is saying, "I made a wise choice to live here and embrace these values." That's what we mean when we chant "USA! USA!" during international sports events and the pride we feel when one of our own wins.

The downside to this tribal instinct is that if we aren't vigilant in fighting it, it can breed social intolerance. This fanaticism argues that the only way to ensure their group's survival is to get rid of any who don't agree. Like the Borg on *Star Trek*, they assimilate all organisms into one hive mind with the mantra "resistance is futile." That is why in early practice, religions such as Islam, Judaism and Christianity considered blasphemy, defined as any breach of orthodox teachings, to be a most serious sin, often punishable by death or eternal punishment. To question the group's beliefs, they argued, could destabilize the entire community and result in social chaos.

That kind of blind loyalty—to anything, including family, race, country, religion (even to the Lakers)—is not the credo of America, because it negates using rational thinking to improve our situation. It relies on popularity and fear of not belonging. Like the old Dr Pepper commercial that seduces the listener into joining: "I'm a Pepper, he's a Pepper, she's a Pepper, we're a Pepper, wouldn't you like to be a Pepper too?" The danger: "I'm an Aryan, he's an Aryan, wouldn't you like to be an Aryan too?"

Rejection of blind loyalty is what the U.S. is founded on. The Founding Fathers realized that the people here were a culturally diverse group who shared the common value of leaving somewhere else that demanded blind loyalty—to a religion or monarch. The U.S. would demand loyalty to principles, not dogma, and to a democratic process, not powerful people. We would pledge allegiance to reason, not a ruler. This diversity of ideas would make us stronger than those who tolerated only one way of thinking and living.

A few years ago, Kid Rock performed a song called "Warrior" to recruit for the National Guard. One line proclaimed, "So don't tell me who's wrong or right when liberty starts slipping away." The problem with that line is that if we don't ask what's right or wrong, then we are *causing* liberty to slip away. Doing the right thing is what we stand for. Not asking those questions is what our enemies stand for. Once we become the enemy, we have killed liberty. That lyric is about as unpatriotic as any could be.

That is the kind of irrational thinking that nurtures racism.

APPROPRIATION OF BLACK CULTURE: HURTFUL BUT INEVITABLE

It's a cruel irony to many African Americans that the very system oppressing them is exploiting their culture for profit. One controversy concerns the popularity of cornrows, the traditional African hair braids. But is it much hairdo about nothing, or a gateway crime against black culture that includes stealing everything from music to art to clothes to language? Cornrows are just the tip of the follicle, but because so many white celebrities have adopted this hairstyle, it has become the public platform to discuss the broader topic of cultural appropriation. Celebrities who have exhibited cornrows include Fergie, Gwen Stefani, Heidi Klum, Christina Aguilera, Paris Hilton,

Justin Timberlake, Jared Leto and David Beckham. More recently, Lena Dunham, Kendall Jenner, Kylie Jenner and Kim Kardashian have taken some heat for popping the cornrow. This has prompted some African Americans to accuse the dominant white American culture of stealing cherished icons of identity from the subjugated black culture. Kind of like wearing the teeth of your pillaged enemy as a necklace.

Most white Americans would agree that the influence of black culture on America is significant. Without the black musicians who pioneered swing, blues and jazz, there is no Elvis or Jerry Lee Lewis or rock 'n' roll. This influence is evident in all aspects of American culture, from fashion to food, from language to literature. Again, most Americans would agree that this is true. What most won't agree with is that there is anything wrong with that. In fact, they would argue that such assimilation of ethnic influences has occurred with every immigrant group in America, whether Latino or Irish or Vietnamese. They would argue that it is a symbol of American inclusion that we so readily embrace these foreign influences into our culture. The melting pot and so forth. American culture is not stealing anything; it's honoring black culture through homage. America acknowledges the influence and gives it full credit. And after all, isn't weaving black culture into mainstream American culture the best way to end racism? Are cornrows the ambassador to racial equality or just another version of Al Jolson mammying in blackface?

One very legitimate complaint is economic. In general, when blacks create something that is later adopted by white culture, white people tend to make a lot more money from it. Certainly, one can see why that's both annoying and disheartening. Through everything from banking to education, systemic racism has created a smoother path to economic success for whites who exploit what blacks have created. It feels an awful lot like slavery to have others profit from your efforts.

Loving burritos doesn't make someone less racist against Latinos. Lusting after cornrow-sporting Bo Derek in *10* doesn't make anyone appreciate black culture more. So the argument that appropriation is the same as assimilation doesn't hold up. Appreciating an individual item from a culture doesn't translate into accepting the whole people. While high-priced cornrows on a white celebrity on the red carpet at the Oscars are chic, those same cornrows on a little black girl in Watts are, to whites, a symbol of her ghetto lifestyle. A white person looking black gets a fashion spread in a glossy magazine; a black person wearing the same thing gets pulled over by the police. One can understand the frustration.

Ripping black styles out of context aggravates the offense. What white culture deems worthy to borrow is often so narrow that it perpetuates negative stereotypes rather than increases racial appreciation. Underwear sticking out of pants? Hip-hop language? Twerking? An unintended by-product is that white people, feeling aglow in the one-worldness brought on by taking a hip-hop exercise class, forget about all the other baggage that comes with being black, especially the serious state of racial inequality that needs to be constantly addressed. In the face of being shamed and persecuted, African Americans have cultivated art and fashion to maintain pride in who they are, so to see other cultures take this and profit from it while allowing the shame and persecution to persist makes us want to holler.

Yet here's the harsh reality. Whether we call it cultural appropriation, assimilation, exploitation, homage, plundering or honoring, it will continue to happen unabated by complaints and protests. Some products, like those involving the Confederate flag, can't seriously claim they are an homage, so public outcry can be effective in eliminating them. But for the most part, culture is a ravenous beast that consists of many commercial outlets that need to sell consumer goods. Music, movies, clothes, books and art need fresh ideas in order to keep the beast alive; products have to evolve in order to keep selling. Because of that, all non-mainstream cultures are open to being looted for inspiration to create new goods to sell.

It is some consolation that, on a smaller scale, African Americans have been able to do some cultural appropriation of their own. Once upon a time, professional sports were all white. Today, more than

76 percent of NBA players and 70 percent of NFL players are black. In 2012, 81 percent of *Billboard*'s top 10 best-selling albums were from nonwhite or mixed-race groups of artists. And this shift will continue over the coming decades. Currently, only 16 percent of Americans ages 85 and older are in an ethnic minority group, but 50 percent of those from newborn to age 4 are in an ethnic minority group. With each subsequent generation, cultural icons truly will be based on assimilation and not appropriation.

"Almost cut my hair," Crosby, Stills, Nash & Young sang in 1970 about a long-haired boy suffering from an identity crisis. Cutting his hair would be to turn his back on the cultural revolution happening at the time in order to seek comfort in rejoining the social norms he doesn't believe in. In the end, he doesn't cut his hair because "I feel like I owe it to someone." It's just hair, but, like cornrows, it becomes symbolic of a cultural identity that does not want to be homogenized like Pat Boone's sleepy 1956 version of Little Richard's dynamic "Tutti Frutti."

Wop bop a loo bop a lop bam boom, indeed!

GUNNING FOR BLACK AMERICA: GUN VIOLENCE IS KILLING THE COMMUNITY

Feb. 1, 2013, was one of the most moving and enlightening days of my life. I was attending the NAACP Image Awards when singer Harry Belafonte, 85, came onto the stage to receive an award for his nearly 60 years of civil rights activism. On an evening that was almost exclusively about celebrating achievements in the arts, Belafonte's speech was both inspiring and sobering. "In the gun game, we are the most hunted," he told the mostly black audience. "The river of blood that washes the streets of our nation flows mostly from the bodies of our black children. Where is the raised voice of black America? Why are we mute?"

The audience's collective passion was movingly expressed by Jamie Foxx, who took the stage after Belafonte to receive his own award. His voice shaking slightly with emotion, Foxx said, "I had so many things I wanted to say [about myself], but after watching and listening to Harry Belafonte speak, sometimes I feel like, like somehow I failed a little bit in being caught up in what I do . . . But I guarantee you I'm going to work a whole lot harder, man." It was an evening of such raw and honest feeling that everyone left feeling elated by the eloquence and commitment of both men. It was one of the only awards shows that was more like a community coming together than a bunch of entertainers congratulating themselves.

But here we are three years later, and gun violence in black communities is unrelenting. African Americans are eight times as likely to be murdered as whites. For whites, the murder rate is 1 per 40,000; for blacks, the murder rate is 1 per 5,000. To put that in an international perspective, the murder rate for blacks in America is about 12 times as high as among all people in other developed countries. Worse, gun violence is the leading cause of death for black children and teens.

It's a heavy burden to raise children who know that the color of their skin makes them walking targets.

This is a burden carried by the entire black community, because gun violence isn't just about the immediate threat of bullets flying; it's about the lasting effects that cripple the ability of the community to protect itself and to heal from the damage inflicted.

Often overlooked are the survivors of gun violence who struggle to return to some form of normalcy. In New York City during the first half of 2012, 96 percent of gunshot victims, whether they survived or not, were black or Latino. Danielle Sered, the director of Common Justice, has been researching the differences in the government's response to violence when the victim or shooter is white versus when they are of color. Sered concludes that very little is done to help the black survivors of violence. In an interview with *New Yorker* journalist Sarah Stillman, Sered said that had victims Trayvon Martin, Eric Garner and Michael Brown—whose deaths launched nationwide protests—survived but been left with disabilities, nothing would have been done to help them adjust to their lives. As dead martyrs, they're inspiring, but as wounded survivors they would have been inconvenient and invisible.

The constant threat of gun violence and the responsibility of caring for the many wounded victims has taken an emotional toll on the black community. Studies reveal high rates of post-traumatic stress disorder (PTSD) in poor, mostly African-American communities in large cities. Researchers at Chicago's Cook County Hospital found that 43 percent of its patients and more than half of its victims of gunshot wounds, stabbings and other violence showed signs of PTSD. Kerry Ressler, the lead investigator researching inner-city residents in Atlanta, said, "The rates of PTSD we see are as high or higher than Iraq, Afghanistan or Vietnam veterans. We have a whole population who is traumatized." The long-term damage of PTSD to the black community can be more devastating than actual bullet wounds. Sufferers can be more prone to violence and depression, have more trouble forming relationships and parenting, and find it harder to adjust to a work environment.

The 2015 terrorist shooting in San Bernardino that killed 14 people mobilized the country into action. Fear of terrorism rose to become the No. 1 concern of Americans. The president addressed the nation from the Oval Office to announce stepped-up attacks on ISIS and to assuage public fear. That's after a single attack on U.S. soil. Well, that same fear of attack is a daily reality in black communities with high gun violence. Where's the outrage? The demand for substantive action? The address from the Oval Office?

For many white Americans, what happens in the ghetto stays in the ghetto. As if people of color live in a sealed snow globe of swirling violence that affects only them. If gun violence were the leading cause of death among white children, as it is among black children, there would be a whole lotta shakin' going on. And demands for immediate action.

I could wave the gun-control flag, as so many have done every time there's a mass shooting, but we are several generations away from overcoming the personal paranoia, irrational justifications and political greed that prevent even the most basic gun protections from being passed. If the fact that children and teens in America are 17 times as likely to die from gun violence as their peers in other high-income countries doesn't convince us, nothing will. If the fact that the U.S.

has one of the highest rates of gun-related deaths in the world doesn't convince us, nothing will. If the fact that toddlers in the U.S. are shooting themselves and others at the rate of once a week doesn't convince us, then nothing will. Perhaps postmillennial generations will be more logical and less willing to blindly trade the real security of less gun violence for the false security of feeling like Bruce Willis.

Poverty breeds violence. People with little or no hope of a secure future for themselves or the safety of their family don't have much investment in the values of those who do have hope and money. So addressing the extreme scarcity of jobs for minority youths would be a high priority in decreasing gun violence. An announcement from the Oval Office that we're intensifying our attacks on poverty to save lives, strengthen the economy and give hope to other Americans who need it now would be welcomed. More PTSD screening in hospitals and treatment of those diagnosed would be welcomed. A judicial system that focuses on rehabilitation rather than retribution would be welcomed.

America is in the business of hope, and we have fallen short in supplying that service to many of those who need it most. When hope has a showdown with the estimated 300 million guns in the U.S., I don't like hope's chances.

WALLPAPER RACISM: FINDING FACES IN THE PATTERNS

Since earlier in this chapter I made the case that most people aren't overtly racist, the average white person might ask, "Then what the heck is the problem? Why all the street protests and op-ed pieces calling America racist?"

Because we're talking about the other white racism.

There are two main kinds of racism: explicit and implicit. Explicit involves bullying, shaming, shunning and using hurtful language or violence. Since explicit racists tend to be blind followers, there's not much to be done to alleviate that problem. Logic is useless, since they often take great pride in denouncing logic, reason and evidence in favor of gut feelings. All we can do is pass laws restricting and punishing their behavior and create a society that will help their children think for themselves.

More destructive to the core values of America is implicit racism. Implicit is more like wallpaper: it's in the background, not glaringly noticeable to most but still creating an undeniable tone and mood. And like the thousands of wallpaper types that contain heavy metals and poisonous chemicals, this one is toxic to all who come in contact with it. With implicit racism, no one is using the N-word or even consciously imposing racist control, but it's happening nevertheless. The introduction of *Racism in the Academy: The New Millennium* describes this phenomenon: "We can speak of race and racism as a 'worldview' because the tenets of black inferiority and white superiority are so deeply imprinted in most Americans' minds that they have become second nature. Racism is indeed a mind-set that is rarely openly articulated but is pervasive throughout our culture." This is the institutional or systemic racism that is hiding in plain sight, almost invisible to us because it has been around for so long.

The Confederate flag I mentioned earlier is part of this implicit, wallpaper racism. It's not screaming, "Get to the back of the bus!" but it's implying that any state that would fly it on government property still approves of the values it represents: the willingness to revolt against their country to keep slavery. It doesn't matter whether there are other values involved. In 2010, 55 percent of all African Americans in the U.S. lived in the South, and the flag was a daily reminder that when it came to how they felt about the flag (75 percent saw it as a symbol of slavery), they were indeed expected to sit quietly at the back of their community bus.

This wallpaper racism appears even in our most prestigious institutions. For 80 years, Harvard Law School's official seal was the family crest of a slaveholder who had once ordered 77 African slaves to be burned alive for an insurrection on his family's sugar plantation. Student protests forced the seal's removal, but the other more than 70 universities around the country under attack for their statues and memorials honoring wealthy racists are holding firm. Imagine what it would be like for Jewish students to attend classes in Hitler Hall or for Christian students to eat in the Judas Iscariot Cafeteria.

Here's what the view from the back of the bus looks like through the dirty windows of implicit, institutional racism:

ECONOMICS:

► In 2015, Honda agreed to repay $24 million that it had over-charged minority borrowers. The company had authorized dealers to mark up interest rates for minorities by up to 2.25 percent regardless of their creditworthiness.

► During the recent recession, blacks and Latinos were more than 70 percent more likely than whites to have their properties fore-closed. Even high-income black families were 80 percent more likely to endure foreclosure than whites in the same income bracket.

EDUCATION:

► A U.S. Education Department survey in 2014 concluded that students of color in public schools are punished more and receive less access to experienced teachers than white students. The same study showed that this leads to lower academic performance for minorities, putting them at greater risk of dropping out of school.

► In 2015, McGraw-Hill Education publishers said they would rewrite a ninth-grade geography textbook because it referred to slaves brought to America as "workers."

JOBS:

► There are only five black CEOs in America's *Fortune* 500 companies, down from a peak of seven in 2007.

► Unemployment among blacks is twice as high as among whites. This figure holds true as well for recent college graduates: 12.4 percent of blacks are unemployed, versus the 5.6 percent general unemployment rate.

► An *American Economic Review* study found that applicants with black-sounding names received 50 percent fewer callbacks than those with white-sounding names. As a result, some black applicants are modifying their applications to remove anything that might indicate their race.

▸ A 2014 study by the National Bureau of Economic Research reported that black job applicants were denied jobs more than any other group based on the assumption that they were using illegal drugs.

VOTING:

▸ From 2010 to 2014, 22 states tightened voting restrictions in ways that made it harder for minorities to vote. In 18 of the 22 states, Republicans led the charge for voter restrictions. The real reason is that minorities tend to be registered Democrats, and by making it harder for them to vote, Republicans can tilt elections in their favor. Although the populations of these 22 states make up 46 percent of the country's population, they represent 57 percent of the U.S.'s black population. The hilariously inadequate reason politicians give the public for enacting these measures is to prevent voter fraud. Yet according to one study, "virtually all the major scholarship on voter impersonation fraud . . . has concluded that it is vanishingly rare, and certainly nowhere near the numbers necessary to have an effect on any election." In Texas during the 2008 and 2010 elections, there were only four complaints of voter impersonation out of the 13 million votes cast.

▸ In September 2015, Alabama closed every driver's-license bureau in counties in which at least 75 percent of registered voters were black, making it nearly impossible for them to get IDs in order to vote. After public outcry, the governor reversed the decision, claiming, "To suggest the closure of the driver's license offices is a racial issue is simply not true, and to suggest otherwise should be considered an effort to promote a political agenda."

THE JUDICIAL SYSTEM:

▸ A 2015 study by the Women Donors Network found that 95

percent of elected prosecutors—those who bring charges, negotiate plea deals and can recommend how much time will be served—are white. More important, since many district attorney positions are elected, with the candidate being chosen by the outgoing DA and often running unopposed, there is very little opportunity for black prosecutors to break this chain.

▸ Black profiling has led to many abuses by police, as highlighted by the numerous deaths of unarmed blacks during 2014–15. Between 2002 and 2015, New York City police stopped and frisked 5 million people, with 80 to 90 percent of them being innocent of any crime, according to the New York Civil Liberties Union. During most of those years, 80 percent of those frisked were black or Latino, with 9 to 12 percent being white.

▸ A 2016 study from Duke University and the New School concluded that rich black kids are more likely to go to prison than poor white kids. "Race trumps class," said one of the study's authors.

HEALTH:

▸ A 2015 study in the *Journal of the American Medical Association*'s *JAMA Pediatrics* concluded that pediatricians treated black children differently than white children. Even when the physicians determined their pain levels to be similar, black children suffering from appendicitis were less likely than white children to receive pain medication.

▸ African-American children have a relatively high rate of exposure to lead poisoning from paint, which puts them at risk of attention-deficit disorders, behavioral problems and irreversible brain and central-nervous-system damage. In 2015, House Republicans sought to cut a third of the budget of the U.S. Office of Lead Hazard Control and Healthy Homes, which would make the agency even less effective at stopping this problem.

▸ A 2015 study in the *American Journal of Public Health* claimed that those living in a community with high levels of racism suffered worse health. This was true regardless of the wealth or education of the communities, and regardless of whether the individuals were the majority or the minority. The whole community suffered.

▸ A Northwestern University study showed that racial discrimination toward 12-year-olds had a lifelong effect on their levels of cortisol, a stress-related hormone. The short-term symptoms included grogginess in the morning and difficulty sleeping at night. The long-term effects included cardiovascular disease, diabetes, depression and chronic fatigue.

This is not an exhaustive list and is meant to reveal only a small sample of the background din of racism that drones in the ears of minorities all day and night. Yes, minorities know very well that the world's not fair and doesn't owe anyone anything. But in the U.S., we proclaim that our main political philosophy is to make our country fair, to fight every inequity so *all* our children can face their future with the same amount of hope, limited only by their own vision and determination. Racism prevents that from being true.

Even black children who overcome all those obstacles to achieve success pay a higher price than their white counterparts. A 2015 study from Northwestern University and the University of Georgia discovered what they call "skin-deep resilience." When they measured DNA methylation in these successful students, they found that the cells in kids from disadvantaged communities aged faster than those in kids from more-mainstream communities. The surprising outcome: kids from poor communities who exhibit this extraordinary self-control go on to have worsening health, while the kids from advantaged backgrounds who overachieve go on to have better health. Overcoming racism to succeed can be devastating to a black child's long-term health. "Do you do well in school . . . or do you have good physical health?" asks Gregory Miller, a psychology professor at Northwestern and the lead author of the study. Even in success, the black child pays a high price.

The successful black student who grows up to achieve a well-paying job at a great company faces obstacles that white employees don't face and are probably unaware of. In his article "What It's

Actually Like to Be a Black Employee at a Tech Company," Mark S. Luckie described his sense of isolation while working at Twitter. He estimated that only 2 percent of the employees are black (similar to the numbers at Facebook and Google), which is why upon seeing a new black person at the company, he and the other black employees would gleefully email one another to discover the identity of the new "blackbird." This kind of racial seclusion can make it much more stressful for black workers. They feel the burden of representing their entire race, and any mistakes they make could affect the hiring of more blacks.

Maybe the most egregious and saddest result of growing up in a world wallpapered with racism is the effect it has on black children's self-image. The infamous "doll test" that has been variously conducted since the 1940s reveals an early level of self-loathing. In this test, young black children are presented with a white doll and a black doll and asked to choose which doll they like best or would rather play with. A majority of children choose the white doll. When asked which is the nicest doll, the white doll is often chosen. When one black girl was asked why she chose the black doll as the "bad" one, she said, "Because she's black." A similar experiment conducted by *Good Morning America* in 2009 with 19 black girls resulted in 47 percent of them choosing the white doll as prettier. One 7-year-old girl said she chose the black doll as bad because "it talks back and don't follow directions." Commenting on this experiment, Harvard University professor William Julius Wilson said, "There's still the problem, the overcoming years, decades of racial and economic subordination."

NOW WHAT DO WE DO TO FIX THIS THING?

Let's start by lowering expectations. Because the harsh truth is that there will never be an end to racism.

Even if all the "races" are eventually swirled into a mixed fruit smoothie of blended features and cultural behavior, humans will find ways to categorize according to appearance—just as children do from elementary school on up—and to judge certain differences as inferior. That cruel impulse feeds the need for many to feel signifi-cant, as if being somehow taller, shorter, thinner, wider, blonder or darker than someone else means you have more worth in the grand scheme of the universe and aren't just another grain of sand in the infinitesimal dunes of a great galactic desert.

Rational people accept their disagreeable impulses but learn to dis-miss or control them. We realize that not every thought that pops into our head should be expressed, nor every urge acted upon. We learn how to be selective in what we say and do, not just to conform to a social norm but because everything we say and do defines who we really are—not the random, even disturbing thoughts cascading through our mind. Unfortunately, many people aren't consistently rational and are controlled by thoughts and impulses implanted in them by family or friends. Because we can't curb this impulse toward racism—this fear of differences—we have to attack the behavior itself.

1. Teach public awareness.

Clarify for people what is considered racist. Remember that most peo-ple want to do the right thing, want to be kind and compassionate, and may not even be aware that despite their best intentions, they are perpetuating racist attitudes. Sensitizing them will help them to understand what might be offensive or oppressive. It's unfair to expect people to automatically know what is culturally insulting when they aren't a part of that culture. The best way to teach is by being tolerant and forgiving. Respond to what's in people's hearts, not what's on their lips. Someone asking to touch your hair may be offensive to you, but it's probably meant as a compliment, a gesture of reaching out and bonding. Use that kind of event as a teaching moment.

2. Apply social pressure.

We can start by creating sufficient and consistent social pressure that shows that our community disapproves of any expression of racism, whether implicit or explicit. A favorite movie of mine is *Gentleman's Agreement* (1947), in which Gregory Peck plays a reporter who pretends to be Jewish in order to write a story about anti-Semitism. He is socially ostracized, his son is threatened, and his engagement is nearly destroyed. Defending her own lack of bigotry, his fiancée explains how she was at a dinner where a man told an anti-Semitic joke. The man she's telling the story to, a close Jewish friend, asks her, "What did you do?" She replies, "I wanted to yell at him. I wanted to get up and leave. I wanted to say to everyone at that table, 'Why do we sit here and take it when he's attacking everything that we believe in?' " "What did you *do*?" her friend persists in asking—to which she replies, "I just sat there." The "gentleman's agreement" is that when people say things that create an atmosphere of fear, hatred and exclusion, nobody speaks up. In order to end it, to send the pretenders of patriotism back to their caves, we all need to speak up. We never want to have to answer the question "What did you do?" with "I just sat there." If someone says anything racist (or anything -ist or -phobic), everyone should point it out as unacceptable. Without the fertilizer of implicit acceptance, racism can't flourish.

3. Pass and enforce anti-racist laws; block enactment of racist laws.

The best way the government sends a clear message that racism won't be tolerated is by passing and enforcing laws that prohibit racist behavior. Especially heinous are the drug laws and bail laws that have targeted blacks. Our prisons are filled with black men and women serving long sentences for selling or holding the same amount of drugs that whites rarely get prosecuted for. Some are doing life sentences for selling as little as $20 worth of pot. Our byzantine bail laws prevent the poor (often blacks and Latinos) from making bail for even minor crimes.

We can't allow governments, employers, businesses, organizations or individuals any loopholes that permit discrimination based on color, ethnicity, gender, sexual orientation or religion. At the same time, we have to be vocal in our opposition to the kinds of laws that are clearly aimed at restricting the political power of minorities, specifically voter registration and gerrymandering laws. We have to support organizations, such as the NAACP, the Brennan Center for Justice, FairVote and the ACLU, that are at the forefront of this battle.

4. Peacefully protest every racist action.

Mass gatherings of outraged people peacefully demanding change is a very effective tactic. It's worked throughout history, securing rights for workers, women, veterans and minorities, as well as bringing pressure to end unpopular wars. In addition to peaceful demonstrations, protests should focus on boycotts of businesses, states and politicians. When Indiana passed a "religious freedom" bill in 2015 that gave businesses the right to discriminate against same-sex couples based on vaguely defined religious beliefs, the public outcry created a coalition of businesses and other organizations boycotting the state, including the NBA, Angie's List, Disciples of Christ, Eli Lilly, Indiana University, Levi Strauss and Co., Nascar, the NCAA, Twitter and Yelp. The state quickly reversed its stance.

5. Support affirmative action.

This is a policy in which members of a disadvantaged group are given some form of preference in order to create long-term fairness. Yes, it does mean that there will be cases of reverse discrimination. Sometimes a perfectly qualified white person may be overlooked for a job, an internship or admission to a school in favor of an equally or less qualified minority. No one wants the policy to remain in place forever. Yet right now it is necessary to fix the many generations of inequity that have put minorities at an economic and educational disadvantage. The eventual goal is to no longer need affirmative action because everyone will have the same shot at success. But that time isn't now, and to create the society we envision and brag about, we have to make some uncomfortable sacrifices. Maybe it's not fair to some individuals, but it's fairer on the large scale of creating a more American community. And that's what patriotism and religion and Disney films teach us: to sacrifice small personal gains for greater social gain.

6. Press for more minorities in TV and movies.

Americans watch a lot of television (among 35-to-49-year-olds, 33 hours a week, almost as much as a full-time job). And while there are many people of color on news, sports and reality shows, there are very few dramatic programs in which a person of color is the lead character. Most of the time they are the black cop partner to the brilliant white protagonist (see *Elementary, iZombie, The Mysteries of Laura, Sleepy Hollow*) or the by-the-book boss (*Blindspot, Quantico, The Blacklist*). It's important that children of all ethnicities see not only their own group portrayed as the hero but other groups as well. If white children rarely see a black man or woman playing the clever, witty, brilliant, admirable hero, how will they associate those qualities with members of those groups? Although there has been significant progress recently with popular shows like *Scandal, How to Get Away with Murder* and *Empire*, it's not enough.

When *Straight Outta Compton* and *The Perfect Guy* dominated the box office for five weeks in 2015, people heralded it as proof that Hollywood had embraced blacks as lead characters and acknowledged the power of black moviegoers. The truth is that the films were released in the movie-scheduling ghetto of late summer and early fall, when no major big budget films are released because of the start of school. The *Los Angeles Times* reported that a black female filmmaker was told by sales reps that the market could not support even two "black films" a year.

In 2015, Viola Davis became the first black woman to win an Emmy for lead actress in a drama. Again, such an event is a start, but it can also inadvertently become another Obama Effect. Hollywood can point to her win as proof of diversity without addressing the most egregious lack of diversity: behind the cameras. In her acceptance speech, Davis said, "The only thing that separates women of color from anyone else is opportunity. You cannot win an Emmy for roles that are simply not there." For those roles to be there, we need black writers, directors and producers. According to a 2015 Writers Guild of America report, only 13.7 percent of writers during the 2013–14 season were minorities, a decline from 2011–12.

For African-American artists and moviegoers, the situation is reminiscent of what Ralph Ellison wrote about being black in America in *Invisible Man*: "I am invisible, understand, simply because people refuse to see me. Like the bodiless heads you see sometimes in circus sideshows, it is as though I have been surrounded by mirrors of hard, distorting glass. When they approach me they see only my surroundings, themselves, or figments of their imagination—indeed, everything and anything except me." It's not enough to see diversity on camera; we need to hear the different voices and see the unfamiliar perspectives in their own words and stories. Showing we value those voices and stories proves we value those people.

NOW YOU SEE RACISM, NOW YOU . . . STILL SEE RACISM

The poet Charles Baudelaire wrote, "The Devil's best trick is to persuade you that he doesn't exist." The metaphor is clear: not seeing the evil lurking in our lives allows us to unknowingly succumb to that evil's influence. The problem is that everyone thinks they can see evil coming and are therefore protected. And that's exactly how the devil wins. Racism is one such evil that seems invisible to those who don't experience it daily and who don't feel racist in their hearts. But just because we turn the channel when it shows starving children in Africa, that doesn't mean those children aren't still starving.

In this case, the pundit and politician's dirtiest trick is to persuade white Americans that racism doesn't exist so that it can continue to fester among those whom they don't care about anyway. They dismiss the black community's concerns and reduce their hope for meaningful change. Not all that far from slavery after all.

Change doesn't come about merely from complaining or even from being morally right. It comes from focused, persistent, intense confrontation of the problem. Remember that the most effective improvements in civil rights have come about from blacks and whites working together. That is the America we are meant to live in.

3
—

Religion
WORSHIP AT YOUR OWN RISK

"People hand in hand
Have I lived to see the milk and honey land?
Where hate's a dream and love forever stands
Or is this a vision in my mind?"
—STEVIE WONDER, "VISIONS"

WHAT DOES GOD WANT?
It is a question as old as humanity, with answers nearly as numerous as the millions of gods who have been worshipped throughout history. Those waving holy books or sacred scrolls proclaiming they have divine answers have formed the foundation for most civilizations, often by destroying any other civilizations that proclaimed different divine answers. That's a whole lot of death, destruction and turmoil when we realize that, when it comes to objective proof, no one's answers have any more authority than anyone else's. The history of religion is a buffet of blind faith, with individuals heaping all-you-can-believe helpings onto their spiritual plates.

But then, that's the point. Religion requires faith, and the definition of faith is to believe strongly in something even though there is no objective evidence. To seek, offer or need physical proof of the existence of one's god or gods or the legitimacy of specific divine teachings could be considered heresy, a display of lack of faith. Which is why we currently have an estimated 4,200 religions in the world—most of them defiantly certain of their own superiority over all others. The *World Christian Encyclopedia* estimates there are more than 33,000 denominations of Christianity, the world's most popular religion. That's at least 33,000 different interpretations of the same 783,137 words in the King James Version of the Bible. Some may see these numbers as proof of how ludicrous and petty religion is. But I think it's proof that people, despite their stumbling and faltering, want to be good and want to do good. And for some, religion is the best way to achieve that.

Which still leaves us asking, "What does God want?" Really, really want?

This question has put America in the midst of an identity crisis. On the one hand, we see ourselves as the great international melting pot that welcomes huddled masses of all religions and ethnic backgrounds. On the other hand, we're terrified that too much diversity mixed in the pot will dilute our white Christian majority. The resulting American stew might be a little darker in appearance and a little less likely to display a nativity scene at Christmas. Statistics support this perception: over the past 50 years, many denominations of Christianity in the U.S. have seen their share of the U.S. population decrease, while the percentage of Muslims has increased, making Islam the third-largest religion in the U.S. From 1928 to the present, the share of religiously unaffiliated people increased from 11 percent to 36 percent. According to the Pew Research Center, the percentage of nonreligious people in the U.S. will continue to climb over the next few decades.

Concurrent with the shift in religion, our cultural identity is transitioning from a large white majority to a more mocha-shaded complexion. The non-Latino white majority (63 percent in 2012) has been decreasing every year. Four states—Hawaii, New Mexico, California and Texas—already have nonwhite majorities. By 2050, some 29 percent of the U.S. population will be Latino. The African-American population, currently at 12 percent, or 39 million, is also increasing faster than the white population. The fastest-growing population is that of Asian descent, which from 2000 to 2010 grew 43 percent, from 10.2 million to 14.7 million; by 2050, it's expected to increase to more than 34 million. In true melting-pot tradition, America is becoming less white and less Eurocentric. According to the U.S. Census, by 2044 the white population will be in the minority.

The speed of change is disorienting for most Americans, especially those of us over 60 who are still aggravated over the closing of Blockbuster and the cancellation of *Law & Order*. But change is a constant strong wind at our backs nudging us along the sidewalk a little faster than we find comfortable. Fighting against it is like trying to use an umbrella to hold off a tidal wave. The ethnic composition of the country in 1800 was vastly different than it was in the 1700s. The ethnic makeup in 1900 would have been inconceivable to those in 1800. People from 1900 walking down Fifth Avenue in New York today would be shocked by the diversity of their fellow pedestrians. Some might even be horrified, but for those who believe in the inclusive principles of the Constitution, it is merely America striving to reach its promised potential.

For better or worse, religion has been a major influence on America's values since the beginning. The country was founded by religious outcasts running for their lives from persecution for their beliefs. Which is why the founders directly addressed religious freedom in the Constitution by forbidding Congress to promote one religion over another or to restrict an individual's religious practices. Today, there are several hundred religions and denominations in the United States. With so many different points of view, the challenge we face is to discover the role religion should play not just in our lives but also in our laws.

Abraham Lincoln said, "When I do good, I feel good. When I do bad, I feel bad, and that's my religion." Oh, Honest Abe, if life were only that simple. The moral struggle all humans face is that one person's good deed is another person's bad deed. Hand $20 to a homeless man, and we're told that we're in fact harming him because we're keeping him from seeking the institutional help he needs. Lying is wrong, but if someone gives you a present you hate, do you tell her? Were the vandals of the Boston Tea Party terrorists or freedom fighters?

The complexity of moral decision-making is why most people seek guidance in some formal religion that teaches a code of ethical behavior. The promise is that by following those teachings, a devotee will find true happiness. But there are thousands upon thousands of religious denominations and nonreligious philosophies claiming they have the one true path to happiness. Where things get complicated is when followers believe that traveling the one true path means destroying all other paths. In this way, religions can behave like any business: they want to crush their competition before their competition crushes them. Survival, not salvation, becomes the driving motivation, even if it means contradicting the core values of the religion. We've witnessed this hypocritical behavior with followers of every world religion throughout history. But we shouldn't condemn a belief simply because the believer is corrupt. Because who among us could cast the first stone?

HOLY TERRORS VERSUS THE REST OF US

To most Americans, there are only two religions: Christianity and Islam. It's the Super Bowl of religion, with the beloved home team versus the unwelcome visitors. Sure, we're aware of those other runner-up religions, like Judaism, Sikhism and Buddhism, but the Final Showdown—encouraged by all the political, cultural and media hype—is Christians versus Muslims. Within the U.S., it's a pretty lopsided battle, with some 250 million Christians versus 3.3 million Muslims. Worldwide, the 2.2 billion Christians outnumber the 1.6 billion Muslims, with the Hindus coming in third at 1 billion. But ISIS, Al Qaeda, 9/11, San Bernardino and Orlando have created a frightening narrative loop that has Americans focused on what they perceive to be a threat to their survival.

But how accurate is that perception?

Certainly, our lives are assaulted by acts of terrorism in the name of God. Around the world, terrorist acts of one kind or another happen almost daily, yet in the U.S. they remain a rare occurrence. That perspective is ignored by the media pundits and fearmongering politicians who have pounded it into our brains like a garage band next door that won't stop practicing "Stairway to Heaven." Some politicians have exploited our anxiety for their own gain. They promise to make the problem go away, and people are so grateful that they don't bother asking how that will be done or what the cost is—whether to our finances or our dignity and humanity. This is a familiar historical pattern. Hitler consolidated power by creating the Jewish Menace, McCarthy by creating the Red Menace, FDR with the Yellow Menace of the Japanese. A 1944 poll had 13 percent of Americans in favor of killing all Japanese. In 1945, the head of a federal commission advised "the extermination of the Japanese in toto." Since the near-extermination of the Native Americans, genocide has always been on the table in America.

Now we have a gang of politicos stumbling over one another to shake their fists at the Muslim Menace. And it's working. In 2014, 39 percent of Americans in a survey expressed great concern about being the victim of a terrorist attack; that figure rose 12 points, to 51 percent, in 2015.

Yet the figures don't match the fear. Despite the horrific attacks in Paris and Belgium, the majority of terrorist attacks worldwide and in the U.S. are not committed by Muslims. According to Europol, between 2009 and 2013 less than 2 percent of terrorist attacks in the European Union were religiously motivated. Most were from separatist groups. The Daily Beast reported that in 2013, the number of Americans killed by Muslim terrorists totaled three—all in the Boston Marathon bombing. That same year, toddlers killed five people through accidental shootings. In 2015, 19 Americans were killed by terrorists claiming Islamic affiliation. In that same year, 20

Americans were killed by cows and 58 were killed by bees, hornets and wasps. "These incidents get much more attention because of the rhetoric of Islamist extremism that's used," says Ken Sofer, a senior policy adviser for national security and international policy at the Center for American Progress.

Part of the reason for our disproportionate fear is that there's a lot more media coverage when attackers are Muslim, so people think it happens much more often in America than it actually does. Muslims are the celebrities of terrorists, guaranteed to both spike the fear factor in Americans and draw eyeballs to media screens and newspaper pages. They are ratings gold. Which is, of course, the terrorists' goal, because the more coverage they get, especially the alarmist kind, the more they are romanticized by the malleable youth who are their recruiting targets. The media, politicians and terrorists have a symbiotic relationship in which their success depends on each other.

Another reason for our exaggerated fear is that we are afraid of what we don't understand, and Islam is a mystery religion to many Americans. In a 2015 poll, 56 percent of Americans (and 76 percent of Republicans) said they believe the values of Islam are "at odds with American values." But that's only because they have no idea what Muslim values are. Spoiler alert: they are very similar to Christian values, including a do-unto-others clause and a warning not to focus on worldly gain. This is basic boilerplate stuff common to the scriptures of Christians, Muslims and Jews, who share an ancestor in Abraham. The Quran, Islam's holy book, reveres Jesus as a great messenger of God, describes his virgin birth and acknowledges the miracles he performed: "I have come to you with a sign from your Lord," Jesus said. "I make for you the shape of a bird out of clay, I breathe into it, and it becomes a bird by God's permission. I heal the blind from birth and the leper. And I bring the dead to life by God's permission. And I tell you what you eat and what you store in your houses . . ." (Quran, 3:49).

The teachings *don't* involve acts of terrorism, unless—as with every other religion—leaders manipulate the teachings to fit whatever they want.

If that's true, then why are people so convinced that Islam teaches aggression and violence? Because passages have been cherry-picked from the Quran and spread by those who have a lot to gain by agitating fear against Muslims. The same tactic has been used against most other religions for hundreds of years.

HOW MOST MUSLIMS VIEW EXTREMISTS

America's double standard regarding religious violence is revealed in a 2015 survey by the Public Religion Research Institute in which Americans were asked, "When people claim to be [Muslim or Christian] and commit acts of violence in the name of [Islam or Christianity], do you believe they really are [Muslim or Christian], or not?" Their response was telling: 75 percent believe that self-identified Christians who commit acts of violence in the name of Christianity aren't really Christians, yet 37 percent said that self-identified Muslims who commit acts of violence in the name of Islam really are Muslims. This disparity is based on most Christians not knowing that the Quran's teachings are just as much against violence as the Bible's. In fact, in a 2013 Pew Research Center poll, 81 percent of Muslims in America said they believe violence against civilians is never justified—an overwhelming rejection of terrorism. By comparison, Christians are greater proponents of violence. A 2011 Gallup poll showed that only 38 percent of Protestants and 39 percent of Catholics believed violence against civilians is never justified.

A major part of the problem is that most Americans (53 percent, in one poll) believe that American Muslims have not done enough to oppose extremism in their own communities. Every time there's another horrendous act of terrorism, people like me who are on media speed-dial under "Celebrity Muslims" are thrust into the spotlight to angrily condemn, disavow and explain—again—how these barbaric acts are in no way related to Islam. And every time we do just that, people say we aren't doing enough.

Yet no Christian American would expect to be taken to task for not doing more when Jim David Adkisson, a devout Christian, fired a shotgun in a Knoxville, Tenn., church, killing two and wounding seven, because of the church's liberal teachings. Or when Dylann Roof, a member of a Lutheran church in Charleston, S.C., allegedly slaughtered nine African Americans during a service at another Christian church in the city. Or when Anders Breivik massacred 77 people in 2011 in Norway, defending his actions in his anti-Muslim, anti-immigrant and pro–"Christian Europe" manifesto. When the Ku Klux Klan burns a cross in a black family's yard, prominent Christians aren't required to explain how this isn't really a Christian act. Most people already realize that the KKK doesn't represent Christian teachings. Like ISIS followers, these white-supremacist murderers have concocted a fantasy scenario in which they can be glorified through violence but which has nothing to do with the religion they pretend to follow. So how can those who do follow the religion be condemned for not stopping them?

For me, religion—no matter which one—is ultimately about people wanting to live humble, moral lives that create a harmonious community and promote tolerance and friendship with those outside their own religious community. Any religious rules should be in service of this goal. The Islam I learned and practice does just that.

Violence committed in the name of religion is never about religion—it's ultimately about money. The 1976 movie *All the President's Men* got it right when it reduced the Daedalus maze of the Watergate scandal to the simple phrase "Follow the money." Forget the goons who actually carry out these deadly acts; they are nothing more than automated drones remote-controlled by others. Instead of radio signals, their pilots use selective dogma to manipulate their actions. They pervert the Quran through omission and false interpretation, just as every religion has done with holy texts throughout history.

How is it about money? When one looks at the goal of these terrorist attacks, it's clearly not about scaring us into changing our behavior. The Twin Towers attacks of 9/11 didn't frighten America into embracing Islam or giving in to extremist demands. The fatwa against Salman Rushdie didn't stop sales of *The Satanic Verses*. Like all terrorist attacks on the West, they just strengthen our defiant resolve. So the attacks on the capitals of Europe, as with most others, aren't about changing Western behavior; they are about swaggering into a room, flexing a muscle and hoping to elicit some admiring sighs. In this case, the sighs are more recruits and more donations to keep their organization alive. They have to keep proving they are more relevant than their competing terrorist groups. As the Mafiosi in *The Godfather* are always saying, "It's strictly business."

Nor should we blame America's foreign policy as the spark that lights the fuse. The autocratic, dictatorial regimes that rule in so many Muslim-majority countries are much more to blame. The spark in these countries is poverty, political oppression, systemic corruption, lack of education, lack of critical thinking and general hopelessness. Yes, we've made mistakes that will be used to justify recruiting new jihadists. But it seems unlikely that reports detailing America's extensive and apparently ineffective use of torture produced any kind of mass-terrorist volunteers. The world knew we tortured. The only news was how bad we were at it. More important, if recruits were swayed by logical idealism, they would realize that the fact that the U.S. conducted, released and debated such a report is one of America's strengths. We don't always do the right thing, but we strive to. We admit our faults and make adjustments. It may be glacial, but it's still movement forward.

Knowing that the terrorist attacks are not about religion, we have to reach a point at which we stop bringing Islam into these discussions as an unthinking reflex. I know we aren't there yet, because much of the Western population doesn't understand Islam's teachings. All they see are brutal beheadings, kidnappings of young girls, bloody massacres of children at schools and these random shootings. Naturally, people are frightened when they hear the word "Muslim" or see someone in traditional Muslim clothing. Despite any charitable impulses, they also have to be thinking "Better safe than sorry" as they hurry in the opposite direction.

It's difficult to overcome such knee-jerk prejudice, as was illustrated when two Dutch comedians conducted an experiment to gauge the extent of this bias. They covered a copy of the Bible to look like the Quran and read passages to people on the street and asked for their reactions. The passages included "But I suffer not a woman to teach, nor to usurp authority over the man, but to be in silence" (1 Timothy 2:12). Another admonished a wife that if her husband is being beaten by another man, she may not help him by grabbing the assailant's genitals, lest she face a cruel punishment: "Then thou shalt cut off her hand, thine eye shall not pity her" (Deuteronomy 25:12). Those interviewed reacted with horror, calling the Quran violent and aggressive but praising the Bible by comparison as being "more positive" and "more peaceful." One interviewee suggested banning the book. Of course, they were shocked to learn the passages they were condemning came from the Bible.

What I and other Muslims long for is the day when these terrorists praising Muhammad or Allah's name as they debase their actual teachings are instantly recognized as thugs disguising themselves as Muslims. It's like bank robbers wearing masks of presidents; we don't really think Jimmy Carter and George W. Bush hit the Bank of America during their downtime.

We can't end terrorism any more than we can end crime in general. Ironically, terrorism is actually an act against the very religion the terrorists claim to believe in. It's an acknowledgment that the religion and its teachings aren't strong enough to persuade people to follow them. Any religion that requires coercion is not about the community but about the leaders wanting power.

I look forward to the day when an act of terrorism by self-proclaimed Muslims will be universally dismissed as nothing more than the criminal attack of a brutal political organization wearing an ill-fitting Muslim mask. To get to that point, we will need to teach our communities what the real beliefs of Islam are.

WHY I CONVERTED TO ISLAM

While I don't feel qualified to describe all the nuances of Islam, explaining why I chose to become a Muslim might be one small step for me to nudge one giant leap for American religious unity. This is not intended to encourage anyone else to follow in my path; we all have to experience our spiritual journey on our own. For some, it leads to religion; for others it does not. I'm reminded of that powerful song of forgiveness and redemption by Johnny Cash, "Reverend Mr. Black": "You gotta walk that lonesome valley. You gotta walk it by yourself. There ain't nobody here can walk it for you. You gotta walk it by yourself."

This was the path I walked:

I used to be Lew Alcindor. Now I'm Kareem Abdul-Jabbar.

The transition from Lew to Kareem was not merely a change in celebrity brand name—like Sean Combs to Puff Daddy to Diddy to P. Diddy—but a change of heart, mind and soul. Mine was not just a simple conversion but also a spiritual transformation. I used to be Lew Alcindor, pale reflection of what white America expected of me. Now I'm Kareem Abdul-Jabbar, the manifestation of my African history, culture and beliefs blended with my American upbringing.

For most people, converting from one religion to another is a private matter requiring intense scrutiny of one's conscience. But when you're famous, it becomes a public spectacle for one and all to openly debate. And when you convert to an unfamiliar or unpopular religion, it invites aggressive scrutiny, not just of one's conscience but of one's intelligence, patriotism and sanity. I should know. Even though I became a Muslim more than 40 years ago, I'm still defending that choice.

I was introduced to Islam while I was a freshman at UCLA. Although I had already achieved a certain degree of national fame as a basketball player, in my personal life I tried hard to fly under the radar. Celebrity made me nervous and uncomfortable. I was still young, so I couldn't really articulate why I felt so shy in the spotlight. Over the next few years, I started to understand it better.

Part of my restraint was the feeling that the person the public was celebrating wasn't the real me. Not only did I have the usual teenage angst of becoming a man, I was also playing for one of the best college basketball teams in the country and trying to maintain my studies. Add to that the weight of being black in America in 1966–67, when

James Meredith was ambushed while marching through Mississippi, the Black Panther Party was founded, Thurgood Marshall was appointed as the first African-American Supreme Court justice, and a race riot in Detroit left 43 dead, 1,189 injured and more than 2,000 buildings destroyed.

I came to realize that the Lew Alcindor everyone was cheering wasn't really the person they wanted me to be. They wanted me to be the clean-cut example of racial equality. The poster boy for how anybody from any background, regardless of race, religion or economic standing, could become an American success story. To them, I was living proof that racism was a mythological beast, like the jackalope.

I knew better. Being 7'2" and athletic got me there, not a level playing field of equal opportunity. But I was also fighting a strict upbringing of trying to please those in authority. My father was a cop with a set of rules, I attended a Catholic school with priests and nuns with more rules, and I played basketball for coaches who had even louder rules. Rebellion was not an option.

Still, I was discontented. Growing up in the 1960s, I wasn't exposed to many black role models. I admired Martin Luther King Jr. for his selfless courage, and later I admired Shaft for kicking ass and getting the girl. Otherwise, the white public's consensus seemed to be that blacks weren't much good. Either they were needy, downtrodden folks who required white people's help to get the rights they were due or they were radical troublemakers wanting to take away white homes and jobs and daughters. The "good ones" were happy entertainers, either in show business or sports, who should constantly show gratitude for their good fortune. I knew this reality was somehow wrong. That something had to change. I just didn't know where I fit in.

Much of my early awakening came from reading *The Autobiography of Malcolm X* as a college freshman. I was riveted by Malcolm's intimate story of how he came to realize he'd been the victim of institutional racism that had imprisoned him long before he landed in an actual prison. His story resonated with me. That's how I felt: imprisoned by an image of who I was supposed to be. The first thing he did was push aside the Baptist religion in which his parents had brought him up. To him, Christianity was a foundation of the white culture responsible for enslaving blacks and the racism that permeated society. His family had been attacked by the Christianity-spouting Ku Klux Klan and his home burned by a KKK splinter group, the Black Legion. He chose to study Islam as a new path.

Malcolm X's transformation from petty criminal to political leader inspired me to look more closely at my own upbringing and forced me to think more deeply about my own identity. His explanation of how Islam helped him find his true self and gave him strength, not only to face hostile reactions from both blacks and whites but to fight for social justice, led me to study the Quran.

This decision set me on an irrevocable course to spiritual fulfillment. But it definitely wasn't a smooth course. I made serious mistakes along the way. Then again, maybe the path isn't supposed to be smooth; maybe it's supposed to be filled with obstacles and detours and false discoveries in order to challenge anyone's belief. As Malcolm X said, admitting he'd made mistakes along the way, "I guess a man's entitled to make a fool of himself if he's ready to pay the cost."

I paid the cost.

As I said earlier, I was brought up to respect rules—and especially those who enforced the rules, like teachers, preachers and coaches. I'd always been an exceptional student, so when I wanted to know more about Islam, I found a teacher in Hamaas Abdul-Khaalis. During my years playing with the Milwaukee Bucks, Hamaas taught me his version of Islam, and it was a joyous revelation. Then in 1971, when I was 24, I converted to Islam and became Kareem Abdul-Jabbar ("the noble one, servant of the Almighty").

The question that I'm often asked is why I had to pick a religion so foreign to American culture and a name that was hard for people to pronounce. Some fans took it very personally, as if I'd fire-bombed their church while tearing up an American flag. Actually, I was rejecting the religion that was foreign to my black African culture and embracing one that was part of my racial heritage (15 to 30 percent of slaves brought from Africa were Muslims). Fans also thought I had joined the Nation of Islam, an American Islamic movement founded in Detroit in 1930. Although I had been greatly influenced by Nation of Islam member Malcolm X, I chose not to join, because I wanted to focus more on the spiritual than the political aspects of the religion. Eventually, Malcolm rejected the group, not long before three of its members assassinated him.

As you might imagine, my parents were not pleased by my conversion. Though they weren't strict Catholics, they had raised me to believe in Christianity as the gospel. But the more I studied history, especially of the Catholic Church, the more disillusioned I became with the role of Christianity in subjugating my people. I knew, of course, that the Second Vatican Council in 1965 declared slavery to be an "infamy" that dishonored God and was a poison to society. But for me, it was too little, too late. The earlier failure of the Church to use its might and influence to stop slavery, instead justifying it as somehow connected to original sin, made me angry. Papal bulls of the Middle Ages (e.g., *Dum Diversas, Romanus Pontifex*) condoned enslavement of natives and the stealing of their lands. And while I realize that many Christians risked their lives and families to fight against slavery, and that it would not have ended without them, I found it hard to align myself with the cultural institutions that had turned a blind eye to such outrageous behavior in direct violation of their most sacred beliefs.

The adoption of a new name was an extension of my rejection of all things in my life that related to the enslavement of my family and people. Alcindor was a French planter in Trinidad who owned my ancestors. My ancestors were Yoruba people, from present-day Nigeria. Keeping the name of my family's slave master seemed somehow to dishonor them. His name felt like a branded scar of shame.

My devotion to Islam was absolute. I even agreed to marry a woman whom Hamaas had suggested for me, despite my strong feelings for another woman. Ever the team player, I did as "Coach" Hamaas recommended. I also followed his advice to not invite my parents to the wedding, a mistake that took me more than a decade to rectify. Although I had my doubts about some of Hamaas's instruction, I rationalized them away because of the great spiritual fulfillment I was experiencing.

But my independent spirit finally emerged. Not content to receive all my religious knowledge from one man, I pursued my own studies. I soon found that I disagreed with some of Hamaas's teachings about the Quran, and we parted. In 1973, I traveled to Libya and Saudi Arabia to learn enough Arabic to study the Quran on my own. I emerged from this pilgrimage with my beliefs clarified and my faith renewed.

From that year to this, I have never wavered or regretted my decision to convert to Islam. When I look back now, I wish I could have done it in a more private way, without all the publicity and fuss. But at the time, I was adding my voice to the civil rights movement by denouncing the legacy of slavery and the religious institutions that had supported it. That made it more political than I had intended, and it distracted from what was, for me, a much more personal journey.

Many people are born into their religion. For them it is mostly a matter of legacy and convenience. Their belief is based on faith, not just in the teachings of the religion but also in the acceptance of that religion by their family and culture. For the person who converts, it is a matter of fierce conviction and defiance. Our belief is based on a combination of faith and logic because we need a powerful reason to abandon the faith of our family and community to embrace the beliefs foreign to both. Conversion is a risky business, since it can result in losing family, friends and community support. I know, because I lost all three. For a while.

Some fans still call me Lew and then seem annoyed when I ignore them. They don't understand that their lack of respect for my spiritual choice is insulting. It's as if they want me to exist only as an idea of who they want me to be to decorate their world, rather than as an individual. Like a toy action figure.

Kermit the Frog famously complained, "It's not easy being green." Try being Muslim in America. According to the Pew Research Center, the U.S. public has the least regard for Muslims among all believers, slightly less than it has for atheists. This lack of regard, based on unfamiliarity and fear, has resulted in a sustained campaign against Muslims in America, the kind of religious persecution that drove the founders of this country from their homes to create America, a place they wanted to be free of religious persecution.

Muslims, Christians and Jews do worship the same God, just as they share beliefs in daily prayer and divine assistance, admiration for Jesus and charity for the needy. They just express their devotion to God differently. Those differences can make each group wary of the other, until they realize that a fundamental teaching in all three religions is to coexist in peace with others. True, we can all dig into one another's holy texts for isolated quotes that seem to contradict this, and we can all air one another's historical dirty laundry when each acted contrary to this teaching. But all of our faiths remind us that what really matters is how we behave toward each other here and now.

A California State University research group, the Center for the Study of Hate and Extremism, has reported alarming increases in hate crimes against Muslims in America, including physical assault on the streets, arson and vandalism at mosques, and shootings and death threats targeting Muslim-owned businesses. In California, more than half the Muslim students in a survey reported incidents of bullying, twice that of non-Muslim students. In January 2016, the New York City Police Department settled two federal lawsuits that alleged Muslims were targeted for surveillance and investigations based only on their religion. The previous month, the private evangelical school Wheaton College had begun the process of firing a black political-science teacher for stating that Muslims and Christians worship the same god. The school ended up withdrawing the charge, and the professor resigned. Ironically, she had been repeating what Pope Francis had already said. In the month after the Paris attacks of November 2015, the average number of monthly suspected hate crimes against Muslims in America tripled. A Muslim cabdriver was shot in the back; a hijab-wearing student was punched; a Muslim woman at a car wash was threatened by a man with a knife. Among the instances of vandalism, a bullet-riddled copy of the Quran was left outside a mosque. A New Jersey Muslim high school teacher claims she was fired for showing a film about Nobel Peace Prize winner Malala Yousafzai, even though a non-Muslim teacher had shown the same film. The teacher brought a lawsuit against the school district alleging she was told not to mention Islam or the Middle East in class. The district, though, has stated that her firing was not related "to religion, national or other improper factors." So much for educating our children to think rationally.

The worst perpetrators of anti-Muslim propaganda are also the ones who hope to benefit most from amping up the paranoia level to DEFCON 1. The politicians' alchemy is to transform fear into votes. GOP presidential candidates in 2016 battled one another for the most atrocious and un-American proposals, including barring Muslims from entering the U.S., registering those already here and assigning extra patrols to keep watch on Muslim-American neighborhoods, even though New York City police commissioner William Bratton rejected the latter idea as "politicians seeking to exploit fear." It's as if the country has a bruised rib and politicians keep poking the bruise while claiming that only they can make the pain stop. (Well, yeah, by no longer poking it!) They've gotten America so riled up that when a 2015 poll asked Republican voters, "Would you support or oppose bombing Agrabah?," 30 percent of Republican voters endorsed such attacks. Agrabah is the fictional kingdom in the Disney movie *Aladdin*. In the same poll, 54 percent agreed with barring Muslims from entering the U.S. and 46 percent agreed with forming a database of Muslims in the country. Both proposals are so unconstitutional that they would do America more harm than the actual terrorists would.

This kind of thinking is a prime example of global dumbing, which is much more dangerous to our survival than global warming. When politicians and the media constantly stimulate the fear center in the minds of Americans, they are deliberately manipulating them to react emotionally rather than rationally. Humans like to proclaim that rational thinking is what makes us superior to other animals. But not using rational thinking when you have it is like celebrating having opposable thumbs but keeping them shoved up your butt. Proverbially, of course.

It's difficult to sustain outrage at the sad individuals conducting these attacks on Muslim Americans, because they clearly don't understand the impotence of their contradictory behavior. They don't realize that each attack on Muslims is like donating money directly to ISIS, because it helps them recruit more jihadists, even while harming the very people here who are most opposed to the terrorists: true followers of Islam.

Part of my conversion to Islam is accepting the responsibility to teach others about my religion. Not to convert them, but to coexist with them through mutual respect and support. "One world" does not have to mean one religion, just one belief in living in peace.

GIMME THAT OLD-TIME RELIGION— WHATEVER THAT WAS

Can you consider yourself an American if you don't follow the teachings of the U.S. Constitution? That may be the most important question Americans should ask themselves, but most don't. They assume geography is identity, that being here equals citizenship. Legally, yes, but is that all that being an American is about? If someone doesn't follow the teachings of the Republican Party or the Democratic Party, then would they be considered a Republican or a Democrat? The presidential candidacy of Donald Trump put the GOP through an identity crisis for that very reason.

Still, everyday people who staunchly wave flags, declare their unwavering patriotism and weep at Fourth of July speeches talk and act in ways that are clearly un-American. I believe the only way to be American is to act in accordance with America's Constitution and, when we disagree with that document, to legally petition to change it or challenge laws in the judicial system. When the government deliberately refuses to live up to its constitutional obligations despite all legal challenges, then people in their frustration might take to the streets to march peacefully to put pressure on the authorities—local, state and federal—to fulfill their responsibilities.

But when it comes to religion, a lot of Americans aren't acting American. In a 2015 poll, 82 percent of Americans in the survey believed that preserving religious freedom for Christians was important. (Just based on the guarantees of religious freedom expressed in the Constitution, that should be 100 percent, or at least the high 90s. So 18 percent of those polled are by this measure anti-American.) But in that same poll, only 61 percent thought those same religious protections should be afforded to Muslims. Jews and Mormons fared slightly better, at 70 percent and 67 percent. Anti-Semitism is also on the rise, but, ironically, incidences of it in 2013 were more frequent among African Americans (36 percent) and foreign-born Latinos (20 percent) than among all Americans (14 percent). It's as if the more that white Americans show bias against blacks and Latinos, the more that blacks and Latinos turn around and show bias against Jews. As with the legacy of child abuse, the abused become the abusers.

This is not the religious tolerance that Thomas Jefferson envisioned for America when he said, "The legitimate powers of government extend to such acts only as are injurious to others. But it does me no injury for my neighbour to say there are twenty gods, or no god. It neither picks my pocket nor breaks my leg." In fact, every vote cast against religious tolerance for Christians, Jews, Muslims or the followers of any other religion—or any nonbelievers—is a vote against what the country stands for and undermines America. Can we even call them Americans, or are they just delusional houseguests?

One reason many Americans act un-American is that they haven't read the whole Constitution. The same is true with religion. Most followers of religions do not adhere to all the teachings of their religion, in part because they don't know what the teachings are. According to a study by the polling organization the Barna Group, titled *The Books Americans Are Reading*, only 20 percent of American adults have read the entire Bible—about the same percentage as those defined as practicing Christians who have read *Fifty Shades of Grey* and *Game of Thrones*. That's a pretty small percentage, considering Christianity is the dominant religion in America. It's also pretty small when one considers that, as Christians, they believe the Bible was given to them by the most powerful being in the universe, yet they don't have time to read it for themselves. This would be true of any religion practitioners who have a text that they claim is the direct word of God. Not reading the text suggests they don't really believe it to be the word of God.

The other reason most people don't follow the teachings of their religion is that they consider the rules to be too strict. For example, in the Sermon on the Mount, Jesus says, "But I say unto you, That ye resist not evil: but whosoever shall smite thee on *thy* right cheek, turn to him the other also. And if any man will sue thee at the law, and take away thy coat, let him have thy cloak also." Jesus is explaining the core concept of Christianity: everything in this world is temporary, but the soul is immortal. People should not do anything that damages the soul in favor of what is temporary. Caring for the soul by not committing violence or being aggravated over the loss of mere goods, rather than favoring anything material, is the main goal. So if someone hits you, you don't hit him back. If he takes your TV, give him the remote.

Very few people find this teaching to be practical, so they ignore it. But by ignoring it, they are eating from the Tree of Knowledge of Good and Evil and choosing which teachings are convenient or practical for them to follow, regardless of what God wants. Even though Jesus, in that same sermon, said, "Whosoever therefore shall break one of these least commandments, and shall teach men so, he shall be called the least in the kingdom of heaven."

And that has always been humanity's problem with religion. It seems impossible to reconcile the spiritual demands of nurturing the soul with the practical demands of feeding the family.

Which is why most Americans aren't really orthodox believers willing to follow every teaching in our preferred religion. Americans are mostly "cultural believers," meaning we usually embrace whatever religion we were raised in because it's a familiar and comfortable part of our culture. Rather than being sticklers for our holy books, we follow Crosby, Stills, Nash & Young's advice: "You, who are on the road /

Must have a code that you can live by." So we distill some general wisdom in a CliffsNotes version of our religion and, using that simple map as our guide, traverse the moral complexities of the road of life. We want to achieve spiritual fulfillment but also material success.

The problem is, of course, that doing so is the exact thing religions tell you not to do. Once you start choosing which teachings to follow and which not to follow, you are saying that human convenience should dictate what to follow, not God's commandments. Now anyone can choose to follow or abandon any teaching based on personal preference. Holy texts become "choose your own moral adventure" books.

This is the point of the story of the Garden of Eden in the Old Testament. God forbids Adam and Eve to eat from the Tree of Knowledge of Good and Evil. A lot of people think it's just the Tree of Knowledge, which wouldn't make sense because the God of the Bible has no reason not to want people to learn. What God doesn't want is for humans to question his plan (I'll use the male gender for simplicity's sake), in which he alone knows what is good and what is evil because he alone is omnipotent (all-powerful), omniscient (all-seeing) and omnipresent (existing in all times at once). If humans eat the fruit from that tree, then they will believe they know good from evil and will act accordingly. They will make themselves god-like, but without God's knowledge. This attempt to be godlike, to decide what is good and evil outside God's teachings, is why Adam and Eve were punished.

The parable tells people to follow God's teachings without variation or interpretation. To do anything else is to demonstrate a lack of faith in God and his plan.

The biggest enemy to following God's teachings is rationalization. A conversation in *The Big Chill* explains how it sneaks into our lives:

> **Michael:** "I don't know anyone who'd get through the day without two or three juicy rationalizations. They're more important than sex."
> **Sam:** "Ah, come on. Nothing's more important than sex."

Michael: "Oh yeah? Ever gone a week without a rationalization?"

It's the one thing we can't live without in order to feel good about ourselves. If we fall short of the teachings we've committed to, we rationalize: "I'm only human." Or "I'll do something nice tomorrow to make up for it." Or "That's what everyone else would do." It's hard to be moral when we have so many excuses not to be.

Part of our rationalization is that we should be judged by what's in our hearts rather than by our actions. We imagine the good, upstanding, kind person we want to be and then think that's who we really are because that's who we want to be. Certainly the fact that I want to be that person reveals that I am at heart that person.

Not really. No one accepts that reasoning any more than we accept the murderer's plea of "I didn't mean to." Religion insists that we are judged by our actions, our choices, not by our fantasies. The person who lies a lot but feels guilty because he believes lying is wrong is still a liar. We mistake guilt for a redemptive quality: because I feel bad, I must be good. No, a person is good or bad based on their actions alone.

The worst manifestation of this rationalization is when leaders deliberately pervert teachings in order to manipulate an unquestioning populace into following them. Slavery was justified by Christians citing biblical passages: "Servants, be obedient to them that are your masters according to the flesh, with fear and trembling" (Ephesians 6:5) and "Exhort servants to be obedient unto their own masters and to please them well in all things" (Titus 2:9). Slaveholders argued that because Jesus never explicitly condemned slavery, it was permissible. They further rationalized that they were actually liberating blacks from their savage ways by forcing Christianity upon them.

Terrorists claiming to be Muslim often use this quote from the Quran to justify violence: "So let those fight in the cause of Allah who sell the life of this world for the Hereafter. And he who fights in the cause of Allah and is killed or achieves victory—We will bestow upon him a great reward" (An-Nisa, 4:74). The quote is taken out of context from the story of Joseph's betrayal by his brothers, which is nearly identical to that in the Hebrew Bible. Most Islamic texts identify this not as a call to violence but as a reminder that Muslims must struggle within themselves to follow the teachings of God, even if they are difficult in this world, because they will reap benefits in the next world.

There are many more examples in which kings, presidents, popes and clerics have contradicted the spiritual teachings of their religions through strained rationalization, all in an effort to enrich their own power and finances. In America, election time is a potpourri of rationalizations that twist religions' teachings in an effort to gain votes. Sadly, people are too often and too easily misled by these holy hucksters.

The key to manipulating people is to prey upon their fears, of which we have no shortage. A 2015 study published in *Social Cognitive and Affective Neuroscience* found that when medical researchers used magnetic stimulation to shut down the brain's threat perception, 32.8 percent fewer participants expressed a belief in God, angels or heaven. Also, 28.5 percent were more positive toward immigrants who criticized their country. Of course, we don't want our fear perception to be shut down, or else we could easily put ourselves in danger. But allowing fear to dominate reason puts us in even greater danger of becoming enslaved by others' manipulating that fear.

"SIRI, GIVE ME DIRECTIONS TO SALVATION"

Believers and nonbelievers alike are looking for the same thing in life: maximum pleasure, minimum pain. What complicates this quest is we don't all agree on what happiness is, or even what pain is. For some, pleasure involves instant gratification of their senses, such as eating, drinking and partying whenever possible. For others, pleasure is focused on delayed gratification, perhaps even delayed until after death. For some, the main source of pain is anything that inhibits them from getting what they want as soon as they want it. For others, the worst pain is caused when their loved ones suffer. Most of us bounce like a pinball among these positions.

We hope that religion will give us guidance and strength to do the right thing and wisdom to know what the right thing is. We struggle to translate divine teaching into daily practice, good intentions into good acts. Sometimes we treat the process like a diet, with its trade-offs: if I do this good thing for Mom, then I can splurge on two bad things that go against my religion's teachings. For some, religion is just a disguise they wear to fit in with their families and communities. They "believe" because everyone they know does and they don't want to stick out. Their moral code is cobbled together from scraps of scriptures overheard in church or in movies. Whether they follow this code or not doesn't matter; for them, goodness comes from professing belief, not necessarily following it. Or as Calvin explains to Hobbes in the cartoon, "A day without denial is a day you've got to face."

I'm not in a position to tell anyone else what faith to follow or to follow any at all. I have found a religion that works for me, just as billions of adherents of various religions around the world are satisfied with their choice. Even so, it would be simplistic to say that all religions are basically the same, because there are some fundamental philosophical and cultural differences. But it's like choosing a model of car. They may look and perform differently, but most of us want the same basic results from our selection: that the trip is pleasant and that we arrive safely.

All societies seek domestic safety, which in many cases is achieved through conformity—getting everyone to believe the same thing. Imposing sharia law (laws based on the Quran's teachings) on an entire country is a way to enforce conformity, but it's a practice that many Christians rightly condemn when Islamic countries follow it. In the same way, America has a long history of legislators trying to impose Christian laws: prayer in school, using the Bible to swear in officials, bans on same-sex marriage, restrictions on abortion. In a 2011 poll, 53 percent of Americans said they believe the Constitution "establishes a Christian nation." Ironically, it does just the opposite. A Public Policy Polling national survey in 2015 found that 57 percent of Republicans want to establish Christianity as the national religion. To do this would make us much more like the totalitarian enemies to whom we brag about our freedoms. How can you consider yourself an American when you are against religious freedom, the very thing that caused the country's creation? And finally, it would be an admission that people have to be legally forced into Christianity because they wouldn't choose it for themselves.

The big difference between the U.S. and Big Brother countries that demand conformity is that we continue to fight against efforts to impose religion-based laws that are contrary to the Constitution. America has always valued its nonconformity, from its rebellion against England to its Wild West frontier to its garage-based inventors, iconoclastic artists and *Shark Tank* innovators. We know the value of dissenting opinions and ethnic diversity because they have enhanced and enriched our economy and culture.

So how do we decrease religious animosity and improve interfaith relations?

1. Make and enforce strict hate-crime laws.

Local, state and federal hate-crime laws must be strongly enforced to send a message that the country stands united in its defense of freedom of speech and freedom to worship. We have to demonstrate our commitment to protecting religious minorities with the same vigor that we target suspected terrorists.

2. Speak up.

When Donald Trump held a town-hall meeting during his presidential campaign, a man in the audience said, "We have a problem in this country. It's called Muslims . . . When can we get rid of them?" The response of a national leader defending the Constitution as well as the lives of Muslim Americans would have been, "Muslim Americans are a valued part of our community. Our problem is ignorance. When can we get rid of that?" Instead, Trump pandered: "You know, a lot of people are saying that, and a lot of people are saying that *bad things* are happening out there. We're going to be looking at that and many other things." A few months later Trump announced he would like to bar Muslims from entering the country, among other anti-Islamic measures. Other Republican candidates and their supporters agreed. This assault on religious freedom in America was one of the most blatant in our country's history.

The most important weapons against religious prejudice in this country are the Americans who will stand up against it. When those around us make biased statements against people of other faiths, our silence is taken to mean support, and that gives the bigots confidence to continue. To them, silence is agreement. But when we cut them off with "I take offense at such bigotry" or even a simple "I disagree," we are stamping out small fires before they grow. We must not cower in a corner when people verbalize their prejudice, because it emboldens them and others.

Neither can we stand by and do nothing when legislators attempt to pass laws that interfere with religious freedom. The most prominent and insidious form is the misleadingly named Religious Freedom Restoration Act (RFRA). Congress passed a version of this in 1993 that stated that the religious liberty of individuals could be limited only by the "least restrictive means of furthering that compelling government interest." The U.S. Supreme Court decided that this law applied only to the federal government, which opened the door for individual states to pass their own versions, mostly intended to allow Christians to discriminate against others. When Indiana passed such a law in 2015, there was a national backlash and a call for boycotts. Angie's List, Salesforce.com, the state of Connecticut, the cities of San Francisco and Seattle and others threatened to cancel construction projects, travel conventions and other business enterprises in Indiana. The bill cost the state at least $60 million in lost tourist revenue.

Some questioned why all the attention was suddenly on Indiana when more than 20 other states and the federal government have passed similar laws. Here's why: Indiana's RFRA was similar to the other laws but had two fundamental differences from almost all the others. Indiana's law allowed for-profit businesses the same right as an individual or church to use this law to discriminate. And it allowed for-profit businesses to fend off a private lawsuit claiming discrimination.

The law was clearly a pouty response to the legalization of gay marriage in the state. The legislators would show government not to interfere with certain private moral choices by passing a government law that interfered with certain other private moral choices. Because this took place before the Supreme Court decision allowing same-sex marriage, it represented an attempt to defy a cultural awakening across the country in support of LGBT equality. In the face of the unexpected national uproar, scrambling Indiana politicians suddenly explained that the law's intention was not to discriminate. In fact, that was its *only* reason to exist. Even if no one actually used the law, it was still a loaded and pointed weapon with one intended victim: anyone who isn't *us*.

Why bring up the past? Because in 2015, 17 states introduced legislation to create or alter an existing religious-freedom law. In 2016, the Georgia and North Carolina legislatures passed similar "religious freedom" bills that allowed discrimination. Once again, institutions including Coca-Cola, the NFL, the city of San Francisco, Walt Disney and various Hollywood studios threatened to boycott many of those states. Even Indiana was back, a few months after the original debacle, trying to slip a revised version of the original act through the legislature.

3. Create more interfaith activities.

Fortunately, there are many Christian organizations that still live by their religious principles as a guide to what Christianity stands for. World Relief, a nonprofit organization started by a group of evangelical churches, is helping to relocate Syrian refugees in the U.S. "Jesus commanded us to love our neighbors," explained Amy Rowell, director of the Moline, Ill., office of World Relief. "The parable of the good Samaritan comes to mind, making it absolutely clear that our neighbors cannot be limited to those of our same ethnicity or religious traditions." The Roman Catholic archdiocese of New Orleans also discussed church support for the refugees: "Today, we face new challenges as we answer the Gospel call to welcome the stranger and care for the vulnerable . . . Catholic Charities is a grantee agency that receives refugees from many parts of the world, including the Middle East." Pope Francis even warned U.S. politicians, "To imitate the hatred and violence of tyrants and murderers is the best way to take their place."

One Sunday in 2015, a group of 200 Muslims, Jews and Christians in Washington, D.C., walked together in what they called "Faith over Fear: Choosing Unity over Extremism." Led by Imam Lyndon Bilal, Rabbi M. Bruce Lustig and Cardinal Donald Wuerl, the head of the Archdiocese of Washington, the group walked from Washington Hebrew Congregation to Washington National Cathedral to the Islamic Center, stopping at each to offer prayers for interfaith unity and asking at the Islamic Center, "Compassionate God, free us to love."

These faithful remind us all of our spiritual—and patriotic—duty. The more activities the various faiths do together, the more exposure each religion has to the other to demystify it. And the stronger each community will become.

THE LOVE YOU GIVE

The world has always been beset by the self-righteous, who are determined to force everyone to think as they think and do as they do. Religion is supposed to teach humility, but it often breeds arrogance and paranoia. Instead of seeing an opportunity for demonstrating tolerance and friendship, zealots see demons and enemies.

In the face of so much religious strife around the world, it's easy to become cynical about religion. Yes, it is used as a tool to brainwash the ignorant and the gullible unwilling to think for themselves. But it's also a commitment by millions of others to seek a path of harmony within themselves and with the world outside. To behave in a way that is worthy of their god and not an insult. To accept the challenge of being better than their base fears and desires. To celebrate what they have in common with one another rather than obsess over the differences. And to unite against those, even within their own faith, who would take that freedom away from anyone, even those of other faiths.

We could do worse than to follow the elegance of the Dalai Lama's statement "My religion is very simple. My religion is kindness."

4

Gender

THE VIEW FROM THE
FRONT YARD

"I've stayed in the front yard all my life.
I want a peek at the back
Where it's rough and untended and hungry weed grows.
A girl gets sick of a rose."
—GWENDOLYN BROOKS, "A SONG IN THE FRONT YARD"

I N THE 1960S, THE BRA BECAME THE SYMBOL IN A WITTY BUT
subversive crusade to show how women are confined by an oppressive society. Just being female was enough to get you rejected for a
job, a credit card or admission to college. In general, pay was meager,
respect was less, and the glass ceiling was so low women could barely
stand up, let alone rise through the executive ranks. Bras represented
a device designed to push up breasts—or to "lift and separate," as one
bra company promised—as if to display them as a woman's best asset,
representing their primary roles first as an object of lust and then as
an inevitable mother. To call attention to this implicit stereotyping of
women, some feminists chose to go braless in a "Ban the Bra" movement, prompting one Illinois lawmaker to call those seeking equal
rights "braless, brainless broads." This didn't mean that most women

stopped wearing bras, only that they didn't want apparel necessary for their daily comfort to be turned into a collar of submissiveness.

Today, the tampon is the needle on our cultural compass that points to the true status of women in America. In movies and TV shows, it is always a source of snickering humor, as strong men melt into squirming lumps of embarrassment or repulsion at the mere mention of one. It's often treated like a *Harry Potter* villain: That Which Must Not Be Named. Or a hilarious symbol of the defining but endearing differences between men and women.

Except that there's a much more sinister symbolism to the modest tampon as a statement of economic injustice. Food, clothing and medical supplies are among the items that are deemed necessities by the government and are therefore exempt from sales tax, but most states tax tampons and other feminine-hygiene products as nonnecessities. Why? Because it brings in a lot of money. California takes in $20 million a year taxing menstruation. In 2016, Utah convened an all-male panel of legislators who decided to continue the tax because the state needed the money. A *Los Angeles Times* editorial calling for the continuation of taxing tampons also cited the need for tax revenue. The argument that constitutional rights and dignity take second place to state budgets echoes every dark moment in our past, from slavery to child labor to union-busting.

Opponents of this tax refer to it as a "womanhood penalty," assessed for no reason except gender. It's hard to argue with that point, given the evidence: nearly 40 states and the District of Columbia tax menstrual products, yet Wisconsin does not tax Viagra, New York does not tax Rogaine, Michigan has an exemption for certain farm equipment, and Indiana does not tax barbecued sunflower seeds. Asked about the "tampon tax," President Obama commented, "I have no idea why states would tax these as luxury items. I suspect it's because men were making the laws when those taxes were passed."

Sadly, the U.S., which prides itself on equality for all, is way behind in actually doing something about this clear inequality. While more than a dozen states have rejected the tax and others are introducing similar legislation, Canada has already banned it, and the European Union is following suit. Some states are also considering legislation to make tampons available for free in schools, because girls who might be unprepared for an unexpected period choose to stay home from school or cut class. Those who can't afford tampons sometimes use toilet paper, which can cause infection.

It's great that states are finally reviewing their arcane and sexist laws. But the real issue is, Why did it take them so long in the first place? And why hasn't every state already just admitted it was a bad—and unconstitutional—idea and fixed it? Because discriminating against women is an ancient tradition. Women have been economically exploited for centuries, and the general indifference over it being done today is the real revelation. And national shame. First Lady Michelle Obama expresses the experiences of many women when she describes her personal journey as a woman in America: "As I got older, I found that men would whistle or make comments about how I looked as I walked down the street, as if my body were their property, as if I were an object to be commented on instead of a full human being with thoughts and feelings of my own. I began to realize that the hopes I had for myself were in conflict with the messages I was receiving from people around me. Messages that said that, as a girl, my voice was somehow less important. That how my body looked was more important than how my mind worked. That being strong and powerful and outspoken just wasn't appropriate or attractive for a girl."

As a Muslim, I am well aware of the various harmful practices against women that are done in the name of Islam, just as we are all aware of similar practices endorsed by the Old and New Testaments and in the Vedas of Hinduism. Orthodox traditionalists will always insist on following religious texts to the letter, even though they were more the reflection of unenlightened cultures than the theologies of salvation. But many modern Christians, Jews, Muslims and Hindus are fighting to change that way of thinking by applying the core principles of their faith—treating others with kindness, humility and equality—to a contemporary culture.

My own journey from being a traditionalist, at the time of my conversion when I was in my 20s, to being a committed advocate for women's rights is like any spiritual journey—filled with obstacles and mistakes from which we must learn in order to mature. Sometimes when I look back at myself as a young man and the smug opinions I held, I'd like to hop in a time machine and go back to kick my own ass. But as all men should, I learned and grew through my relationships with women, especially with my daughters. Seeing the challenges they faced because of their gender, I realized I had to champion them in order to create a world in which they would not need a champion because they would be their own advocates. Today, my goal, as with many people of various faiths, is to focus on ways to bring all people together in harmony and tolerance in a world in which every person has an equal opportunity to achieve happiness and success.

THE EASIEST S.A.T. QUESTION EVER: WHAT DO WOMEN WANT?

Sigmund Freud once famously wrote to his psychoanalyst colleague Marie Bonaparte, "The great question that has never been answered, and which I have not yet been able to answer, despite my thirty years of research into the feminine soul, is 'What does a woman want?' " Since Freud's admission of failure and frustration, we've had eight decades of lively discussion regarding that question.

But Freud was wrong. The great question isn't "What do women want?" They've been telling us very passionately and articulately what they want for years. Articles, books, songs and movies abound with answers. Television shows, from *Sex and the City* to *Oprah* to *The View* to *Younger* to *Girlfriends' Guide to Divorce*, as well as all the *Real Housewives* reality shows, attempt to answer this question from multiple perspectives of age, ethnicity and economic status.

The *real* great question is, Why are so many people—including other women—determined to keep them from having what they want? A 2016 *Washington Post*/Kaiser Family Foundation poll found that 94 percent of adult Americans believe that men and women should be social, political and economic equals. If 94 percent of Americans are for equality for women, why doesn't America have it?

A clue can be found in another statistic: only 18 percent of Americans consider themselves "feminists." That severe disconnect Americans have between the term "feminist" and the ideal of gender equality gets to the heart of why we are still arguing over a topic that should have been settled long ago.

Many people just don't like the word *feminist*. For some males, it echoes the word *feminine*, which they think would be unmanly to be associated with. According to social convention, they are not wrong. The main way boys insult one another is to accuse each other of being somehow like a girl. To have characteristics of a girl, to do things the way a girl does, to like things girls supposedly like—these are the worst epithets boys can wield. For a male to call another male a bitch is to say he is submissive or whiny or nagging. In other words, girly.

Sports coaches do a lot to perpetuate this dangerous and dumb attitude by using gendered insults to motivate their athletes. "Pick it up, ladies!" "Hit the ball harder, Alice!" "My daughter can jump higher!" "Where's your purse?" "Did your skirt get in the way?" These early role models who most embody the male mystique to impressionable boys are often perpetuating misogyny. Using the term "pussy" to accuse someone of being afraid or weak spreads the idea that those are typical female traits. The ever-popular insult of calling someone a "douchebag" suggests that the device is somehow odious because it cleans the vagina, which perpetuates the idea that vaginas are inherently unclean. More insulting and accurate, and less derogatory to women, would be to call someone an "enema bag." As long as we continue to use language that identifies females with negative traits, gender equality is impossible.

The widespread use of disparaging language shows how trapped we are in the swamp of gender definitions and stereotypes. Some men are more afraid of being labeled feminine than they are of undoing a constitutional and moral wrong that affects half the country, including their own mothers, sisters and daughters. Worse, these destructive stereotypes are enforced just as much by some women as by men.

Certain people argue that feminists would be more successful if they rebranded their name as something more consumer-friendly by being gender-neutral, such as "humanist" (which is already taken) or "equalist" (which sounds like an advocate of artificial sweetener) or "genitalist" (which sounds like you've been banned from being within 300 yards of any schools). There is a practical side to that suggestion. The civil rights movement would have faced a lot more resistance if its participants had called themselves "blackists." But in the end, I disagree with de-gendering the name to accommodate the skittish. Embracing the name acknowledges that we are overcoming the stigma attached to being female; changing the name perpetuates that stigma.

Others who shun the feminist label include men and women who identify feminists as extreme radicals who want more rights for women than men have. They are similar to those who reject Black Lives Matter in favor of All Lives Matter because they argue that we shouldn't consider one group's lives to matter more than another's. Absolutely true, but the point is that white lives are not in danger because of the color of their skin. Same principle here: men certainly have problems that are gender-specific and that need to be addressed, but their civil rights are not restricted as women's are.

Some women argue that feminists demand that all women must have high-powered jobs as well as manage families in order to be fulfilled. They worry that making any other life choices—to be a housewife or a model or childless or raising many children—will result in their being judged by feminists as stupid or shallow or a gender traitor.

None of that is accurate. The Merriam-Webster definition of feminism is simple: "the belief that men and women should have equal rights and opportunities." There is nothing there about women receiving preferential treatment or that job standards should be lowered to accommodate women. Just equal rights and opportunities. So if you are one of the 94 percent for equality for women, then you should be, by the definition of the word, a feminist. All the other fears about manliness, radical rights demands or having-it-all role models have nothing to do with the basic goal of feminism.

The fact that most Americans claim they are for gender equality and yet only 1 in 5 define themselves as feminists is a triumph of cultural brainwashing by industries, corporations, religions and politicians who monetarily profit from that discrimination. Morality in America is often a marginal note next to the financial bottom line. If a company can get away with paying workers less, then it will. Multiply that by millions of workers, and we're talking about billions of dollars going into private jets and mansions in the Hamptons.

This same discrimination spills over to Americans with gender identities that differ from those of the mainstream, including gays, bisexuals, transgenders and transsexuals. Gender identity is an integral part of the feminist movement because of the general prejudice in our culture that anything tainted with being female is inferior and that those not satisfied with their gender roles (as defined by society) are perverse. To persecute anyone because of what gender they are or what gender they want to be or what gender they identify with is the same type of bigotry that is used to justify all other discrimination. The simple truth is that no one's free unless everyone's free, because permitting any prejudice encourages all prejudice.

ARE WOMEN TREATED EQUALLY IN AMERICA?

If you believe women are treated equally to men in America, then either you are under 5 years old or you don't follow the news, watch TV or observe the world around you. Entire books and websites are dedicated to cataloging in great detail all the ways in which we undervalue women in the workplace and at home and demean them in society. But a small sample of news items will give an overall perspective of the status of women in America today:

MONEY AND JOBS:

▸ Women make about 13 percent less in federal jobs than men. In part, this is because they occupy jobs on the lower end of the pay scale. But a 2014 study found that federal agencies more often set higher starting salaries when hiring men than women, even for the same jobs.

► In 2015, author Catherine Nichols decided to submit her novel to agents under her own name as well as under a male name. Under the male name, she sent 50 queries and received 17 manuscript requests. Under her name, she sent the same letter and manuscript pages to 50 agents and received only two manuscript requests.

► A 2012 study echoes the above results, but in the field of science. Male and female scientists who were given identical application materials for a lab-manager position, some with a male name and some with a female name, ranked the "female" applicants significantly lower than the "males" in competence and suitability for the role. When females were chosen, they were offered less money than males for the same position: an average of $26,507.94, compared with $30,238.10.

► A 2015 report from McKinsey & Company and LeanIn.org found that, contrary to conventional wisdom, women do not drop out of corporate jobs more often than men but are actually more loyal to their companies. Despite that, in the year the study was released, there were only 24 female CEOs of *Fortune* 500 companies in the U.S. The study concluded that gender bias was the main reason for this disparity. "Some of the biggest barriers are cultural and related to unconscious biases that impact company hiring, promotion and development processes," said Dominic Barton, global managing director of McKinsey & Company. At the current rate, the researchers estimated, it would take 100 years to achieve gender parity.

► A lifetime of wage discrimination or forced gender roles has serious repercussions in retirement. Older women generally receive $4,000 less annually in Social Security benefits than men.

► After the New York City Department of Consumer Affairs compared almost 800 products that were virtually the same but packaged differently for marketing to males and females, they found that females paid a "gender premium" of an average of 7 percent more for the same product. Urban Outfitters charged 24.6 percent more; Levi's, 24.3 percent more. Other studies confirm this finding in other areas. Women pay 25 percent more for haircuts that require the same amount of labor and 27 percent more to launder a white cotton shirt. According to Lea Goldman in an article in *Marie Claire* magazine, "on average women pay $151 billion in extra fees and markups that men don't have to pay."

▸ Many people take comfort in reports that large corporations are instituting diversity policies. However, according to an article in the *Harvard Business Review*, these efforts are not really working. Mostly, the effect of such programs is to make white men in management feel as if women and minorities are being treated fairly, even when they aren't. In addition, white men at companies with diversity programs tend to feel as if they might be discriminated against, even when they aren't.

▸ According to a University of Southern California study, only 1.9 percent of the directors of the 100 top-grossing movies from 2013 to 2014 were women. In fact, the number of female directors of big-grossing movies has declined over the past 12 years. Films directed by women tend to feature more female roles and women working behind the cameras. And the issue isn't just jobs in show business. Having fewer women involved in Hollywood means having less of their voice and perspective as a part of our culture.

SAFETY:

▸ According to the U.N., 95 percent of all aggressive and denigrating behavior in online spaces is aimed at women. This results in women being afraid to share opinions and comments, which silences valuable voices and excludes them from cultural exchanges.

▸ More than 70,000 rape kits have gone untested nationally, a situation that will take years to clear. Not only does this prevent justice from being done for rape victims, it also allows rapists to continue to assault women.

EDUCATION:

▶ A 2014 mega-study of more than 300 studies from around the world concluded that girls do better in school than boys in all subjects, including math and science, all over the world—and have done so since 1914. Susan Voyer, one of the study's authors, concluded, "The fact that females generally perform better than their male counterparts throughout what is essentially mandatory schooling in most countries seems to be a well-kept secret, considering how little attention it has received as a global phenomenon." However, the perception that girls are less capable in math and science has resulted in women being offered fewer jobs and less grant funding within STEM professions. One female postdoctoral scientist said that it wasn't until she began adding male colleagues' names to her research papers and grant applications that she suddenly received more funding and was published more often.

▶ The governing body of college sororities prohibits them from drinking alcohol in the sorority house or hosting parties that serve alcohol; if sorority sisters want to throw a party where they can drink, they have to co-host with a fraternity at whose residence booze is allowed. This results in fraternities controlling the sororities' social status on campus, making the women dependent on the men.

SOCIAL STATUS:

▶ The United States is one of the few democratic countries in the world that has refused to ratify the United Nations' Convention on the Elimination of All Forms of Discrimination Against Women. This sends a signal to American women that they are valued less here than in other democratic countries.

▶ A study published in the *Proceedings of the National Academy of Sciences* in 2014 found that hurricanes named after women killed more people than those named after men because people who lived in affected areas took them less seriously. The study said that changing a hurricane's name from male to female could result in the death toll tripling.

What makes this fight so difficult to win is the constant backlash against women each time they make progress. It's as if America is at war with its own conscience. We know what the right thing to do is, but we're afraid of the changes that come with doing the right thing. According to Pulitzer Prize winner Susan Faludi, who documented this phenomenon in her remarkable 1991 book *Backlash: The Undeclared War Against American Women,* "The anti-feminist backlash has been set off not by women's achievement of full equality but by the increased possibility that they might win it. It is a preemptive strike that stops women long before they reach the finish line." Not much about that has changed in the 25 years since it was written.

This backlash manifests itself in people actively opposing gender parity, but more damaging is when it shows up as ignorance and indifference. That seems to be the case now: a 2016 survey from the Fawcett Society found that older Britons were more concerned than younger Britons about equality between men and women. Ninety-two percent of men over 65 said they want equality of opportunity. Many young people seem to take all the progress for granted, unaware that the forces of resistance must be constantly challenged. So if we're counting on the next generation to carry on the fight, we may be in for some disappointment.

HOW IS GENDER DISCRIMINATION EVEN POSSIBLE?

The math just doesn't add up. How can females, who make up 50.8 percent of the population in the U.S., be socially and economically enslaved when they have the sheer numbers to stop it?

Part of the reason is that most of the country—men and women—is yoked by archaic notions of gender roles that are detrimental to everyone. Men are big, strong protectors and providers; women are submissive nurturers. In the media, we've tinkered with those Ken-and-Barbie ideals through the portrayal of tough, smart, independent women who can kick ass physically and professionally. But not that much has really changed on Main Street.

A 2015 study in the *Personality and Social Psychology Bulletin* suggested that although men might say they like smart women, in reality they prefer not to date such women. In the first phase of the study, a questionnaire, 86 percent of the men said they would feel comfortable dating someone smarter than them. However, by the second phase of the study, in which the men were told they would meet their female counterparts, men felt uncomfortable and less masculine around smarter women and even tried to distance themselves physically. There's a difference between what men might like on the TV or movie screen and what they want at home. So while men applaud these new-millennial women in fiction, in real life they just can't seem to take that leap of faith.

This study reveals a damaging dynamic in male-female relationships. In the past, men's fear of smarter women prompted women to act less smart in order to attract men. Or worse, girls would value education less because guys didn't want them to be too smart, so they didn't pursue education or a career, leaving them financially dependent on men. This behavior perpetuates the social stigma that women aren't as smart as men, and it makes it harder for them to earn the respect and rights they deserve.

Evidence shows that these cultural biases are persistent in other developed countries as well as the U.S. A U.K. study of 14-year-olds for the University of Warwick's Centre for the Study of Women and Gender found that gender stereotypes had a detrimental effect on the girls and boys being observed. Girls put themselves on restrictive diets in order to be thinner, though they were all of a healthy weight, and tended to avoid sports so as not to appear too boyish. Boys exerted their manliness through daily physical contact, from friendly smacks to actual fights. Some of these young teen boys drank alcohol to excess. But when the children were interviewed alone, each said they didn't like the gender roles they were expected to follow.

Part of the problem in America is that the War on Political Correctness gets in the way of understanding what's best for our children. That term is so loaded that to most people it stands for an elitist push for liberalizing social rules and labels and thus a relentless attack on the comforting traditions we were raised on. But much of what is labeled PC amounts to practical adjustments to ways in which society has already changed. This is an emotional journey every generation has had to go through. The raw sensitivity to this challenge was apparent in the angry response among many to Target's 2015 decision to stop the gender-specific labeling of toys and certain bedding. The outrage that followed, which often included the phrase "too politically correct," was almost entirely because the angry patrons *didn't understand what Target was doing or why.* The company had made the changes because of earlier customer complaints for the opposite reason: toy labels that seemed stuck in the 1950s. Target decided to stop labeling toys as gender-specific so that the children and parents could decide for themselves which toys best suited the children's interests. If a girl wanted a building set, she wouldn't be dissuaded or stigmatized by a "Boy's Building Set" label on the toy. The decision actually gave parents and children more options and control, but parents were so consumed with hatred of the concept of political correctness that they couldn't think straight about it. Some on Fox News said they'd be too confused and not know what to buy for a child. If you need a label from Target to tell you what to buy for your kid, you're so removed from that child that buying any toy isn't going to help. Plus, as we noted earlier, some toys labeled for girls are automatically more expensive than the same toys labeled for boys.

The big reveal is that those fixed notions of what a woman is and what a man is aren't even scientifically accurate. Although many people are convinced that most men and women are hardwired with specific traits that define that gender, recent scientific studies tell us that many of those assumptions are false. The idea that women are from Venus and men are from Mars in the way they think and behave may have more to do with cultural foot-binding to force mangled conformity than with actual brain chemistry. A 2015 Israeli study using MRI scans of 1,400 brains of men and women confirmed what other studies have suggested: at most 8 percent of the subjects had brains that were composed of all "male" or "female" structures. More than half contained a mix of structures, suggesting that most people, rather than being clustered around either the male or female end of the gender spectrum, fall somewhere in between, sharing characteristics traditionally assigned to one gender. Much current research indicates that gender identity is molded through the interaction of genetic, hormonal, experiential and environmental influences. "The idea of a unified 'masculine' or 'feminine' personality turns out not to describe real people," explained Daphna Joel, one of the authors of the Israeli study.

Gender identities are so rigid in America that any variation or attempt to step outside their confines is often condemned. Sometimes it results in physical and emotional abuse. Sometimes it involves job discrimination or social ostracism. More than 40 percent of gay employees said they were harassed and discriminated against at work, while nearly 90 percent of transgender individuals reported the same experience. The personal cost to each of those people is immeasurable, but the financial cost to America is measurable. According to a 2012 report, workplace discrimination against employees because of race, gender or sexual orientation results in a cost to businesses of $64 billion annually in terms of such factors as lost business and impact on employee health and well-being.

The story of pink and blue reflects our confused and panicky relationship with gender identity. Currently, many males refuse to wear pink because it's so clearly a female color, while many females champion pink for its feminine allure. Historically, it's just the opposite, as this 1918 article from a trade publication explained: "The generally accepted rule is pink for the boys, and blue for the girls. The reason is that pink, being a more decided and stronger color, is more suitable for the boy, while blue, which is more delicate and dainty, is prettier for the girl." A 1927 TIME article noted that some felt there was no consensus. The fashion reversal started in the 1940s and holds fast to this day. Even in today's more enlightened times, many American males refuse to wear pink out of fear it would undermine their masculinity in the eyes of others. Sadly, they might be right.

The point is that much of the behavior and preferences that we think are natural to specific genders are merely cultural conventions unrelated to gender. Some are commercially driven in order to make money. This is not to suggest men and women don't have fundamental physiological and psychological differences. Science will sort out the minutiae of what those differences are and why. The issue isn't really whether there are differences but rather that we have declared, through how we treat women, that the differences demonstrate one gender to be superior to the other and therefore more deserving of rights and opportunities. From jobs to reproductive rights, women are still reminded on a daily basis that they are not as valuable as men.

The heart of this justification that one gender is superior comes down to the most primitive reason of all: physical strength. I'm reminded of a powerful scene in the second season of *True Detective* in which detective Ani Bezzerides (Rachel McAdams) explains why she carries so many weapons: "Could you do this job if everyone you encounter could overpower you? I mean, forget police work. No man could walk around like that without going nuts. The fundamental difference between the sexes is that one of them can kill the other with their bare hands."

The physical danger for women is very real. A third of all women murdered in the U.S. are killed by male partners; only 2.5 percent of murdered males are killed by their female partner. Women are the victims in 85 percent of domestic-violence incidents. More than 18 percent of women in the U.S. have survived a rape or attempted rape. Of all women raped or sexually assaulted in the U.S. in 2010, the attackers in 48 percent of the cases were friends or acquaintances, and 17 percent were intimate partners; only 25 percent were strangers. The physical threat alone makes it difficult for women to trust men, but the knowledge that society conspires to restrict their rights and opportunities makes it difficult to trust anyone.

WOMEN ON CAMPUS: DEGREES OF SAFETY

Imagine you lived in a neighborhood in which 1 in 5 people was violently assaulted. And that the officials chose not to bother investigating 40 percent of assault victims' complaints. Would you continue to live in that neighborhood? Probably not. Especially if you had children.

That dangerous neighborhood actually exists. It's called college.

This year American parents will send more than 20 million of their 18-to-24-year-old daughters to attend colleges and universities. Besides the ivy-covered walls, homecoming bonfires, administrative support and lifelong friendships we hoped for them, we'll be sending some of them into groping hands, drug-laced drinks, administrative indifference and lifelong trauma. As Vice.com reported, "it's more likely that a woman will be sexually assaulted during college than it is that she will get the flu."

Go, Tigers.

California recently enacted legislation to make it easier to prosecute offenders. SB967, popularly known as the Yes Means Yes law, obliges those engaging in sexual activity to first give "affirmative conscious and voluntary agreement." That means they have to specifically say "yes" before any sexual contact. This is an improvement over the previous No Means No protocol, because sexual aggressors could claim a woman didn't say no to their advances, even though the woman might have been incapacitated through drink or drugs (whether self-administered or given to her without her knowledge) or because of being frightened by threatening or violent behavior on the part of the male. Apparently, some males believe that being passed out is a woman's coy consent.

Such legislation is especially necessary in light of the widespread negligence of our colleges and universities to protect their students by educating them about consent and especially by thoroughly investigating *all* claims of sexual assault. When it comes to both those necessities, college administrators today receive an F-minus. And those administrators and campus security personnel who neglected their duty to launch earnest investigations of sexual-assault claims should, at the very least, be fired from their jobs, if not sued or charged with criminal negligence.

Maybe that sounds harsh, but they've been entrusted with our children and the future success of our society. Their negligence is the result not of ignorance but of greed: protecting their brand so they can lure more unsuspecting students, grants and alumni donations. How is this so different from some primitive tribe sacrificing its children to the gods in hopes of a better harvest? Worse, how is this so different from the behavior of sexual predators?

The danger is magnified by the widespread college policy of allowing students accused of sexual assault to simply withdraw before their disciplinary hearings and transfer to another school, with no specific record on their transcripts that they might be a threat. Though there are dozens of such cases known, the most egregious involves Jesse Matthew Jr., who was convicted of murdering a University of Virginia student and a Virginia Tech student. Numerous times, he had been accused of sexual assault at a college, only to leave that school and enroll in another. Each time he transferred, officials from the school Matthew left did not discuss the accusations against him, though they legally could have. It's a severe case of Not My Problem, which has already killed more people in this country than Ebola.

Colleges that ignore the problem are encouraging it to grow. As institutions of learning, they aren't charged with just teaching the nuances of mathematical equations and the uses of metaphor in poetry; they are supposed to be teaching social values, at least by their own example. Any tolerance of sexual assault teaches those students that women are somehow deserving of less protection than men in society, that sexual aggression by men is perfectly OK, and that even if we huff and puff about how it isn't OK, nothing much will be done about it. It's not enough to provide panic buttons around campus or train female students how to be alert to predators. We must attack the bros-before-hoes mentality as not cool or high-five-worthy.

As a former college athlete, I'm especially aware of the culture of entitlement that some athletes feel as they strut around campus with the belief they can do no wrong. A study by researchers Jeff Benedict and Todd Crosset cited on the website of the National

Coalition Against Violent Athletes (ncava.org/statistics) concludes that although male student-athletes make up only 3.3 percent of the campus population, they constitute 19 percent of sexual-assault perpetrators and are responsible for 1 in 3 college sexual assaults. While the general population has a conviction rate of 80 percent when tried for such crimes, the conviction rate of college athletes is only 38 percent. When you add to that the statistic that indicates that a rapist on a college campus will have raped seven times before being caught and, if not convicted, will probably continue his behavior, you have the makings of a horror film.

Schools should play a role in changing male behavior and self-image, but the process must start in other areas, including in the home and in the media, because these are where our children learn about gender identities. Where do guys get the idea that it's OK to pursue sex even when the woman isn't interested? They get the idea from testosterone thrumming through their brains, but they get the entitlement from subtle social cues. Having a biological impulse is not a license. Every time we tolerate the unironic use of the word "bitch," we're encouraging this view of women as inferior. Every time we tolerate phrases like "don't be such a girl" as put-downs, we're promoting the notion of the woman as prey. Every time we see a movie or TV show in which a woman tells a man she hates him and he then forces a kiss on her, which she at first resists but then melts into, we're advocating sexual assault as being "romantic."

Legislating romance is a tricky business. And California's bill is not without some word-definition problems. But it's a giant leap for humankind in doing what our colleges have been irresponsible in not doing: protecting students. Some opponents complain that stopping to say "Yes, I want to have sex with you" will somehow kill the mood. Do they really think that two college students who are about to have sex will be deterred by having to articulate their desire? With 57 percent of college students being female, it's time that other states enacted legislation similar to California's, not just to protect women but also to promote the ideals of equality that these schools teach in the classrooms but don't enforce on the campuses.

A few years ago, I saw a *60 Minutes* interview with the singer Mary J. Blige in which she talked of her sexual molestation at age 5 as well as the brutal violence men in her neighborhood committed against women. "Men . . . didn't have any mercy," she said. Of course, she didn't mean all men; she was commenting on a child's view of the world through observing ceaseless assaults. That phrase has resonated with me. I don't want one more child to see the world that way. This legislation won't solve the problem, but it's a step. A step toward mercy.

"DANCE: 10; LOOKS: 3": WHAT WE SEE WHEN WE SEE WOMEN

In her novel *The Bluest Eye*, Toni Morrison writes, "Along with the idea of romantic love, she was introduced to another—physical beauty. Probably the most destructive ideas in the history of human thought." Setting aside the romantic-love idea for another time, Morrison's harsh assessment of social ideals for physical beauty as destructive is accurate. We have established a definition of beauty for women so narrow that almost no one can live up to it. We display these paragons of attractiveness on billboards and magazine covers and in Victoria's Secret ads with the full knowledge that because of the use of photo enhancing, lighting, makeup and other morphing techniques, the women shown are as real as the computer-generated Hulk in the *Avengers* movies. It doesn't matter that they aren't real; we demand of women to try, damn it, to live up to these images.

There is plenty of evidence of how harmful this notion is to society, with women struggling to fit within social expectations of thin, youthful sexuality as constricting as a Victorian corset or Spanx shorts. One of the most poignant moments in the musical *A Chorus Line* is when one of the dancers explains to the other dancers why she chose to have silicone implants. Frustrated that she wasn't booking dance jobs, she swiped her assessment card after an audition and saw that they had graded her "Dance: 10; Looks: 3." As she struts in front of her competitors, she brags, "Tits and ass / Had the bingo-bongos done / Suddenly I'm getting national tours." As an added bonus, pre-surgery she was able to date only "strays and losers," but now her life has turned into an endless medley of guys in love with her. When this song first appeared in 1975, during the height of the women's liberation movement, it was a cautionary tale about the sad desperation and self-deception of a woman changing her looks to fit an arbitrary and ultimately destructive model of beauty. Today it might be cheerfully (and misguidedly) embraced as proactive advice for empowering a woman to get what she wants.

That shift in attitude, mistaking enslavement for empowerment, is today's biggest obstacle to gender equality. The reason it's such a powerful enemy is that few are willing to admit to the delusion. Why? The usual reason: money. It is because of those who profit from perpetuating the unrealistic emphasis on physical beauty as the main measure of a woman's worth. This would include the American cosmetic-surgery industry, which every year rakes in $13 billion from more than 15.1 million cosmetic surgeries and minimally invasive procedures such as Botox. Doesn't it seem absurd that so many American women have had cosmetic surgery? That some 400,000 liposuction procedures, which involve sucking fat deposits from the body, are performed annually in the U.S.? That the death rate for this procedure, according to a study in *Plastic and Reconstructive Surgery*, is 20 in every 100,000 patients, higher than the annual death rate for car accidents? Fame and money do not protect anyone from the dangers. Liposuction and breast-reduction surgery contributed to the death of Kanye West's mother, Donda, and Olivia Goldsmith, the author of *The First Wives Club*, had a fatal reaction to anesthesia before she was to undergo a chin tuck.

A co-conspirator in perpetuating female insecurity is the cosmetics industry. The result is that American women far outspend those in all other countries: about $60 billion a year (up from $30 billion in 2003). Typically, a woman will spend about $215 a year on cosmetics. That adds up to about $15,000 over her lifetime; had she put the same amount of money into a standard retirement plan, she could retire at 70 with an extra $100,000.

Money is only a small part of the real cost. The more significant and harmful cost is the dismantling of women's self-esteem. Even though Americans spend the most on cosmetics overall in the world, we are ranked only 12th in "satisfaction with life." Sweden and the Netherlands, two countries that spend a lot less on hair care, skin care, fragrances and makeup, have higher rankings in the Satisfaction with Life Index.

Under the guise of helping women feel better and more confident, the "beauty" industry actually makes women feel worse because it creates a dependency on those products. Female preoccupation with appearance is a reaction to growing up being told that looks are their main asset in attracting men. Pop songs, TV shows, movies and young-adult literature mostly confirm this. And the dozens of women's magazines featuring svelte models whose images have been artificially manipulated establish the impossible standards they struggle to meet. Aliens browsing through these covers might think "Flatten your stomach and firm your thighs!" was a religious mantra for our culture.

Even pop songs that purport to dismiss these standards are actually enforcing the same basic idea. Meghan Trainor's song "All About That Bass" rejects the notion that only skinny girls are attractive, but it still links girls' self-worth to their physical attractiveness to boys: "I got that boom boom that all the boys chase." The harm in all the "real women have curves" and "All About That Bass" talk is that it's self-deceptive. It perpetuates the idea that a woman's worth is based on physical attributes, whether those are curvy or skinny. If a woman is troubled about weight, it should be based on her concern for her health, not what she's told that men want. If a man prefers you when you've shoved some squishy bags into your breasts, is that really the kind of man you want to spend your life with?

Part of the problem is that many women have been brainwashed to think their dependence on this image of beauty is their own idea, despite all the evidence to the contrary. We have several multibillion-dollar industries that are dependent on women feeling insecure about their looks and age and that do everything possible to encourage that insecurity to sell more products. And those industries grow larger every year. Women spend more of their money on beauty products and fashion than men and therefore have less money to spend on other things, which keeps them economically oppressed. Worse, the products can be detrimental to their health. Makeup can cause skin problems. High heels cause permanent issues such as irreversible damage to leg tendons, shortened calves, osteoarthritis, and knee and back injuries. Eight out of every 10 women say their shoes are painful, which parallels a study by the American Orthopaedic Foot and Ankle Society that concluded that *88 percent of American women wear shoes that are too small*, probably in an effort to conform to the wacky idea that smaller feet on women are more attractive. In spite of all that information, the average height of a high-heeled shoe has increased over the past few years from 3 to 5 inches, and complaints of foot pain have grown accordingly. Which shows how much in denial we are.

Women often defend their "beauty" choices by claiming they feel more empowered, more confident and more attractive by using all these products and restricting fashions. We have raised generation after generation of girls who are taught the joys of makeup from an early age until they become hooked. At first we think it's cute to see them sitting beside their mothers at the mirror giggling as they awkwardly apply lipstick. But then there comes a time when they are reluctant to ever leave the house without lipstick. We hear the self-deceptive cries of "It's my choice" and "I can stop anytime I want."

What exactly is the ideal image of beauty that women are chasing? Let's add it all up. First, let's put her in tight dresses that show her figure but restrict her movement. Second, let's put her in high heels that make her feet look smaller and display her butt but restrict her movement. Third, let's shave her body hair in places that define an adult female. What we are promoting as the paragon of beauty is the image of a prepubescent little girl whose movements are restricted and who is therefore in need of someone to take care of her. According to author Susan Faludi, "The 'feminine' woman is forever static and childlike. She is like the ballerina in an old-fashioned music box, her unchanging features tiny and girlish, her voice tinkly, her body stuck on a pin, rotating in a spiral that will never grow."

This stunted feminine ideal is just as destructive to males, who unnecessarily heap burdens of responsibility on their shoulders that result in them dying younger and living in worse health than women. Men's obliviousness to the problem is perfectly illustrated in the 1971 film *Carnal Knowledge*, directed by Mike Nichols, in which the two male characters (played by Jack Nicholson and Art Garfunkel) discuss their romantic problems while behind them a female ice skater twirls gracefully. She is the idealized version of a woman whom their pursuit of has ruined their ability to fully love the real women in their lives. For their part, women's obliviousness is illustrated in the Paula Cole song "Where Have All the Cowboys Gone?," in which a young woman dreams of a traditional male lover in the mold of tough, swaggering John Wayne–type cowboys: "Where is my John Wayne? . . . Where is my happy ending?" The reality is that the cowboy she married drinks at the bar every night while she is home with the children and doing the laundry, unnoticed by her husband.

Perhaps the worst aspect of this emphasis on beauty and youth is that it makes women more like perishable produce with a limited shelf life. If we keep pounding the cultural drumbeat that the most important aspect of a woman is physical beauty, then we condemn women to an early expiration date. On her show *Inside Amy Schumer*, the titular star satirized this in a skit called "Last Fuckable Day." In it, Schumer is picnicking in the woods with Tina Fey, Patricia Arquette and Julia Louis-Dreyfus, commemorating Louis-Dreyfus's last day as an actress men want to have sex with. They discuss how Sally Field went from being Tom Hanks's love interest in 1988's *Punchline* to playing his elderly mother six years later in *Forrest Gump*. The idea is that a Hollywood actress is valuable only as long as the males in the audience want to have sex with her—a reflection of women's worth in general in the rest of society.

Age makes Hollywood actresses less employable, but it also affects women in other fields. A recent study on long-term unemployment from the Federal Reserve Bank of St. Louis found that after the Great Recession a few years ago, employment prospects for women over age 50 worsened considerably. In 2006–07, right before the recession began, less than a quarter of the unemployed women over 50 had been out of work for more than six months. Six years later, more than half of the jobless women over 50 had joined the ranks of the long-term unemployed.

The valuation of a woman to society mostly based on her sexual desirability, which is in turn dependent on her youthfulness, is what drives the cosmetic, plastic-surgery and fashion industries. Without the insecurity that comes with them, these industries would go broke. Many of the women on the *Real Housewives* shows are prominent examples of living with this pressure. The first thing they say to each other almost every time they meet is a variation of "You look pretty." Many of them relied on their looks for work when they were younger, as actresses or dancers or models. Now, in middle age, they battle against aging the way Don Quixote fights the windmill giants—hopelessly. The reliance on makeup emphasizes their age rather than disguises it. It would be revolutionary if they just went about their days without all the fussing over hair, makeup, figures, spa treatments and Botox injections and announced to the world that sexy is not related to age but to attitude, to intelligence, to wit, to wisdom.

Hollywood both reflects and maintains this status quo, with aging male actors playing men with love interests played by actresses 10 to 20 years younger. This is rarely the case in reverse—just as it is a rite of passage for actresses to appear topless yet not for males to appear bottomless, which is the nearest comparable level of personal exposure. Oscar winners Halle Berry, Angelina Jolie, Jennifer Connelly, Charlize Theron and many others have done nude scenes. In fact, according to the new *Report on the Status of Women and Girls in California*, female characters are three times as likely to appear nude or partially nude in films as male characters. Nothing wrong with nudity in film, but it shouldn't be used as a device to confirm women's value as sexual beings first.

Yes, we value our mothers and grandmothers and female executives, artists and scientists, but we also put them through a lifetime of marginalization, taunts, insecurities and depression based on looks. We live in a culture wallpapered with images of sexualized young women, which makes women in general feel inadequate and men feel justified in asserting control. In 2015, during the presidential campaign, Donald Trump mocked GOP candidate Carly Fiorina's looks: "Look at that face! Would anyone vote for that? Can you imagine that, the face of our next president? I mean, she's a woman, and I'm not supposed to say bad things, but really, folks, come on. Are we serious?" True, he isn't "supposed to say" that—because it's offensive to all women to reduce their intellectual worth to their beauty as measured by anyone, let alone a man who has married two models and an actress, his current wife 24 years younger than he is. Or a man who tweeted a professionally lit photo of his wife in glamorous makeup next to a candid photo of his rival's wife to prove he's the superior candidate.

WOMEN IN SPORTS: WE LIKE STRONG WOMEN, BUT NOT TOO STRONG

The controversy surrounding women in sports is an example of forcing women to fit a narrow definition of beauty and body-shaming them if they don't. In 2015, Serena Williams won her 21st Grand Slam title at Wimbledon. This marked the 17th time in a row that she defeated Maria Sharapova. Yet Williams's status as the world's top female tennis player, which has earned her more prize money than any other female player in tennis history, has been continually overshadowed by the marketplace dominance of the woman she consistently beats. Sharapova earned $29 million from 2012 to 2013, $23 million of it from endorsements. Serena earned $20.5 million, but only $12 million in endorsements, about half of the amount earned by the woman she's now defeated 17 times in a row. How's that possible? Because endorsements don't always reward the best athlete. In this case, they reward the most presentable in terms of the Western cultural ideal of beauty.

In 2015, Misty Copeland became the first African-American

woman to be named principal dancer at the American Ballet Theatre. But when she was 13, she was rejected from a ballet academy for having the wrong body type: "Dear candidate, Thank you for your application to our ballet academy. Unfortunately, you have not been accepted. You lack the right feet, Achilles tendons, turnout, torso length, and bust," read the letter. At 13? The criticism of her body being too muscular and "mature" has followed her throughout her career. "There are people who say that I don't have the body to be a dancer," Copeland said in response, "that my legs are too muscular, that I shouldn't even be wearing a tutu, that I just don't fit in."

This translates in sports to women being more concerned with a marketable image than athletic ability. Tennis pro Agnieszka Radwanska is 5'8" but only 123 pounds. This is a conscious decision by her coach "to keep her as the smallest player in the top 10. Because, first of all, she's a woman, and she wants to be a woman," he said. Highly ranked tennis pro Andrea Petkovic said she hates seeing photos of her bulging arms when she hits a two-handed backhand. "I just feel unfeminine," she said. "I don't know—it's probably that I'm self-conscious about what people might say. It's stupid, but it's insecurities that every woman has, I think . . . I would love to be a confident player that is proud of her body. Women, when we grow up, we've been judged more, our physicality is judged more, and it makes us self-conscious," Petkovic was quoted saying in a 2015 *New York Times* piece. This reluctance to push themselves physically because doing so reduces their marketability as women results in their never striving to be the fully realized athletes they could be.

Sharapova, at 6'2" and 130 pounds (Williams is 5'9" and weighs 155 pounds), has confessed that she wishes she could be even thinner: "I always want to be skinnier with less cellulite; I think that's every girl's wish." (Is it? Should it be?) She does no weight training: "I can't handle lifting more than five pounds. It's just annoying. And for my sport, I just feel like it's unnecessary." Yet she has been beaten 17 times in a row by someone who has added the muscle necessary to excel. Her goal seems to be to look the part of the ideal woman in order to be the highest-paid female athlete rather than to be the *best* female athlete. In June 2016, Sharapova was banned from professional tennis for two years after she tested positive for use of the drug meldonium, which she said was to treat a magnesium deficiency but can also enhance athletic performance. Was she relying on medicine instead of muscle?

"I sing the body electric," Walt Whitman declared in his poem from *Leaves of Grass*. In that poem, he expresses Renaissance delight over the physical body as a source of pleasure, spirituality and achievement. If Americans are to similarly celebrate the body, we must question our current ideals of physical beauty. We need to overcome the brainwashing and make sure our ideals are healthy ones, not just convenient marketing images to create insecurity that will sell products. The fact that humankind's ideals of beauty have changed throughout history tells us that they aren't all hardwired into our brains. By broadening them, we can encourage females of all ages to strive confidently to reach their full potential.

HOW DO WE ACHIEVE GENDER EQUALITY?

We have the numbers: 85 percent of Americans want gender equality. The fact that we don't yet have it despite the majority's preference is an insult to the American political system. It's rejecting the spirit of the Constitution as well as the will of the people.

We know who the enemy is: industries that seize on and perpetuate impossible beauty standards in order to sell unnecessary products and services, corporations that deliberately charge women more than men for the same product, and mostly our own compliance in denying the problem and its effects.

We need to recognize that gender equality may be the most important issue facing our society, because it cuts across all races, religions and economic strata and negatively affects the entire population. If Americans can't respond to this problem, how will we be able to unchain ourselves from other destructive ideas and behavior, no matter how steeped in tradition they are? It is a proving ground for rational thought over unthinking, traditional bias.

Some specific things we can do to bring about gender equality:

1. Convince people of the causes of inequality.

Americans often treat gender equality as an afterthought because most of its advocates are articulate and civilized in stating their case and calling for action. This may be an instance in which calmly and rationally discussing why women are invisible keeps them invisible, as if reason is more easily dismissed than fiery rhetoric. There are 157 million women in this country, and each one is in some way unconstitutionally denied rights and opportunity. For some, this leads to abuse, poverty, depression, unfulfilled dreams, eating disorders and even death. But as the rest of the world's prominent democracies progress in gender equality, in the U.S. it still remains a back-burner issue.

In October 1975, Iceland's women took it off the back burner. Frustrated with their lack of rights, 90 percent of Icelandic women went on strike in what they called Women's Day Off. They chose not to cook, clean or go to jobs. Instead, they took to the streets to protest. Stores and factories closed, and men were responsible for child care. The following day, they returned to their usual routine, but not everything was the same. Five years later, in 1980, Iceland elected its first female president. In 2005, another Women's Day Off took place. Today, Iceland is ranked the No. 1 economy in the world for gender equality. The U.S. is No. 20.

Rational discourse is important, but the issues can be more dramatically and effectively illustrated through overt actions. Public rallies and boycotts of stores that overcharge women would let the public know we think this issue is important. In the late '60s, stickers with the words THIS EXPLOITS WOMEN! were slapped wherever appropriate. It was an effective way to publicize disparity and shame some offenders into change. The issue must become more prominent and our response to abuses less laid-back. This includes not tolerating comments or terms that disparage women. Do we really want to wait for several more generations before we finally eliminate the harmful gender stereotypes that we are tethered to?

2. Pass new laws and enforce existing ones that protect gender identity.

The feminist movement needs to continue to fight alongside the LGBT community in pursuing equal rights. The heart of the discrimination is against gender identity, not just physical gender. As long as anything (or anyone) associated with the female gender is referred to as inferior in any way, the bias will continue. This does not mean we shouldn't acknowledge physical differences, but we shouldn't allow those differences to define people's capabilities or opportunities.

Many Americans are uncomfortable with accepting variations in gender identity—such as gay, lesbian, bisexual, pansexual, transgender, transsexual—because they see them as a threat to "traditional families." But America's idea of the traditional family has been evolving for the past six decades. In the past 56 years, the number of children living in households with two married heterosexual parents in their first marriage has dropped by 27 percent. The largest change is the increase in single parents, who constituted 9 percent of parents in 1960 and 34 percent today. Of those single parents raising a child, 83 percent are women. Although the families are different than they were back in the days of *Father Knows Best*, people still fall in love and raise children to the best of their ability. It's America's mission to make sure every individual has the option and support to do just that.

"Engraved on the front of the Supreme Court is the phrase EQUAL JUSTICE UNDER LAW, but as long as any Americans can be legally discriminated against, there is not equal justice in this country," said Representative Bob Dold in January 2016 when he became the first Republican to back federal equal-rights legislation for the LGBT community. The Equality Act, which amends the Civil Rights Act of 1964, bans discrimination on the basis of sexual orientation, gender identity and gender. But as we've seen with racial discrimination, having a law isn't enough. Law-enforcement agencies have to be motivated to enforce the laws. That occurs only when there is public pressure.

Similar laws need to be passed at the state and local levels to ensure broader enforcement. Business owners who charge women more than men for the same products should be fined significantly as well as face criminal penalties. These corporate executives steal millions from women and should be punished as thieves as they would punish a shoplifter in one of their stores. Currently, there is no federal law that requires businesses to set gender-equal prices on products.

3. Reduce the emphasis on physical beauty.

"Makeup is an apology for my face" is a pretty accurate expression. Some feminists argue that they use makeup as a way to express their power, sometimes through ironically exaggerated use. But a chain around the neck is still a chain, even if you bedazzle it. The act of purchasing and applying makeup itself is confirmation that however one looks is not good enough. And the only way to measure up to an artificial and unreachable standard is by spending time and money pursuing it.

Makeup is not the only oppressive beauty standard. A few years ago, a photo appeared in *People* magazine showing Julia Roberts waving to the crowd, exposing her unshaved underarms. *People* reported that British tabloids expressed outrage and dismay. Again, women who shave their underarms and legs claim they do so because it makes them feel cleaner and smoother, but the main reason is that men have been trained to prefer the malleable image of the forever young prepubescent girl. And women perpetuate this self-destructive fantasy every time they try to emulate it.

About 99 percent of women remove hair, 85 percent regularly, even daily. According to American Laser Centers, this adds up over a lifetime to $10,000 and two months of their lives. Because there is money to be made, hair-removal industries have persuaded many men that they, too, need to manscape. However, the practice of women shaving their legs and underarms wasn't common in the U.S. until around 1920–30, when fashions began revealing more skin. Several current movies and sitcoms joke extensively about the importance of women cutting or removing pubic hair in order to be more attractive to men. Why would looking less like an adult woman be more attractive? Justifications and rationalizations abound about how personal grooming is about being playful or taking control, but in the end it's about chasing a manufactured ideal that leaves women in perpetual fear and self-loathing.

We don't have to accept this. If women stopped shaving, stopped wearing restrictive fashions, stopped putting on makeup and stopped surgical and chemical enhancement, they would be healthier and happier. And so would men.

In her song "Mrs. Potato Head," Melanie Martinez compares women seeking plastic surgery to the Mrs. Potato Head toy, with interchangeable parts: "Kids forever, kids forever / Baby soft skin turns into leather / Don't be dramatic, it's only some plastic / No one will love you if you're unattractive."

Oddly, before it became mandatory for women to scrape off hair, slather on makeup and wobble on high heels, men found unshaved, makeup-free, low-heeled women sexually attractive. They fell in love with them, raised children with them and grew old together.

4. Include all classes of women.

Sheryl Sandberg's 2013 book *Lean In* advised women to be less docile and people-pleasing in pursuing their careers. That's great advice. But it's important to remember that the fight for female equality is not just about the mostly white middle- and upper-class woman. Even in new-wave feminism, which uses social media to discuss issues, the majority of women taking part in the discussion are from families with higher incomes and education levels. That's why it's important that the concerns of lower-income women are also addressed, such as increased day care at work, a higher minimum wage, access to medical services, grants for education, and increased public services to help with housing, food and employment. There is no female empowerment unless all women are included.

THE WAR OF THE WORLDS

People often refer, with a bemused grin, to a continuing "war between the sexes," as if it were a saucy parlor game in which the "combatants" end up giggling in an intimate embrace. All fun and games. But the phrase is much more revealing of a deeper issue. The word "war" implies a ferocity of differences between the two sides, as if no quarter can be given nor expected. However, it's not really a war when both sides benefit from the triumph of one particular side. Nor is it a war when one side is not trying to defeat the other side but merely to free itself from injustice, the way the colonists did during the American Revolution. In that way, it's not a war between the sexes but a war of independence, in which both sides are freed from harmful and limiting gender roles. Not a war between the sexes but a war *of* the sexes.

A war requires an army to meet the threat. And there's a question as to who is willing to face the enemy. Certainly, it will require both men and women fighting together. But it will also require massive support from the next generation, who will most reap the benefits of increased equality. However, some young women today think the war is over and that they have already won. The *Washington Post* started a new-wave-feminism project that the editors described in a troubling way: "This project explores how young women are taking a decades-old movement and making it their own. Their expression of feminism is more an embrace of individual freedoms than a shared struggle against oppression, more an online sprawl of dialogues than a political mission led by activists."

Unfortunately, there are no "individual freedoms" to embrace without a focused mission of activists. Laws don't just change; inequities aren't uncovered on their own; exploiters don't just see the light and stop. The civil rights movement, the women's liberation movement, the labor movement and the LGBT movement did not produce revolutionary changes in our society by discussions alone; they organized like-minded people to action, through protest, through pressing for legislation, through spotlighting bigotry wherever they found it. That's how real change occurs.

5

Class Struggle
ANOTHER DAY IN PARADISE

*"First feed the face
And then talk right and wrong."*
—"HOW TO SURVIVE," *THE THREEPENNY OPERA*

AMERICA'S MOST IMPORTANT PRODUCTS ARE NOT THE machines, electronics, aircraft and automobiles that are our country's top exports. Our most important product, the one that defines us to ourselves as well as to the rest of the world, is the star-spangled American dream. It's our uplifting promise that anyone from any background, no matter how humble, can rise to unlimited heights based on talent, drive and hard work. It is our Michelin-star signature dish, and it entices hundreds of thousands of people to our country, fuels a million high school and college valedictory speeches and inspires endless rags-to-riches movies, books and songs. We have all been blasted with the "land of opportunity" playlist from birth, like children in the backseat on a long drive forced to listen to their parents' oldies nostalgia. The million-to-one success story has become a song we can't get out of our heads.

Unfortunately, that song may be just a nostalgic oldie that sounds better sweetened through the filter of years than a realistic anthem of American beliefs. Recall the aforementioned polls from the *New York Times* (in 2014) and the Harvard Institute of Politics (in 2015) that indicated a declining belief in the American dream, particularly among America's youth. According to the *Times* poll, only 52 percent of Americans think our economic system is fair, with 45 percent believing it to be unfair. Not surprisingly, the higher the respondents' income, the more likely they were to believe the system is fair.

Most disturbing is that, according to a 2014 poll by CNN/ORC, 63 percent of Americans surveyed believe that most children will eventually be worse off than their parents. That's saying a lot, considering how bad off many Americans see their own future. In a 2012 Pew Research Center poll, 38 percent of Americans thought they would not have enough money to retire. How much worse off do they fear their children will be? The parents' concern for their children's future reminds me of one of my favorite films, *The Magnificent Seven*. A group of bandits is constantly raiding some poor Mexican villagers, stealing their food and killing them. No one protects them, so the villagers hire seven gunfighters who have fallen on hard times to train the villagers to fight to get rid of the bandits. When some village boys tell one of the gunmen, Bernardo O'Reilly, that they are ashamed of their fathers for being cowards, O'Reilly scolds them:

> "You think I am brave because I carry a gun; well, your fathers are much braver because they carry responsibility—for you, your brothers, your sisters and your mothers. And this responsibility is like a big rock that weighs a ton. It bends and it twists them until finally it buries them under the ground. And there's nobody says they have to do this. They do it because they love you, and because they want to . . . Running a farm, working like a mule every day with no guarantee [anything] will ever come of it. This is bravery."

The bravery of those who work so hard every day must be rewarded with at least the hope of their children having a better life. But that's not the case today.

There is much inequality in America—by race, gender, sexual orientation, gender identity, physical ability—but the most destructive of all is economic disparity, because the other inequities don't have a chance of being fixed until there is a realistic hope that hard work can lead to a substantially better life. Without that hope, those who are unfairly marginalized by society will continue to be pitted against one another and will fail to come together as a large, powerful force of change. Petty bickering over who is most aggrieved will distract us from the larger cause. And that's just the way those in power want it, because, while things have gotten economically worse for most Americans, they've gotten better for the top 10 percent. According to federal data, from 2010 to 2013, only those wealthiest 10 percent of Americans saw their median income rise. Those in the middle-income bracket experienced very little change in average real income, while those at the bottom 30 percent saw substantial declines. In 1989, the richest 3 percent of Americans possessed 44.8 percent of the country's wealth; by 2013, that figure had risen to 54.4 percent. During that same period, the share of America's wealth held by the bottom 90 percent declined from 33.2 percent to 24.7 percent.

The super-rich got super-richer; the rest got poorer.

Looking at these figures, one can understand the frustration of struggling Americans over the inaction of our millionaire politicians, who take donations from even wealthier millionaires and billionaires while slashing benefits and support programs for the neediest Americans. The median net worth of a member of Congress is $1.03 million, while the median American household has a net worth of $56,355. So while politicians blather on about "American exceptionalism," about our country having a special status and privilege in the world, do they have any idea what is going on inside our borders? That poor people actually pay more for many goods than do the rest of Americans? Take the humble toilet-paper roll. A University of

Michigan study found that the poor pay nearly 6 percent more per roll of toilet paper because they cannot afford to buy the discounted bulk sizes. Diapers have the same financial impact: they can cost poor families as much as $1,000 per child each year, which to the poorest segment is almost 14 percent of household income, compared with the top fifth segment, who spend 1 percent on diapers. Making the hardship worse, federal assistance programs have a diaper gap: food stamps can't be used on them, Medicaid doesn't cover them, and mother-child nutrition programs don't provide them.

The economic disparity that begins at birth continues throughout the lives of the poor. The substandard levels of life's necessities available to them—in nutrition, health care, education and more—lead to harsh, deprived lives. According to a study by the Brookings Institution, the poor in America live 13 to 14 fewer years than the wealthy, a gap that has doubled over the past 30 years. Condemning inequality on a global scale, Pope Francis declared, "Such an economy kills. How can it be that it is not a news item when an elderly homeless person dies of exposure, but it is news when the stock market loses two points?" American politicians can generally ignore the poor with impunity, since the poor vote less often than other Americans. In the 2016 presidential primary in New York, candidate Bernie Sanders claimed that he lost the state "because poor people don't vote . . . That's a sad reality of American society." He further claimed that in the 2014 election, "80 percent of poor people did not vote." But the dream has faded for working-class and middle-class Americans as well, who let loose their anger and created a populist upheaval in the volatile 2016 campaign.

Americans don't generally see themselves as having the same class conflict as other cultures, because we see our society as more fluid, with people able to transcend their birth status through hard work and diligence. Everybody is one *Shark Tank* pitch away from wealth. However, the real reason many Americans are less concerned about class differences is that they see the lower classes in terms of race more than economics. To America's majority, the poor are mostly black or Latino. According to the Institute for Research on Poverty, only 9.7 percent of the poor in the U.S. are white, while almost all of the rest of the poor are people of color: 27.2 percent are black, 25.6 percent are Latino, and 11.7 percent are Asian. This racial difference, which reassures white voters that the poor are not their people, is why poverty is a back-burner issue for many politicians.

Much of the heated rhetoric has been about casting blame toward immigrants, minorities and other outsiders. What we need instead is a much more positive focus on returning the luster to the American dream by making it a real possibility again—for everyone willing to work hard and sacrifice, not just those lucky lottery winners.

AMERICAN ME

A lot of people might consider me a poster boy for the American dream. I grew up in a working-class family during one of the most dangerous times to be black in America. The civil rights movement instigated a brutal backlash from some angry whites, who responded with beatings, bombings, imprisonment and murder. This social turmoil had a direct effect on me, even as a child. Attending a mostly white Catholic high school opened me to hurtful racial biases, not just from other students but from the curriculum as well. We were taught very little about black people of achievement, which sometimes left me feeling hopeless and worthless. While still a young teenager, I was accidentally caught up in a violent riot in Harlem during which I ran for my life. This further convinced me how disposable blacks were to mainstream society.

True, I went to college at UCLA, where I received an outstanding education while I played basketball, and I then had a 20-year career in the NBA. Fame has allowed me to hang out with some of the most famous and influential politicians, artists, musicians, actors and writers of the past four decades. There was also the opposite of inclusion: the ceaseless racial slurs and death threats from those who felt success belonged only to white people. But they were a small, insignificant group. In my last year in the NBA, thousands came out in every city I played to shower me with gifts and gratitude. After retirement, I've been welcomed as a commentator in major news out-lets. Everything about my life screams *American dream.*

But had I been a foot shorter, I could have been a high school his-tory teacher wondering if I could afford to retire yet. That, too, can be an American-dream success story, but for a lot of Americans, rising to the heights of being a high school teacher is just as out of reach as becoming a professional athlete.

The American dream is not about everyone in America becoming financially successful; it's about everyone in America having a realistic shot at the career of their choice, living in the neighborhood of their choice and raising their children in safety. The reason so many don't have a realistic shot is that higher education—supposedly the great class equalizer—is not a genuine option for those most in need of it to break the poverty cycle. In his book *Reaching and Teaching Students in Poverty*, George Mason University associate professor Paul C. Gorski dispels the myth of American education as the great economic equal-izer. The problem, he says, is that poor students start out at a disad-vantage in the earliest grades and have little chance of catching up:

> Unfortunately, schools as they are constituted today are not the equalizers they are cracked up to be . . . Poor students are assigned disproportionately to the most inadequately funded schools with the largest class sizes and lowest-paid teachers. They are more likely than their wealthier peers to be bullied and to attend school in poorly maintained buildings. They are denied access to the sorts of school resources and opportunities other children take for granted, such as dedicated school nurses, well-stocked school libraries, and engaging pedagogies. In fact, by these and almost every other possible measure, students from poor families, the ones most desperate to find truth in the "great equalizer" promise, appear to pay a great price for their poverty, even at school.

While schools serving poor children have, in general, worse teachers, less money and more-crowded classrooms than schools serving children from the middle class and up, studies have concluded that two thirds of student achievement is the result of factors outside of school, the most influential being economic status. The students often have parents with little education and strained relationships, so they don't receive the help or encouragement at home that students from families with higher incomes do. Poor students may receive subsidized meals at school, but they are less likely to have nourishing meals at home, a problem that starts early. Children growing up in poverty often receive poor nutrition as infants, which can result in their brain not developing at a typical pace. And they are more likely to live in buildings with environmental hazards that affect children's cognitive abilities.

What is significant isn't just that the problem is bad but that it's very rapidly getting worse. Although the U.S. has the largest economy in the history of the world, 22 percent of our children live below the federal poverty line. Many of those live in families that fight on a daily basis to meet the basic needs of food, clothing and shelter. In 2001, only four states had poor children as a majority of their schoolchildren. By 2011, 17 states reported that poor children constituted a majority. In only 10 years, the problem quadrupled. More bad news: the poor in America stay that way longer than in other countries in the industrialized world. Poor children in those countries have a better chance of realizing the "American" dream than American poor children do.

As an American-dream success story, I'm a great booster of the ideal. Yet even as I was reaping the benefits of my triumphs, I realized how many others with much harsher backgrounds wouldn't have the same opportunities. Over the years, I had hoped that as a nation we were moving in the right direction of being more generous, more inclusive, more aggressive in insisting on equal opportunity. However, that's not what has happened.

The American dream has become a fantasy promoted to blame

the poor for their own condition and celebrate the wealthy for their achievement. In his book *The New Class Conflict*, Joel Kotkin describes a modern-day "clerisy" class based on the medieval clergy whose job it was to promote those in power to the rest of the people, like spin doctors in clerical collars. In exchange for the PR hype, they were paid well and occasionally got to dine in their masters' Big House. Today, that clerisy consists of some academics, pundits, politicians and government officials preaching the gospel of "pulling ourselves up by the bootstraps" while fewer and fewer people can afford boots.

IT'S THE ECONOMY, STUPID

Campaign strategist James Carville helped guide Bill Clinton's victory over incumbent George H.W. Bush by focusing campaign workers on three simple messages, the most famous of which was "It's the economy, stupid." This message was so effective that despite Bush's approval rate of nearly 90 percent in 1991, just after the first Gulf War, by the following year 64 percent of Americans disapproved of his performance, leading to his re-election loss. The lesson of "It's the economy, stupid" is the same that Bertolt Brecht understood in 1928 when he penned these lyrics from *The Threepenny Opera*: "First feed the face / And then talk right and wrong." To those in need, the issues of food on the table and job security trump all others. To those not in need, forcing their well-fed morals on others is a priority.

About 46 million Americans (14.8 percent) live in poverty, a group about equal to the populations of New York and Texas combined. The U.S. government's definition of poverty in 2013 was a single person living on $11,490 a year and a family of four living on $23,550. That seems excessively conservative, considering that a study in California found that those with the lowest income spend two thirds of their income on housing. And the housing crunch isn't just for the poor: a 2015 report from Harvard University found that about half of all renters ages 25 through 34 in America are spending more than 30 percent of their income on housing, while a quarter are paying rent in excess of 50 percent of their monthly income. This problem spans all age groups.

With so much spent just to survive in life, there's little left over to have a lifestyle. Certainly not the kind Americans see on prime time. The dark reality of the situation is revealed through the Federal Reserve Board's recent survey that monitors the economic status of American consumers: 47 percent said that in order to cover a $400 emergency, they would need to borrow the money or sell something. Nearly half of Americans don't have a few hundred bucks to handle a crisis.

The statistics showing the level of economic disparity are so overwhelming that those on both sides of the political spectrum can agree for a change—the problem is serious. Presidential candidates in the 2016 campaign have all promised to get America working again and to rein in the Wall Street excess that has banking CEOs pulling in compensation in the tens and hundreds of millions. Even arch-conservative billionaire Charles Koch wrote a *Washington Post* op-ed article describing his agreement with self-described democratic socialist Bernie Sanders:

> The senator is upset with a political and economic system that is often rigged to help the privileged few at the expense of everyone else, particularly the least advantaged. He believes that we have a two-tiered society that increasingly dooms millions of our fellow citizens to lives of poverty and hopelessness. He thinks many corporations seek and benefit from corporate welfare while ordinary citizens are denied opportunities and a level playing field.
>
> I agree with him.
>
> Democrats and Republicans have too often favored policies and regulations that pick winners and losers. This helps perpetuate a cycle of control, dependency, cronyism and poverty in the United States. These are complicated issues, but it's not enough to say that government alone is to blame. Large portions of the business community have actively pushed for these policies.

Koch describes an *X-Files*–worthy conspiracy of government puppets and Big Business despots vigorously perpetuating poverty instead of fighting it. Koch's difference with Sanders, he explains, lies in how to fix the problem. Koch blames expensive but ineffective government programs, while Sanders has argued that the government has a duty to do much more. Yet despite the public braying by such powerful people, little is done to bring economic relief to those most in need.

The effects of the pervasive public hopelessness about the future are far-reaching. A hopeless populace gives rise to demagogues and hucksters who exploit the desperate people by promising instant remedies—at a cost to our American principles. Conservatives often point fingers at immigrants, particularly Latinos and Muslims, as the source of our woes. Though all the evidence contradicts these accusations, historically, people are more easily manipulated when given a common enemy to blame, as Germany did with the Jews during the Great Depression in the 1930s. Poor economic policies by the government, world economic problems in other countries and underhanded manipulations by Wall Street are too complex for most people to grasp. But if we put a human face on our troubles—Jews, Muslims, African Americans, the poor, immigrants—then we don't have to actually do anything to fight the real problem. While these cynical leaders make us accomplices to violating the Constitution, we merrily goose-step behind them while they point at whom to hate.

In 1964, President Lyndon Johnson introduced legislation that became the foundation for his War on Poverty. At the time, 19 percent of Americans were in poverty. By 2000, the rate had fallen to 11.3 percent, but by 2014 it had risen to 14.8 percent. An additional 33 percent, or 97.3 million, are classified as having low income, meaning they earn less than twice as much as the poor. All told, that means nearly half of all Americans are poor or low-income. Even worse is that the ruler for measuring poverty is still based on what it took to feed a family in the 1950s, a formula devised by Mollie Orshansky, a government statistician under Johnson. Each subsequent administration has been afraid to redefine it, because the number of poor would seem to have increased during their presidency. Yet in 2014, a Center for American Progress study found that 61 percent of Americans believe their income is below the cost of living. "Our aim," Johnson said a half-century ago, "is not only to relieve the symptom of poverty but to cure it and, above all, to prevent it." At first, the public supported this lofty goal. But by the 1970s, public sentiment had cooled because of politicians' accusations that we were turning into a welfare state. The War on Poverty turned into the War on the Poor, with Congress adopting a budget in 2015 that cut $5.3 trillion over 10 years (2016–2025), with two thirds ($3 trillion) of the nondefense budget cuts coming from programs for those with low or modest incomes. In the House of Representatives budget, $2.9 trillion was cut in health-care reductions for low- and moderate-income people; $125 billion was cut from Supplemental Nutrition Assistance Programs (SNAP, formerly known as food stamps); $159 billion was cut from tax credits for low- and moderate-income families; $300 billion was cut from other mandatory programs for those families.

The sentiment that justifies these budget cuts was infamously expressed by a software developer in San Francisco who wrote a letter to the mayor in 2016 complaining of having to see poor people around him: "The wealthy working people have earned their right to live in the city. They went out, got an education, work hard, and earned it. I shouldn't have to worry about being accosted. I shouldn't have to see the pain, struggle, and despair of homeless people to and from my way to work every day." Although many Americans would recoil at this statement, the current attitude in Washington seems to be that instead of seeking to cure poverty, we would ignore the poor and hope they stay in their ghettos.

How is it possible to get away with passing a budget guaranteed to make the problem worse? The obvious answer is that the poor don't cast ballots as often as those with higher incomes. A 2015 poll indicated that only 48 percent of those with a family income under

$20,000, below the poverty level, are regular voters. Compare this with the 78 percent who regularly vote among families with incomes over $475,000. The effort to maintain this voting disparity is taking place mostly in Republican-controlled states that have enacted voter ID laws that have little effect on the almost nonexistent voter fraud but an enormous effect on keeping the poor, the elderly and minorities from voting.

Skimping on help for the poor is a sweet deal for politicians because they can look as though they are being fiscally responsible without any repercussions in their cushy jobs. Unfortunately, the reality is that reducing these antipoverty programs has devastating repercussions for millions of Americans living on the edge of survival. A 2014 report issued by the Center for American Progress indicated that without federal programs such as SNAP, Head Start, Pell grants, Medicaid and Social Security, the poverty rate would be double what it is now.

Certain politicians and entrepreneurs conspire to keep the poor just as they are in order to financially exploit their condition. In 2014, on his HBO comedic news show *Last Week Tonight*, John Oliver ran an exposé of the payday-loan business and those who so callously abuse the desperation of the poor. How does an industry that extorts up to 1,900 percent interest on loans get away with it? In Texas, State Representative Gary Elkins blocked a regulatory bill on such businesses, despite the fact that he owns a chain of payday-loan stores. And the fellow Texas legislator who had badgered Elkins about his conflict of interest, Representative Vicki Truitt, became a lobbyist for ACE Cash Express just 17 days after leaving office. In Oliver's report, he showed how the poor are lured into loans in advance of their paychecks, only to be unable to pay back the money and then have to secure yet another loan. This practice is reminiscent of drug dealers giving prospective customers a taste and then hooking them into perpetual dependency.

Fast-food restaurants, with their low-cost fare and lower nutrition, set the table for a lifetime of poor health for the poor. A 2014 study in the *Journal of the American Medical Association Internal*

Medicine concluded that from 2005 to 2010, the diet of low-income Americans worsened while the diet of the wealthiest Americans improved. Contributing factors included the high cost of healthier meals and less access to quality supermarkets in poor neighborhoods. Although two thirds of Americans are overweight, that rate is even higher among the poor. Diseases associated with obesity account for 70 percent of America's health costs and have "a significant economic impact on the U.S. health-care system," according to the Centers for Disease Control. Nobody forces a person to eat a Big Mac, but when there aren't many affordable alternatives, those dollar menus can seem irresistible, despite the long-term cost.

When jobs and education seem out of reach, the American dream of financial security seems less the result of hard work and determination and more like a long-shot lottery: "You're my only hope, Set for Life Scratcher!" In 2014, Americans spent $70 billion on lottery tickets, with 54 percent of the tickets bought by 5 percent of the people, many by the poor. Critics call this a regressive tax, because the poor spend nearly twice as much money overall as those above the poverty level. State governments advertise in poorer neighborhoods to encourage residents to buy lottery tickets with the slim hope of rising out of poverty, which raises enormous revenue for the state but leaves the poor even poorer. In one low-income neighborhood in Chicago, the Illinois Lottery featured a billboard with the hopeful phrase "This could be your ticket out."

John F. Kennedy said, "Those who make peaceful revolution impossible will make violent revolution inevitable." Hopeless people do desperate things, which is how this country was formed. "No taxation without representation" was the colonists' version of "It's the economy, stupid." And while we will probably never face that kind of violent revolution here again, we are facing a revolution in the form of erosion of faith in the government's commitment to unify us. The exploitation of those in need of our help has created an infrastructure of poverty that should not be written off as acceptable losses or "friendly fire."

NOW WHAT DO WE DO TO FIX THIS THING?

A 2014 poll found that 86 percent of Americans surveyed agreed that the government has a responsibility to fight poverty, with 70 percent wanting Congress and the president to cut the poverty level in half within 10 years. The respondents also agreed that the three most important categories in reducing poverty are jobs, wages and education. We've known that for many years. The problem is that our commitment rises and wanes with the overall economy, and it needs to be a consistent policy of reform. We can accept economic fluctuations without changing our principles as Americans.

This list of suggestions is not comprehensive, nor is it meant to be. Experts have dedicated thick books and exhaustive studies to this problem. But the proposals that I make here are practical and will offer some degree of relief.

1. Reduce occupational regulations to provide more jobs.

State boards and commissions regulate about 1,000 types of jobs, from doctors to hair braiders. The idea is that by establishing standards for entry into these professions, consumers will be protected from fraudulent and unscrupulous competitors. However, research shows that the regulations increase the price for services without raising the quality; sometimes they actually lower it. Some states require barbers or hairstylists to have an associate's college degree, even though everything they do can be learned on the job. A number of years ago, Oregon upped its required training hours from 1,500 to 2,500 under pressure from cosmetology schools, enabling them to charge more money. Some states insist on U.S. citizenship or legal residency for licenses, even though they do not add value to the job. Licensing exams are typically designed to limit the number of passing grades in order to restrict competition in the various occupations.

A 2015 report from three federal offices—the Treasury's Office of Economic Policy, the Council of Economic Advisers and the Department of Labor—stated that "the current licensing regime in the United States also creates substantial costs, and often the requirements for obtaining a license are not in sync with the skills needed for the job. There is evidence that licensing requirements raise the price of goods and services, restrict employment opportunities, and make it more difficult for workers to take their skills across State lines." The same report said that licensing increased consumer costs by 3 to 16 percent.

This overzealous regulation hurts the economically disadvantaged in two ways: it effectively keeps them from entering certain professions, because they cannot afford the extensive and sometimes unnecessary schooling; and the reduction in competition drives up the prices so they have to pay more for services.

2. Raise the minimum wage to $15.

Franklin D. Roosevelt championed the minimum wage in the 1930s and warned that "no business which depends for existence on paying less than living wages to its workers has any right to continue in this country." After years of inaction regarding minimum wages, the recent Great Recession knocked millions of people out of their middle-class salaries and into jobs within sniffing distance of the minimum wage. Learning how difficult it was to survive on less, Americans opened up the conversation on raising the minimum wage to something approaching a living wage. In 2015, walkouts from fast-food workers across 270 cities launched the talks into reality. The city of Seattle and the states of New York and California have adopted a $15-an-hour minimum wage. Although some argue that an increase in the minimum wage would cause a spike in unemployment, a 2014 letter to President Obama and congressional leaders from more than 600 economists, including seven Nobel Prize winners, noted "the weight of evidence now showing that increases in the minimum wage have had little or no negative effect on the employment of minimum-wage workers, even during times of weakness in the labor market." Support also comes from many in the business community. A Luntz Global survey of 1,000 businesses across the country concluded that 80 percent of respondents backed raising their state's minimum wage, with only 8 percent opposed to it.

Low wages come at a cost to society, according to a 2016 study by a Florida union, which indicated that underpaying workers costs Florida $11.4 billion a year in corporate subsidies and government assistance programs.

3. Protect unions in order to safeguard jobs and benefits.

Businesses are using economic uncertainty to scare people into abandoning unions. Twenty-five states have adopted "right to work" laws that allow workers to refuse to pay union dues for contracts the unions have negotiated and administered for them. More states are in the process of passing similar laws. The effect will be to seriously weaken unions at a time when many people are so desperate for work that they are willing to give up many of the benefits that have taken decades to win.

In 1983, unions represented 20.1 percent of the American workforce; today they represent 11.1 percent. Although there is something especially irksome to independent-minded Americans about being compelled to do anything, without powerful unions defending workers, we would see less worker safety, lower wages and less job security.

4. Reform the bail system to stop punishing the poor.

We need to support efforts by legislators to decrease the amount of bail currently being set on nonviolent suspects. As it stands, many poor people who are arrested for minor infractions, including speeding, are kept in jail for weeks because they can't afford even a few hundred dollars in bail money. The ripple effect is not just that the state has to pay for housing them (which unnecessarily costs the taxpayers) but also that they can lose their jobs, their homes and their children, all because of a few hundred dollars.

We're not talking small numbers of people. In Benton County, Washington, 25 percent of the people in jail for misdemeanors were there because they couldn't pay the fine. In 2013 in the Tulsa, Okla., jail, 29 percent of the inmates were there for inability to pay fines.

Same for 18 percent in Rhode Island jails in the mid-2000s. The situation got so bad in Ohio that in 2014 the state's chief justice asked judges to stop jailing indigent defendants. Hoping to stem the rise, in 2014 the U.S. Justice Department issued a letter asking courts to seek alternatives to jailing indigents, saying, "In addition to being unlawful, [the practice] can cast doubt on the impartiality of the tribunal and erode trust between local governments and their constituents."

This flawed system forces many innocent people to plead guilty in order to get out of jail sooner than they would if they stayed in jail and waited for a trial. The result is people with convictions on their records that further harm their chances at employment. It's like being trapped in a maze with no exit. In 2015, Connecticut governor Dannel Malloy proposed reforming the state's bail system by eliminating bail for low-risk defendants. This is what all states must do.

5. Provide equal education for all income brackets.
People agree that a good education is one of the best roads to escape the cycle of poverty. But the reality is that this is, for many, a false hope. Children in poverty are absent more often or quit school early because they have to work or care for other family members, either small children or the elderly. The dropout rate among low-income families is seven times that of families with higher incomes. Forty percent of children in poverty aren't prepared to attend primary school. By the end of the fourth grade, African-American, Latino and low-income students are two years behind grade level; by 12th grade, they are four years behind.

Yes, part of the problem is money. Poor kids don't get an equal share of the educational funds. A 2011 report from the U.S. Department of Education concluded that more than 40 percent of low-income schools don't get as much of state and local funds as schools serving higher-income families. Because there are so many more challenges for schools with low-income students, it would make sense for such schools to receive more money, not less.

As important as the money is the educational approach. Students are taught repetitive drills that deaden educational enthusiasm in order to produce better test results. Study after study has concluded that this method of teaching might raise test scores but lowers students' ability to learn. Deborah Stipek, the dean of Stanford University's school of education, rejected this drill-for-testing method: "[W]hy use a strategy to help poor kids catch up that didn't help middle-class kids in the first place?" In higher-income schools, children are taught critical thinking, creativity, questioning and collaboration.

The problem is that there is a public consensus that we need to see quick results, and if those results aren't what we want, then someone has to be held accountable. The pressure to show better test results is enormous because educators' jobs are suddenly on the line. The 2015 conviction of 11 Atlanta teachers for conspiracy to cover up poor student performance on standardized tests is only a part of the cheating epidemic among teachers and administrators that has been reported, extending through 40 states and Washington, D.C. Even the indictment in the Atlanta case called the pressure to meet test scores "unreasonable." Both President George W. Bush's No Child Left Behind and President Obama's Race to the Top unwisely used standardized testing to prove their programs worked. They didn't.

How do we fix it? Let professional educators create the curriculum and judge its effectiveness, not through standardized testing but through more rational measures. That curriculum should be the same for children from all economic levels, but we should include more social and educational support programs to help students from low-income families. The curriculum should be implemented in all states without the judgment of local school boards intent on perpetuating local biases. The distance is long, and some may lag behind at times, but it's important that they finish the race.

6. Increase voting to increase political clout.

Many of those elected politicians vested with the responsibility and power to fight poverty choose not to. Their rationale is "Why work so hard for people who won't vote for me anyway? Where's the payoff for me?" This is why it's important to empower the poor through the ballot box. Fighting voter ID laws is crucial to stopping attempts to keep these voters invisible. Registering voters and transporting them to polling locations will give them a chance to influence the policies that affect their lives. We shouldn't encourage people to vote out of guilt based on civic duty, but rather we should show them the wisdom of voting based on economic self-interest in order to give themselves, their families and their communities more opportunities. When the poor become a powerful voting bloc, politicians will aggressively court them, and laws to help them will become more of a priority.

HE AIN'T HEAVY, HE'S MY BROTHER

In the musical *Fiddler on the Roof,* the impoverished protagonist, Tevye, struggles to feed his large family. Frustrated by his hopeless plight, he addresses God: "Dear Lord, you made many, many poor people / I realize, of course, it's no shame to be poor / But it's no great honor either!" It is even less honorable to let our neighbors and fellow Americans suffer under a system that is growing less and less compassionate and offering less and less hope. To me, the American mantra has always been: "The world may not be fair, but we can treat each other fairly."

6

Sports

ARE YOU NOT ENTERTAINED?

"Just hadda show those creeps and those punks what the game is like when it's great, when it's really great . . . When I'm goin', when I'm really goin' I feel like a . . . like a jockey must feel. He's sittin' on his horse, he's got all that speed and that power underneath him . . . he's comin' into the stretch, the pressure's on 'im, and he knows . . . just feels . . . when to let it go and how much. 'Cause he's got everything workin' for 'im: timing, touch. It's a great feeling, boy, it's a real great feeling when you're right and you know you're right. It's like all of a sudden I got oil in my arm. The pool cue's part of me. You know, it's uh—pool cue, it's got nerves in it. It's a piece of wood. It's got nerves in it. And feel the roll of those balls, you don't have to look, you just know. You make shots that nobody's ever made before. I can play that game the way . . . nobody's ever played it before."
—FAST EDDIE FELSON, *THE HUSTLER*

I DIDN'T START OUT TO BE AN ATHLETE. AS A CHILD, I WAS embarrassed by my gangly body. It felt as awkward as when I tried to ice-skate for the first time. My two-year growth spurt that shot me up 10 inches meant this shy, 14-year-old bookworm was suddenly very popular—if not with girls, then at least with the basketball coach. At first, I wobbled around the court on two bony legs that felt like wooden stilts while my teammates zipped all around me. I quickly discovered that height didn't instantly translate into athletic ability.

But I learned.

I learned how to play, score, win, repeat.

The more I learned about the sport, the more I learned about who I was as a person. I learned how to be an athlete without defining myself as only an athlete. I learned how to become a team player without losing my individual identity. I learned how to use my championship rings to champion social causes. I learned the alchemy of turning celebrity into charity.

It only took about 50 years.

And though I haven't played basketball in decades, I'm still learning how much my life as an athlete taught me how to live as a man, as an African American and as an American.

This transformative power of athletics makes it clear that sports is never "just a game" or a simple form of mass entertainment used to sell beer and potato chips. Given the political and social divisiveness in America, a passion for sports may the one thing that most Americans have in common. According to one study, an astounding 90 percent of Americans watch sports, and we spend about $35 billion on sporting goods and an additional $25.4 billion following professional teams. Most of our children participate in at least one organized sport. Sports is the preferred topic of conversation among many men and boys, who can have lively debates about teams without risking friendships. Watching sports together bonds families and friends.

Sports are among the most effective ways in popular culture to teach moral values. We can teach those moral lessons through actually playing sports or by using sports as a metaphor in art, especially books and movies. Children growing up playing sports learn about discipline, strategy, compassion, teamwork, fair play, conflict resolution, physiology and diet—all while having fun and getting exercise. Showing students *Breaking Away* or *McFarland USA* teaches perseverance and overcoming social barriers caused by class or ethnicity. Whether or not they play a sport, kids tend to understand these valuable lessons by encountering them in art more than by enduring a lecture from their parents.

Humanity is obsessed with pushing the boundaries of what the human body is capable of doing, and sport is one way in which we measure our progress. Before May 6, 1954, running a four-minute mile seemed impossible. Then Roger Bannister did it, and that became the benchmark for all runners to challenge themselves. In the 62 years since Bannister's historic run, the record for running the mile has been lowered by 16 seconds. Eventually that record, like all others, will fall.

When I retired from the NBA in 1989, I held a few world records: points scored (38,387), games played (1,560), minutes played (57,446), field goals made (15,837), field goal attempts (28,307), blocked shots (3,189), defensive rebounds (9,394) and personal fouls (4,657, though 4,650 of those were clearly bad calls from the refs). Since I set those records, most have been broken. And I'm confident that those that remain will also be broken. Like most other sports fans, I look forward to seeing them be broken so I can witness another giant leap for humankind. That's another lesson sports teaches us: the human race is a relay in which we all make our best run and then pass the baton to the next runner. What matters isn't who crosses the finish line but that we did our best to boost the whole team.

Yeah, I know sports metaphors can sound corny, but that's also the effectiveness of them: they are honest, direct and clearly understandable. Sports stories often inspire us to change our lives. *Rudy* sent a lot of smaller kids out onto the football field to try their hardest just because they loved the game. *Rocky* flooded the streets with joggers shuffling along to "Gonna Fly Now." For me, the inspirational power of sports is best explained in a scene in the 1985 film *Vision Quest*. In it, Elmo, an aging fry cook at a hotel, explains:

> I was in the room here one day, watchin' the Mexican channel on TV. I don't know nothin' about Pelé. I'm watchin' what this guy can do with a ball on his feet.

Next thing I know, he jumps in the air and flips into a somersault and kicks the ball in—upside down and backwards. The goddamn goalie never knew what the fuck hit him. Pelé gets excited. He rips off his jersey and starts running around the stadium waving it around over his head. Everybody's screaming in Spanish. I'm here, sitting alone in my room, and I start crying. *[Pause.]* Yeah, that's right, I start crying. Because another human being, a species that I happen to belong to, could kick a ball, and lift himself, and the rest of us sad-assed human beings up to a better place to be, if only for a minute . . . Let me tell ya, kid—it was pretty goddamned glorious.

That is the magic of sports. To see something seemingly impossible, reminding us that if one person can do it, then we all somehow share in that achievement. It is what sends children onto playgrounds to duplicate a Kobe Bryant fadeaway or a Steph Curry three-pointer. Or Mia Hamm inspiring a whole generation of girls to come off the bleachers and onto the field. Millions of children across the country pushing themselves toward excellence because they saw an athlete do something spectacular and they want to do it too. Or at least try. That same kind of drive is behind many of humankind's greatest achievements.

And it's all pretty goddamned glorious.

Or it should be. But whenever there's money to be made, there will be people trying to corrupt what's glorious for venal grubby gain. The more money involved, the greater the venality.

THE GOOD, THE BAD, AND THE REALLY BAD: ARE ATHLETES GOOD ROLE MODELS?

This morning I opened the newspaper and read about an incident at the University of Tennessee in which a football coach allegedly called one of his players a "traitor to the team" for helping a woman he found hyperventilating and crying in a parking lot who said she'd been raped by two of his teammates. The player was reportedly later attacked by several teammates for helping the woman, after which he transferred to another school. The coach denies he made the comment. Since then, eight women have filed a lawsuit claiming they were sexually assaulted by football players at the school.

The worst part of reading that story is that it didn't surprise me.

There have been too many similar cases over the past few years for the public to still hold any illusions about hoisting athletes on our shoulders and parading them around the field as heroes and role models just because of their achievements in sports. A 2014 Rasmussen Reports poll found that only 24 percent of adult Americans surveyed believe professional athletes are good role models for children, while 57 percent said they are not good role models. It seems as if most adults agree with NBA Hall of Famer Charles Barkley's 1993 comment: "I am not a role model . . . Just because I dunk a basketball doesn't mean I should raise your kids."

The problem is that most *kids* disagree. A Kaiser Family Foundation study in 2000 showed that, regardless of their parents' skepticism, most kids see professional athletes as important role models. When kids ranked the most-admired people in their lives, athletes came in second, behind parents. Most kids said they learned from professional athletes that playing fair is as important as winning and that being successful in sports requires hard work. The athletes motivated them and showed them how to be a good sport. That's exactly the kind of things role models should be teaching.

Unfortunately, some of the kids also learned some pretty nasty behavior. Eighteen percent of the youths surveyed said they learned not to worry about the consequences of sex; 13 percent said they learned it was OK to use alcohol and drugs; 24 percent said you don't have to study hard and do well in school if you become a pro athlete. William Gayton, a sports psychologist and the chair of the psychology department at the University of Southern Maine, observed, "This topic is very deserving of our attention because the fact of the matter is, observational learning is one of the primary means in which children learn. And children are going to learn from the models in their life—including their sports heroes." But what happens when these sports heroes are cheaters (Lance Armstrong), domestic abusers (Ray Rice), sexual predators (Mike Tyson) or murderers (Aaron Hernandez)?

When it comes to the influence athletes have on our children, our economy and our culture, we have to examine the situation with our eyes wide open rather than be blinded by the glitz of sports celebrity or the cult of bro-chismo.

We can start by acknowledging the relationship between sports and violence off the field, particularly sexual assaults. We've all seen the viral video of NFL player Ray Rice punching his girlfriend in an elevator. We know boxer Mike Tyson went to prison for raping an 18-year-old beauty queen. Professional soccer player Marlon King punched a college girl in the face and then sexually assaulted her. Soccer star Hope Solo has been charged with physically abusing her half sister and nephew. And those are just a few drops in an ocean of violent offenses.

We have condoned the formalized combat in professional sports because it is strictly governed by rules and the players are adults. But when the players' combative behavior spills out into daily behavior, we have to worry that this is conveying the message that violence is an acceptable way of expressing emotion or solving problems. And when much of that violence is directed at women, we have to be even more concerned.

Just how much violence from professional athletes are we talking about? According to a 2013 article in the *Journal of Science and Medicine in Sport*, violent behavior from athletes is higher than that among nonathletes. Apologists for athletes refer to a report on the website FiveThirtyEight.com that shows that the arrest rate for domestic violence among NFL players is about half the national average. But, as the site acknowledges, that lower rate could be misleading. Pro athletes can avoid arrest because of their celebrity, access to high-priced attorneys and the influence of the powerful sports leagues.

A 2015 University of Texas at Dallas study that was widely covered in the news media showed that NFL players are arrested less often than men in their 20s and 30s in the general population. However, that study focused on three categories of arrests: violent crime (murder, assault, rape), property crime (burglary, theft) and public-order crime (DUI, prostitution-related offenses, public intoxication). Although arrests of NFL players for property crimes and public-order crimes are below the average for the age group (because those crimes are usually committed by those with lower incomes), when it comes to violent crimes, they are arrested at a rate above the average. And it's not just football players. NBA players have an even higher arrest rate than NFL players.

College athletes are even worse when it comes to violent offenses. One analysis of Division I colleges found that although student athletes were only 3 percent of the school population, they were 19 percent of offenders in cases of sexual abuse or violence. A 2011 CBS News/*Sports Illustrated* report found that on the top 25 college football teams, 7 percent of players (1 out of every 14, or more than 200) had a police record or were cited by the police, and 40 percent of those crimes were "serious." Most of the schools had no idea about their players' criminal records because most don't do background checks.

Even when college athletes are accused of a crime, they often receive preferential treatment. An ESPN investigation of crime statistics from 20 colleges between 2009 and 2014 concluded that college athletes are much more likely to avoid prosecution than nonathletes accused of the same crimes. At the University of Florida, male football and basketball players accused of crimes either were not prosecuted, had charges dropped or never faced charges 56 percent of the time. According to the stats, they get off the hook twice as often as male nonathletes. However, this advantage isn't always because of preferential treatment from authorities; it's also because they have access to expensive lawyers and because victims and witnesses may feel too intimidated to accuse well-known campus athletes. Whatever the reasons, membership in the athletic community has its rewards.

Sexual aggression is a particularly warped entitlement. According to the National Coalition Against Violent Athletes, whose founder, Katherine Redmond Brown, is a consultant to the NFL, 1 in 3 college sexual assaults is committed by an athlete. And while the general population has a conviction rate of 80 percent, the conviction rate of athletes is only 38 percent. Experts give several reasons for this abhorrent situation: (1) Athletes are put upon a pedestal in high school and college, often given preferential treatment in terms of missing classes and other privileges that go with popularity. (2) Colleges, universities and pro teams have so much money invested in the success of their team that they are willing to protect their players from charges by ignoring, feigning ignorance of or even covering up violent behavior. (3) Players are trained from an early age to use aggressiveness and violence in their sport, for which they are continually rewarded. Because they are young, it is difficult for them to turn off that behavior outside their sport. This may explain why a vast majority of violent crimes, including sexual abuse, are committed by players in more-aggressive sports, including football, basketball, hockey, wrestling and boxing, as opposed to more individualized, noncontact sports such as tennis, swimming and track.

The relationship between sports and sexual violence doesn't end with the athletes; it extends to the fans as well. A 2016 study by researchers at colleges in Texas, Montana and Australia reported a sharp increase in rapes reported to police whenever the college football team was playing a local game. Home games brought a 41 percent increase, while away games brought a 15 percent increase. When the team had an upset victory, beating a team it wasn't expected to defeat or coming from behind to win, reports of rapes drastically increased. This is not a reflection on the athletes but on our culture of sexual exploitation. It is an example of how sports can, rather than elevate our best instincts for self-improvement and competition, become an inspiration for rape. Sports, then, seem to be a powerful amplifier of our impulses, often for good and sometimes for bad. How do we sort out that influence?

Despite adults proclaiming that sports figures shouldn't be taken as role models, our collective behavior sends mixed signals to kids. We cheer athletes on, talk admiringly about the great plays they made, buy our children clothing with players' names emblazoned across the front or back. This is hero-worship behavior, which to a kid means the player is revered enough by society to be given fame and fortune. To children, that's what a role model is. Unfortunately, as long as there's more money to be made off a role model than just an athlete, the hype will continue. And we will continue to be shocked and outraged every time an athlete is caught punching someone off the field or misusing corporal punishment on his children.

We can't pretend athletes aren't influencing our children's thinking and behavior. So we must demand higher standards from them. Like it or not, the college and professional sports machines are turning them into role models, and if they aren't willing to accept that responsibility as part of the contract, then they should seek another profession.

I feel about sports the way a lot of baby boomers feel about Woodstock. Sure, it's just a game, like Woodstock was just a concert, but it also represents the chaste spirituality of humanity, a ritual in which we focus on human potential, on working together so that the whole is greater than the sum of its parts, and on inspiring others to be their best selves. In her song "Woodstock," Joni Mitchell sings, "We are stardust, we are golden / And we got to get ourselves back to the garden." She means the Garden of Eden, a place of grace and innocence and selflessness, which sports, at their best, can be. It's where people are judged only by performance at that moment and not by anything else. Not by ethnicity, not by education, not by make of car. And not just by how many times they scored but by how generous they were in passing the ball, setting picks, helping up an opponent who has fallen, calling their own fouls, complimenting players for good plays. That's the Garden.

That's the place where role models dwell.

FRIDAY NIGHT LIGHTS OUT: YOUTH SPORTS

We're told that it takes a village to raise a child. But when I look at what's going on in some aspects of youth sports, I'm convinced we need to take another look at those in our village whom we allow to help raise our children. Gone are the innocent days portrayed in the nostalgic film *The Sandlot*, when kids played for companionship and fun. Today's youth sports are driven by invested adults who have their own agenda that often exploits, ignores or harms the kids.

About 45 million school-age (ages 5 through 18) children play in an organized sport in America. That represents a lot of volunteer work by parents—and also a lot of money. Youth sports, generally defined as non-school-related sports activities, generate at least $5 billion a year. Youth sports tourism, which involves families traveling for their children's games and other activities, is the fastest-growing segment of travel, accounting for an additional $7 billion a year. According to the National Council of Youth Sports, parents spend an average of $671 annually on league sports, with 21 percent spending more than $1,000 each year *per child*. Kids Play USA Foundation reports that a sport such as ice hockey, which requires costly equipment and facilities, can run as much as $10,000 annually per child. With so much money and so many jobs at stake, it's not surprising that the kids themselves can sometimes get overlooked.

Which may be why, by the time those kids reach 15, almost 80 percent quit playing.

Why do they quit? Pressure from parents, even when well-meaning and supportive, is cited by children as one of the main reasons they leave sports. Parents create additional pressure by being over-involved in each game, talking about unrealistic college scholarships, pushing for single-sport specialization and emphasizing the goal of becoming a professional athlete.

There's nothing wrong with encouraging children to play a sport with the hope that they may someday get a scholarship or support-ing a kid's dream of becoming a professional athlete. What's wrong is when the parents push the child too hard under the justification of "learning discipline" or "setting goals," or when the parents cling to unrealistic expectations. The NCAA website reveals the very low odds of children getting sports scholarships or turning pro, based on 2013–14 enrollments:

- **Baseball:** Of 482,629 high school players, 6.9 percent will play in college, and 8.6 percent of those players will be drafted by Major League Baseball.
- **Men's Basketball:** Of 541,054 high school players, 3.4 percent will play in college, and 1.2 percent of those players will be drafted by the NBA.
- **Women's Basketball:** Of 433,344 high school players, 3.8 percent will play in college, and 0.9 percent of those players will be drafted by the WNBA.
- **Football:** Of 1,093,234 high school players, 6.5 percent will play in college, and 1.6 percent of those players will be drafted by the NFL.

Despite this stark reality, a 2015 poll found that 26 percent of parents with children in high school sports hoped their child would become a professional athlete. In homes with household incomes under $50,000, 39 percent hoped their child would turn pro. Among parents with a high school education or less, 44 percent pushed for a professional athlete. But among parents with a college education or more, only 9 percent hoped their child would go pro. Clearly, there is an economic factor to sports as a means to a better life, just as the poor make up a large percentage of lottery-ticket buyers who lack hope in conventional routes of success—pathways often denied them by systemic biases—so they play the long shot here. It's often to the detriment of the children. When sports are emphasized over education, many children are less competitive in seeking higher education or in the job market.

Many parents at every economic level drive their young athletes until their child hates the sport and quits or the child becomes injured.

According to more than one survey, a third of children in sports actually wish their parents wouldn't attend their games. One way that parents damage their children's athletic experience is through single-sport specialization, which has been a growing trend among young athletes. Parents fearing their children will fall behind enroll them in program after program in which they play the same sport to the exclusion of others for most of the year. Research has shown that this approach is harmful because it increases risk of injuries, causes kids to burn out and quit, and holds back their overall athletic development. In fact, one-sport kids often don't improve in their specialized sport as much as those who play several different sports. A 2013 study concluded that children engaged in single-sport training were 70 percent to more than 90 percent more likely to be injured than those who played multiple sports. In 2015, dozens of sports organizations, including the NCAA, the NFL, MLB and the U.S. Olympic Committee, ran ads condemning single-sport specialization.

Because parents are among the main reasons kids quit their sports, they can also be a significant factor in kids maintaining their passion for sports. Experts in youth sports suggest that parents should support their children in their sport without being their at-home coach. Don't do postgame analysis with them. Celebrate their victories and see them through their losses without making too big of a deal about either outcome. Encourage children to try different sports, and establish firm limits on how much they can practice. The American Academy of Pediatrics suggests kids take two to three months off every year from a specific sport.

Coaches share some of the blame. A good coach can be the inspiration for a great athlete. But producing great athletes should not be the mission of youth-sports coaches. Instead, they should be producing great teams. For kids, a great team should be defined not only by its win/loss record but also by the athletic skills and social values taught.

Unfortunately, while there are great coaches who will be fondly remembered by their players for their entire lives, there are also plenty of bad coaches out there ruining sports for our children. Issues include:

- Parent coaches favoring their own children on the team
- Not teaching game fundamentals
- Incorporating outdated or inappropriate conditioning skills
- Failing to communicate properly
- Being poor role models
- Committing physical and sexual assault

College coaching includes some of the same problems mentioned above, plus a bunch of its own:

- Permitting academic fraud
- Not stressing the need for academic achievement
- Blocking scholarships of former players attending new schools
- Emphasizing winning at all costs in order to keep their jobs
- Protecting players who commit crimes
- Paying incentives tied to winning

Some kids were born to become professional athletes, and there's nothing that's going to get in their way. Not aggressive parents, not bad coaches, not even injuries. For the rest of our young athletes, sports should not be a means to an end but the end itself: encouraging children to have fun. Teaching them how to better themselves. Instilling values of discipline, hard work and teamwork. Learning how to deal with triumph and disaster and, as Rudyard Kipling said, "treat those two impostors just the same."

More important, to teach them a love of playing that could last a lifetime.

NOW WHAT DO WE DO TO FIX THIS THING?
The reason sports films are so popular—aside from the built-in drama of "Who will win the final showdown?"—is that they are generally uplifting stories about the indomitable human spirit. One of the main themes in sports films is the battle between those who corrupt the sport for selfish personal gain and those who struggle to reclaim the purity of

the sport as an expression of communal responsibility. They compete not just to aggrandize themselves but also to inspire their community. Another popular theme is how sports encourage people to overcome their self-doubts and fears about life to see their potential more clearly. Competing gives them the tools and confidence to succeed.

Clearly, sports in America are much more than mindless entertainment. They're an integral part of how we raise our children, both as participants and as fans. They're also part of our cultural myth-making, the stories we tell one another to convey our deepest moral values. That's why it's crucial that we safeguard their integrity. The more sports become corrupted, the less valuable they are as a symbol of human striving.

It's not my intention here to fix everything that's wrong with sports. That's another, much longer book. Instead, I will address a few aspects that might restore a little of the purity we all want.

YOUTH SPORTS

1. Establish better training for youth coaches.

According to ESPN, 60 percent of boys and 47 percent of girls are on teams by age 6. Our children are being taught at their most impressionable ages by men and women whose hearts might be in the right place but whose teaching skills might not be. Nor might they have the right temperament to teach children. We also have to factor in that 1.35 million kids a year sustain a serious sports injury, so we need to be sure that the coach isn't taking unnecessary risks.

An ESPN/Aspen Institute poll found that over 60 percent of parents surveyed were concerned about the quality and behavior of their children's coaches. They are right to be. Only a fifth of coaches have been trained in age-appropriate motivation and communication, and only a third have been trained in their specific sport. That leaves a lot of coaches who are just winging it. Why entrust your children's safety and happiness to someone so poorly qualified?

Many coaches rely on training methods and drills that they were taught back when they were high school athletes. But since then, a lot of those drills and methods have been proven ineffective in the sport and even physically harmful to the children. Some coaches try to establish authority through yelling, bullying and ridiculing, which not only discourages children from participating in sports but establishes that these are acceptable tools for those in authority to use. Coaches who taunt boys with sexist phrases like "Let's hustle, ladies!" or "Did you drop your purse?" aren't just promoting the idea that ridicule is an effective coaching method; they are also perpetuating the idea that females are weaker and less capable.

One way to ensure better coaching is to require coaches to be certified in a program that teaches the most current knowledge about age- and sport-appropriate training. The program should include a component of sensitivity training about how to address and motivate young athletes without bullying. A few national organizations, such as the American Youth Soccer Organization, USA Hockey and USA Rugby, have certificate programs, but that doesn't apply to all the local organizations and other national sports groups that coach most of our children. If parents demand such certificate programs before signing those checks, we'll see them being instituted pretty quickly.

2. Improve the quality of parental participation.

Just as we want better training for coaches, parents could use some expert training as well. Organized sports should require parents to attend at least one session devoted to teaching the best, most supportive ways for parents to participate in their children's sports. Many parents take prenatal classes to learn the best ways to care for their children from pregnancy through birth. This is just one more step in their parental evolution. They will learn not just courtside etiquette—such as not coaching the coaches, children or referees—but also how best to encourage their children's enthusiasm for sports as well as increase their skill level.

3. Bring the costs down to make sports more inclusive and competitive.

High school varsity sports used to be the gold standard for youth sports. What made sports particularly admirable was that kids from any socioeconomic background were eligible. The only qualifications to play were desire and ability. But the high costs of playing sports have even affected public schools. A 2014 study by the University of Michigan C.S. Mott Children's Hospital found that 61 percent of families surveyed had paid to participate in middle school and high school sports. "The end result," reported NBC, "is that a significant share of lower-income children and adolescents find themselves shut out of team sports." Sports participation in schools is directly related to family income. About 20 percent of Americans have household incomes above $100,000, with an estimated 33 percent of them involved in sports. However, 32 percent of families making less than $50,000 say the costs make it difficult to participate. Low-income families must also factor in the risk of injuries. Sports-related emergency-room treatment for kids ages 6 to 19 costs nearly $1 billion a year.

Additionally, the number of players in public-school programs is so limited that a lucrative market was created for club sports. The problem is that playing on a club team is even more costly than playing on a school team. Kids not only pay for their coaches and court time but are also often involved in weekly tournaments that cost extra. Club teams often travel to other cities for regional and national tournaments, usually with their parents in tow. The expenses add up. One parent totaled the cost of his daughter's club-soccer participation at $18,115 for the season.

As the costs continue to rise, fewer children can afford to join teams. From 2011 to 2012, the percentage of kids between ages 6 and 17 participating in team sports fell from 54 percent to 50 percent. As fewer kids can afford to play, the costs are passed on to those remaining, pushing fees higher and causing even more kids to drop the activities.

The goal should be to create organized sports that are affordable enough to include kids from low-income families. This can be done on the local level, through city and county governments, funded by taxes and donations. This would be a cheaper, more inclusive way to make sports available to kids—and for communities to reap the abundant social benefits.

COLLEGE SPORTS
Emancipate college athletes by paying them.

In 2014, former UCLA linebacker Ramogi Huma attempted, with one modest proposal, to destroy everything that America holds sacred. Were he successful, our glorious cities would have crumbled to nothing more than shoddy tents stitched together from tattered remnants of Old Glory; our government officials would be loincloth-clad elders gathered in the rubble of an old McDonald's passing a talking stick. We would be without hope, dreams or a future.

Or at least that's what you might imagine based on the nuclear reaction to Huma's proposal to unionize college athletes. Huma, the founder and president of the National College Players Association, made a simple argument that college athletes should be classified as employees of the college and should therefore receive certain basic benefits. He did not advocate for player salaries, instead calling for programs to minimize brain-trauma risks among athletes, a raise in scholarship amounts, more financial assistance for sports-related injuries, an increase in graduation rates and several other similar goals.

You would have thought he'd proposed dressing the Statue of Liberty in a star-spangled thong.

But Huma is not alone in his assault on the NCAA's iron-fisted control of all things related to college athletics that might generate income. (The association's motto might as well be: "If it earns, it's ours.") Former UCLA basketball player Ed O'Bannon, along with several other players, is suing for players to have control over the use of their likenesses that earn millions of dollars for the NCAA but not a cent for the players. Two class actions have been filed to challenge the cap on player compensation, which is currently limited to the value of the scholarship athletes receive, on the grounds that it's an illegal restraint of trade.

Predictably, the NCAA is against this, claiming that any move toward unionizing would "completely throw away a system that has helped literally millions of students over the past decade alone attend college." Attend, but not necessarily complete, especially if you suffer any long-term injury. Because if you don't compete, you don't complete.

The NCAA has backing from some powerful Washington politicians who, like Senator Lamar Alexander, a Republican from Tennessee, worry about student-athlete unionization that would "destroy intercollegiate athletics as we know it." Former speaker of the House John Boehner, a Republican from Ohio, chimed in: "I haven't looked at the specifics of this and what would be required, but having formally chaired the House Education and Workforce Committee and worked with the National Labor Relations Act for the last 30 years, I find it a bit bizarre."

Nothing more reassuring than someone who acknowledges he hasn't really "looked at the specifics" but has an opinion anyway.

To put the dispute into context, the NCAA takes in about $6 billion a year. College athletes, who risk their health, education and even lives, are paid zero dollars a year.

When I played basketball for UCLA, I learned the hard way the realities of how the NCAA ban on paying college athletes impacted my daily life. Despite the many hours I put in every day, seven days a week, practicing, playing games, learning plays and traveling around the country to play games, and despite the millions of dollars in revenue our team's efforts generated for UCLA, both in cash and in recruiting students to attend the school, I was always too broke to do much but study, practice and play. It was a vicious cycle perpetuated by the school administration and the NCAA.

What little money I had came from spring-break and summer jobs that I was lucky enough to get. For a couple of summers, Mike Frankovich, the vice president of Columbia Pictures and formerly a UCLA quarterback in the 1930s, hired me to do publicity for his movies, most memorably *Cat Ballou* (1965), which was nominated for five Academy Awards and won one for Lee Marvin. During spring breaks I worked as a groundskeeper on the UCLA campus or in its steam plant, repairing plumbing and electrical problems. No partying in Cabo San Lucas for me. Pulling weeds and swapping fuses was my glamorous life. Living in Southern California was very challenging for someone without a car. Unless you were always tagging along with someone else, you were pretty much stuck on campus, which could be limiting and embarrassing when you wanted to go on a date. Those summer and spring-break jobs allowed me to spend $1,100 on a used car that I could fit into.

Despite my jobs, every semester was a financial struggle. So in order to raise enough money to get through my junior and senior years, I let Sam Gilbert, the wealthy godfather of a friend of mine, scalp my season tickets to his rich friends. This brought me a couple of thousand dollars. Spread out over a year, it was still barely enough to get by. I was walking out onto the court a hero but walking into my home a pauper.

Naturally, I felt exploited and dissatisfied. In my first year, our freshman team beat the varsity team, who had just won the NCAA championship. We were the best team in the country, yet I was too broke to go out and celebrate. Students on academic scholarships were allowed to make money on the side, but not we athletes. The ones bringing in the money. And unlike those with academic scholarships, if we were injured and couldn't play anymore, we lost our scholarships but still had medical bills to worry about. We were only as valuable as our ability to tote that ball and lift that score.

Coach John Wooden told us that there was no changing the NCAA's mind, that it was "immovable, like the sun rising in the East." I never personally encountered any players who cheated or shaved points, which is despicable under any circumstances, but I could see why some players resorted to illegally working an extra job or accepting monetary gifts in order to get by.

The worst part is that nothing much has changed since my experience as a college athlete 50 years ago. Well, one thing has changed:

the NCAA, television broadcasters and the colleges and universities are making a lot more money. A lot more!

- ▶ In 2015, the NCAA basketball playoffs known as March Madness generated $1.19 billion in ad sales for CBS Sports and Turner Sports.
- ▶ That same year, the NCAA president made at least $1.7 million.
- ▶ The NCAA's top 10 basketball coaches earn salaries that range from $3.1 million to $7.2 million.

NCAA management argues that student athletes receive academic scholarships and special training worth about $125,000. While that seems like generous compensation, it comes with some serious caveats:

- ▶ The NCAA allows scholarship money to be applied only toward tuition, room and board, and required books. On average, this is about $5,500 short of what the student will need.
- ▶ Academic scholarships provide for school supplies, transportation and entertainment. Athletic scholarships do not.
- ▶ Athletic scholarships can be taken away if the player is injured and can't contribute to the team anymore. He or she risks this possibility with every game. The recipient of an academic scholarship does not.

The injustice worsens when we consider that the millionaire coaches are allowed to go out and earn extra money outside their coaching contracts. Many do, reaping hundreds of thousands of dollars a year beyond their already enormous salaries.

In that light, not only is the compensation for student athletes inadequate to account for the effort and risk compared with academic scholarships, there is also a real possibility that players might end up without an education and deeply in debt. Players who are seriously injured could technically make use of the NCAA's catastrophic-injury relief. Sounds fair and compassionate. Except that the policy doesn't apply unless the medical expenses exceed $90,000—which most claims don't. So if the student's medical bills are $80,000, he and his family are on the hook for all of it. Let's just hope they can get that second mortgage on their home.

To protect students against career-ending injuries, the NCAA has Exceptional Student-Athlete Disability Insurance. But this pays only if the athlete can't return to the sport at all. The problem is that most injuries can be repaired to some extent, even if the athlete is no longer as good and gets cut from the team. Clearly, this insurance is just for show, since only a dozen such claims have been successful over the past 25 years.

Student athletics is no longer the quaint Americana fantasy of the homecoming bonfire followed by a celebration at the malt shop. It's big business in which everyone is making millions and billions of dollars—everyone except the 18-to-21-year-old kids who in every game risk permanent, career-ending injuries.

It's the kind of injustice that just shouldn't sit right with Americans.

Unfortunately, those with a stranglehold on the profit margin aren't likely to give up money just because it's the right thing to do. Instead, they will trickle some out in a display of fairness and hope that it's enough to keep the peasants from storming the castle. Case in point: there is ongoing litigation over finally paying money to the athletes whose likenesses have been used in sports video games that generate millions of dollars without a cent going to the athletes. Such litigation may bring more progress.

The NCAA's power is eroding thanks to the push to unionize college athletes, a necessary step in securing fair play in the future. Without the power of collective bargaining, the student athletes will have no leverage in negotiating for basic fair treatment. Unions aren't a perfect institution, but they have done more to bring about equal opportunities and break down class barriers than any other institution.

In the meantime, student athletes continue to play Oliver Twist approaching the Mr. Bumble of collegiate sports, begging with empty bowls, "Please, sir, I want some more."

PROFESSIONAL SPORTS

Give athletes freedom of speech on social and political causes.

America has always had a complicated relationship with its athletes. When it comes to game day, athletes are revered warriors whose acrobatic actions on the court or field are emulated by millions of children across the country. Their faces are on clothing, their profiles on video games. But when it comes to Election Day, or any other day that involves expressing personal opinions about social or political issues, they are relegated to a locker-room ghetto and told to keep their politics as private as a jockstrap. From the team owners' point of view, mixing sports and politics is bad for business because fans might be repelled by the opinions expressed. Fans want to indulge in the escapism of the sport without the heavy baggage of real life interfering.

The conventional wisdom seems to be that athletes should never step outside their roles as entertainers to pontificate about topics that they might know little about. This attitude is a cultural throwback to the idea that athletes are muscle-bound morons always on the verge of punching someone. To be fair, some athletes have done a lot to perpetuate that image. The violent behavior described earlier in the chapter has only reinforced public disdain.

So if they are going to be role models to children, whether adults like it or not, athletes have to start acting like role models, and we have to start treating them like role models. The best way to overcome that damaging image is for athletes to use their celebrity to improve their communities.

When some 30 football players from the University of Missouri threatened to boycott their season in protest of the school's failure to address racial-bias problems on campus, their stand on the issue forced the resignation of the college president. This has had a ripple effect, as student athletes at other campuses, including Amherst College, have launched protests demanding changes in campus policies. Kansas City, Mo., station KCTV reported, "Their threat to boycott football-related activities became one of the biggest stories on every American radio and television network and in newspapers from L.A. to London." The real shame in this case is that until the football-team boycott threatened to cost the school $1 million for defaulting on an upcoming game, university officials remained impassive despite other student protests and even a hunger strike.

The University of Missouri football players were not the first athletes in recent years to express their political views on a national stage. Professional athletes have begun to appear in media campaigns on issues ranging from homophobia to gun violence. In December 2014, LeBron James, Kyrie Irving and other NBA players wore I CAN'T BREATHE shirts before a game, calling attention to the death of a New York man named Eric Garner who died after being put in a police choke hold. Five players from the St. Louis Rams took the field before a game with their arms up in a "Hands up, don't shoot" gesture to protest the police shooting of Michael Brown in Ferguson, Mo.

For some Americans, this is a welcome evolution of athletes as activists, using their status in society as a platform to address urgent issues. For others, it's a sign of end times (sports edition), with athletes shattering the fantasy by breaking the fourth wall of sports theater and directly addressing the audience. The significance of this can be measured by the reactions of the presidential candidates. Donald Trump criticized the University of Missouri resignations caused by the athletes' boycott: "When they resigned, they set something in motion that's going to be a disaster for the next long period of time." Ben Carson said it was a matter of people being "so frightened of the politically correct police that they are willing to do things that are irrational in order to appease them."

Clearly, the fear is that now that athletes have found their voice, their opponents on the issues won't be able to shut them up again. The genie is out of the locker, and no amount of ACE bandages will bind him back to mute servitude. The other fear is that what athletes say will be silly, impertinent or simpleminded. That's a reasonable fear, since the behavior of some athletes does not reflect an ability to think through their actions. However, the price of free speech is that we must endure some pretty awful yammering in order to hear words worth listening to.

When it's convenient for governments with an agenda, athletes have long been used as an extension of foreign policy. In 1971, the U.S. Table Tennis Team's friendly exchange with the Chinese team at the 31st World Table Tennis Championships in Japan became known as Ping-Pong Diplomacy. The encounter helped soften relations between the U.S. and China, creating an atmosphere that allowed President Nixon to make his historic visit to Beijing in 1972. In 1980, the U.S. and 64 other countries boycotted the Summer Olympics in Moscow to protest the Soviet Union's invasion of Afghanistan. In retaliation, the Soviet Union led 13 other countries in boycotting the 1984 Summer Olympics in Los Angeles.

When countries use athletes to promote policy, the athletes are given no choice. But when athletes wish to stand up for causes they personally believe in, they are often condemned for using their position as a platform. Muhammad Ali learned that in 1967 when he refused to be drafted on religious grounds and was convicted of refusing induction and stripped of his heavyweight-champion title. The verdict was overturned by the U.S. Supreme Court, but Ali nevertheless lost four years of boxing bouts in his prime, fights worth millions of dollars. Ali's sacrifice inspired me to boycott the 1968 Olympic basketball team to call attention to the rampant racial injustice of the time, which resulted in people calling me "un-American." (Ironically, in 1980, athletes who complained about the U.S. boycott were also called un-American.) Some black athletes who did participate in the 1968 Summer Olympics chose to use the event as a platform to make the same statement I did. Gold medalist Tommie Smith and bronze medalist John Carlos, both African Americans, raised black-gloved fists in the air in a black-power salute during their 200-meter-race medal ceremony. "We were not Antichrists," Smith said. "We were just human beings who saw a need to bring attention to the inequality in our country."

And 48 years later, that's all these athletes are doing now: adding their voices to the national conversation on racial disparity. If sometimes they need to flex their power a little to be heard, well, they're just following in the same tradition as their government. Democracy is not a solo concert; it's a choir of differing voices blending to create a beautiful sound. Sure, there's a discordant note now and then, or someone gets aggressively pitchy, but even those sounds teach the rest of us how to better harmonize. We are hearing the voices of those brave athletes, and it's a beautiful song.

Professional sport has lots of controversies, from massive numbers of concussions in football to accusations of fixed matches in tennis to bribery in international soccer and much, much more. But for me, all issues start with treating individual athletes as being more important than their stats. This gives them the power and the voice to speak up and become not just profiteers but also protectors of their sports.

WE WHO ARE ABOUT TO PLAY SALUTE YOU

If you want to understand how important sports are to America, just imagine if everything sports-related suddenly vanished from our culture and our daily lives. The void would be more powerful than a black hole. I love books, music and art with as much passion as I love sports. But sport is different—it is art in motion. It is the thrum in the blood that begs the body to move, move, move. It is a physical sensation that connects the mind to the body in a way that expresses not only individuality but also our connection to others. It stimulates us to be more, not just as athletes but as human beings.

7

News Media

I READ THE NEWS TODAY, OH BOY

*"This is the West, sir. When the legend
becomes fact, print the legend."*
—JOURNALIST IN *THE MAN WHO SHOT LIBERTY VALANCE*

THE GREATEST THREAT TO THE AMERICAN WAY OF LIFE IS
not from international terrorists blowing up innocent civilians,
runaway Big Government micromanaging our lives, the Wall Street
elite siphoning billions or an economy barely able to create good jobs
and hope for our children's future. No, the greatest threat to our
basic freedoms and to democracy comes from the relentless attacks
on the news media from politicians and business leaders who fear
journalistic scrutiny. They undermine public trust in all news media
when they try to redirect the glaring spotlight on their activities onto
the people shining that light. This is the last refuge of today's scoun-
drels: blame the media.

Just as guilty of blotting out the truth, however, are certain media
outlets whose clearly biased reporting *deliberately* misinforms their
audience for the sake of corporate profits. Their blatant lack of impartiality in exchange for audience loyalty might be good business, but

it's bad for the country. Sadly, they know it and don't care. They remind me of the seven tobacco executives who lied to Congress in hearings in 1994, testifying that cigarettes weren't addictive. They lied to keep making money, despite knowing that their product was killing or harming millions of Americans. In business, the bottom line often trumps morality or even national well-being. The difference is that major news outlets aren't just businesses—they are the bearers of a national trust.

Both of these problems could be solved if Americans, who tend to despise the media for invading their living rooms daily with disturbing news, had a better understanding of the necessity of free speech and a free press to uphold our democratic ideals. Most Americans don't appreciate that in order to maintain their independence, journalists need the freedom to report "without fear or favor," as a wise publisher once declared. That includes the stories that disclose bad news about your favorite presidential candidate, your employer, your church or your sports team. What's equally important to media outlets' journalistic freedoms is their *responsibility* to exercise them in a fair and accurate way. This kind of integrity is easier to maintain if they make huge profits, reach a wide audience and have great influence. Yet what's challenging even the purest-hearted journalists today is the economic disruption of their business, which has forced many newspapers and other media to drastically reduce their staff or close altogether. The news media are trying to maintain a precarious balance between delivering the news the public needs and keeping from falling into bankruptcy. This precariousness has prompted many media outlets to cling desperately to their audiences by telling them what they want to hear. There is money to be made in supplying a comforting echo chamber.

Preventing the news media from becoming mealymouthed sycophants requires the public to take responsibility too. We must demand truth and not settle for seductive sweet talk. A 2010 poll by the First Amendment Center at Vanderbilt University found that barely 18 percent of Americans in the survey knew that the First Amendment protected freedom of the press. A 2013 Newseum Institute survey found that 96 percent of Americans in the poll couldn't name all five freedoms guaranteed by the First Amendment (religion, speech, the press, peaceable assembly, the right to petition the government). Yet 34 percent of those polled thought the First Amendment went too far, a sharp jump from only 13 percent a year earlier. A 2015 national survey from Yale University's William F. Buckley, Jr. Program revealed startling results: almost one third of college students could not identify the First Amendment as the one dealing with free speech, and 30 percent of students who consider themselves liberals say the First Amendment is outdated. "Americans remain generally supportive of First Amendment freedoms. But the inability of most to even name the freedoms, combined with the increase of those who think the freedoms go too far, shows how quickly that support can erode," said Newseum Institute chief operating officer Gene Policinski.

This lack of basic knowledge among Americans about the importance of the press is like not knowing your plants need water to stay alive. The necessity of a free press in a democratic society was forcefully expressed by Thomas Jefferson: "[W]ere it left to me to decide whether we should have a government without newspapers, or newspapers without a government, I should not hesitate a moment to prefer the latter." As we see in a world full of totalitarian regimes, any government without a free press is one that's intent on enslaving its people. It's even worse when the people are manipulated into enslaving themselves by dismantling their own freedoms. Each time we reject the reporter's hard truth for the faux reporter's comforting lie, we are embracing our abuser. As newsman Edward R. Murrow warned, "A nation of sheep will beget a government of wolves."

Those most aggressively attacking the news media seem to have the most to lose from legitimate, probing journalism. When Donald Trump bashed the press during his 2016 campaign, he was simultaneously seeking to discredit reporters, some of whom were scrutinizing his business dealings, and stir the anger of his supporters. Trump consistently badmouthed the press: "They're scum. They're horrible people. They are so illegitimate. They are just terrible people." While reporters waited outside in the Iowa cold amid a mix-up at one of Trump's rallies, his supporters shouted insults as well as "Let 'em freeze." When Senator Ted Cruz's campaign deliberately released a false statement implying that fellow candidate Ben Carson was going to suspend his campaign, Cruz blamed CNN, which he claimed was the source of the report. But CNN had never issued such a report. Democratic candidate Bernie Sanders was no kinder: "The media is an arm of the ruling class of this country. And they want to talk about everything in the world except the most important issues."

Harsh attacks on the media are typically meant to persuade the public to ignore reporting that is damaging to the attackers. It's the typical ad hominem fallacy of confronting the accuser rather than the accusation: "I didn't do any insider trading. Did you see the cheap car the prosecutor is driving? He's jealous of my millions." The reasoning is absurd, but it's clearly effective—and with serious consequences to our country. Confidence in the media has been sliding downward for the past 40 years. A 2016 study by the Media Insight Project found that only 6 percent of Americans surveyed had a great deal of confidence in the press overall, an all-time low. Whom, then, shall we trust to inform us about the fatal side effects of prescription drugs that manufacturers hid? Or the epidemic of child molestation by clergy that had been covered up for decades? Or the criminal conspiracies of government officials, even presidents?

THE NEWS MEDIA: JEDI KNIGHTS OR THE NEW DEATH STAR?

Personally, I've always had a complicated relationship with the press. In many ways, it reflects both sides of the media controversy in America.

Growing up, I had two kinds of heroes. The first was the squinty-eyed gunslinger with a dark past who eventually uses his fast hands and deadly aim for good, like Paladin in *Have Gun—Will Travel*, Lucas McCain in *The Rifleman* or the Man with No Name in *A*

Fistful of Dollars. As I grew older, the rugged Western hero evolved into modern versions of the same kick-ass outsider: Shaft, Dirty Harry, Xena: Warrior Princess, Malcolm Reynolds in *Firefly*, Peter Quill in *Guardians of the Galaxy*. Their stories were romanticized fantasies through which I lived an edgy life of action and adventure—and still did good deeds.

My more realistic heroes, the ones who inspired me, have always been crusading journalists, steely-eyed zealots of uncompromising integrity, like the ones in *All the President's Men, His Girl Friday, The Paper, Kill the Messenger, Broadcast News, Veronica Guerin, Spotlight, Lou Grant* and *The Newsroom*. They are the flip side of my fantasy heroes. They don't punch or shoot or pilot a spacecraft in order to defeat evil. They meticulously ask questions, do bleary-eyed research, slurp cold coffee and reason their way past the labyrinthine defenses of the formidable foes that are much darker than any Hollywood hero ever faced.

Forget the scar-faced villains in tuxedos threatening to annihilate the world with super-lasers. Journalists uncover the real-world evil: the poisons in our food and water, the crooked business deals that rob millions of their pensions, the lies of corrupt politicians who squander our tax money and leave us without crucial services. They give us the facts necessary to make informed choices and question our assumptions about our government, our jobs, our health and our families. Without them getting the word out to the average citizen, we'd still be giving our children "soothing syrups" (which, as a 1910 *New York Times* article reported, sometimes contained morphine, heroin or powdered opium), treating wounds with mercury (one of the most toxic elements in existence) or taking diet pills that were mostly highly addictive amphetamines. Even when journalists get the story right, like most heroes who are fighting the good fight, they have to endure a lot of public disdain and hostility along the way.

My passion for journalism began one summer when I was 17 and joined the Harlem Youth Action Project (Haryou-Act), a city-sponsored antipoverty program meant to teach black kids about their heritage. Our mission was to produce a weekly journal about Harlem life. Entombed in our tiny windowless room, we pecked away on heavy black typewriters just like the journalists I'd seen in old black-and-white films. Except we were black, and the reporters in movies were always white. So were the newspaper readers and the people they wrote stories about. Even the newsboys shouting the headlines.

My life as a writer was ordained the day Martin Luther King Jr. came to Harlem and I was chosen to cover the event as a journalist for our magazine. King was about to be named TIME magazine's Man of the Year and was a few months away from being awarded the Nobel Peace Prize. My journalist credentials gave me access to King's press conference, where I huddled with all the seasoned reporters as we scribbled on our notepads. When I finally dared to ask King a question, my voice trembled and my hand gripping my tape recorder shook. I wrote the story with a mixture of fear of failure and a sense of divine purpose.

I've been writing ever since.

For 50 years I've been writing about one topic in particular: the missing stories of African Americans in our history books and popular culture. Not just where in pop culture were the black cowboys (some 25 percent of all cowboys were black) or black journalists I hero-worshipped, but where in our schoolbooks were the mentions of our contributions to American history and society? Isolating our stories in a media ghetto made us invisible. We were usually portrayed as martyrs or victims, defined only in the context of the racism around us. That wasn't me, and it wasn't any other black people I knew.

The only way for white America to understand us, to empathize with us, to not fear us, was for them to see us beyond stereotypes of sitcom goofballs and cop-drama pimps and drug dealers. And the only way for young African-American boys and girls to grow up seeing themselves as more than historical footnotes or cardboard characters was for us to provide alternative role models. As a result, I wrote books about the black geniuses of the Harlem Renaissance, the all-black tank battalion of World War II and the black inventors who have radically affected our daily lives.

During my five decades as a writer, I also played some basketball. I came to realize that my writing and playing basketball were really part of the same mission. As a writer, I wanted to share stories of achievements of African Americans to provide role models for kids to see that their potential did not have to be limited by society's myopic vision. As a player, I wanted to *be* a role model for achievement: the athlete-scholar to whom education was as important as championships.

But it's a lot easier to write about other role models than to actually be one. As a writer, I controlled the stories I told. As a player, my story was controlled by other writers, who often seemed more interested in my politics, my religion and my moods than in my playing. They were right to be. I used my celebrity to take political stances. That made me fair game for reporters who wanted to question my motives and my opinions. Some things that were written about me were factually wrong, nasty and racist, to which I sometimes reacted with less than graciousness. Being the focus of the media can be like riding a wild bronco: you just hope to get off alive.

Having experienced the media from both sides—participant and subject—I have a healthy skepticism about them. Not all journalists seek truth and justice. Some seek only readers and ratings by any means necessary. I sometimes imagine cynical "journalists" sitting together just before the TV camera is switched on, laughing at the suckers they are about to bamboozle with lies, half-truths and distortions. I also imagine a giant attic where their portraits are stored in Dorian Gray fashion, their pained faces corroding with each deception as their TV faces remain pleasantly bland from layers of makeup and injections of Botox.

And yet.

My childhood admiration and love for the press has not diminished. Without the free flow of information and the exchange of opposing ideas, we would not be able to strengthen a country based on reason. We would be at the mercy of self-serving information and ideas from only those in power. The land of the free would cease to be.

WHY WE DON'T TRUST THE PRESS

When it comes to cherishing free speech, America waves the foam finger: WE'RE NO. 1! A 2015 Pew Research Center survey found that Americans, more than nearly any other citizens in the world, support free speech, free press and freedom on the Internet—71 percent of those surveyed, versus the global median of 56 percent.

However, while we say we want to be given the message, we generally don't trust the messenger. According to a 2015 Gallup poll, 6 out of 10 Americans surveyed do not have confidence that the mass media report the news "fully, accurately and fairly." The Pew poll found that millennials (which it defined as ages 18 through 34), Generation Xers (35 through 50) and baby boomers (51 through 69) all had about the same level of mistrust of news sources. So Americans are united in our lavish love of news and opinion—and our deep distrust of the professionals who deliver it to us.

Why this disconnect between our reverence for the abstract idea versus the actual press? Is it just another example of respecting ideals over practical application? Or have the news media abused our trust by failing to live up to the principles we expect?

In fact, our attitude toward the news media mirrors our belief versus our practice of pretty much most of America's ideals. We patriotically tear up over "all men are created equal," but we sometimes balk when it comes to taking specific steps to make that a reality. We brag about our constitutional freedom of religion, but millions rally behind those who want to register Muslims. We sing that we are "the land of the free" at every sporting event, but states still conspire to end-run the Constitution to pass laws allowing discrimination against gay people. And so on. We often mistake the concept of freedom to mean "freedom to agree with me."

One reason for our slipping confidence in the media is that Americans have become less tolerant of opinions other than the ones they already hold. Many seek news sources that present only information and commentary that support their entrenched political stance. Rather than use the media to gather information on various viewpoints and then reach a reasoned conclusion, we just seek validation that we're right. This has led people to seek alternative sources for their news, abandoning such outlets as daily newspapers and local TV. Only 37 percent of millennials watch local TV news, while 61 percent get their political news from Facebook. This is nearly the reverse of baby boomers: 60 percent rely on local TV news and 39 percent choose Facebook.

The problem with that approach is that it leads to a less-informed population, less able to make rational choices. Because the majority of Americans still get most of their news from television, it's important that we examine the reliability of those sources. Of the six most popular network news shows, Fox News has the most viewers and was shown by a Quinnipiac University poll to have the most-trusted news coverage. The irony is that Fox News has also been criticized for being the least accurate. According to the fact-checking site PunditFact, assertions made on Fox and Fox News are 61 percent Mostly False, False or Pants on Fire (compared with CNN's 21 percent in those categories). Only 10 percent of the selected claims on Fox News are deemed True (11 percent Mostly True, 18 percent Half True). Compare this with CNN's 15 percent True, 42 percent Mostly True, 23 percent Half True. From this study, the "most trusted" news source is the least fact-based. Both liberal and conservative news sources have questioned the reliability of PunditFact's findings. Yet in *The Republican Brain: The Science of Why They Deny Science—and Reality* (2012), *Washington Post* journalist and author Chris Mooney cites numerous surveys, polls and studies that reach the same conclusion: "It really is true that Fox viewers are the most misled based on the evidence before us—especially in areas of political controversy." Which means people trust it because it tells them what they want to hear. They trust a source that substantiates their own beliefs. This is the triumph of what Stephen Colbert dubbed "truthiness"—believing something because it feels good, without regard to facts, logic or evidence.

For the 61 percent of millennials getting their news from Facebook, this can create a similar problem. They can go to Facebook pages sponsored by various news organizations, but they are more likely to go to the sources that most reflect their political and social biases. Or, if they are getting their news from Facebook friends posting news stories that resonate with them, the followers are also getting news that reflects their same tastes. When we read or watch only sources that promote a bias, we never challenge our beliefs. We just stay the same ill-informed people.

That tells us that there are a substantial number of Americans on both sides of the political spectrum whose opinions are so intractable that they want to plug their brain into news sources that just repeat the same point of view over and over. The more partisan we become, the more we dislike anyone who doesn't support our prepackaged, vacuum-sealed opinions. This lack of healthy self-doubt and curiosity about other points of view makes such people easier to manipulate by politicians and special interests. The true believers act more like unquestioning cult members than active participants in a democracy. What's the point of having 24/7 access to some of the greatest news-gathering organizations in the world on your phone, TV, radio and computer if you're only going to listen to the same propaganda loop all the time?

In the case of deeply alienated citizens, like many of Donald Trump's supporters during the 2016 campaign, this can lead to a disconnect not only from mainstream media but also from generally accepted reality. Fellow believers form their own social-media feedback loops. "Mr. Trump's rise is actually a symptom of the mass media's growing weakness, especially in controlling the limits of what it is acceptable to say," wrote Zeynep Tufekci, an assistant professor at the School of Information and Library Science at the University of North Carolina. Talking with Trump backers at a rally, she found that "his supporters and I did not share the same factual universe. At one point, I heard Mr. Trump declare that Congress had funded the Islamic State. I looked around, bewildered, as there was no reaction from the crowd. My social media forays confirm that even that was not an uncommon belief."

Because of this alienation and sharply partisan divide, news out-lets have sprung up to provide news and opinions customized for their audience's narrow point of view. Once that happens, these news outlets can rarely test the loyalty of their audiences with reporting that's dissonant with those hard-set views—or they will risk losing viewers and the advertising dollars that go with them. For example, on Sept. 4, 2014, the *Washington Times*, a conservative newspaper, published an article with the headline FED: UNDER OBAMA, ONLY THE RICHEST 10 PERCENT SAW INCOME RISE. Beneath the head-line was a photograph of a smiling President Obama clinking fancy glasses of what looked like champagne, accompanied by a group of well-dressed, seemingly affluent people. The headline clearly blames the president for the income rise (and the lack of one for the other 90 percent), yet the article offers no evidence suggesting specific policies by the president that might be responsible, beyond the basic statistic from the 2013 Survey of Consumer Finances. Instead of analysis, the newspaper offered only the photograph, which caricatured the pres-ident as having an attitude of "let them eat cake." This is how news gets processed to support a bias among readers. If you are tuning in to a particular media outlet because you hate Obama, then your favorite show can never agree with anything he ever does, even if it's generally beneficial. It's like having your own personal ass-kissers to make you feel important and smart. As the ratings of these shows attest, many people choose *feeling* smart over actually *being* smart.

Further undermining trust in media are the periodic scandals involving deliberately inaccurate reporting. Typically, the cause is misguided ambition in a hotly competitive field. In 2016, Juan Thompson, a reporter for the national-security-focused website The Intercept, was caught fabricating quotes and sources in several arti-cles. Peabody Award winner Brian Williams of *NBC Nightly News* was suspended by the network after he concocted tales about being in a helicopter that was shot down in Iraq and seeing a body floating past him in New Orleans in the aftermath of Hurricane Katrina. Fox's Bill O'Reilly has been inconsistent in describing his experiences in the 1982 Falklands War. *Rolling Stone*'s investigative article about a supposed rape at the University of Virginia was cited in an article titled "The Worst Journalism of 2014" by the *Columbia Journalism Review*. The *New York Times*'s Jayson Blair, Fox's Mike Tobin, Fox's Sean Hannity, the *New Republic*'s Stephen Glass, the *Chicago Sun-Times*'s Paige Wiser and many more people from reputable media outlets have been caught misrepresenting the truth.

There is no excuse for journalists lying. In this profession, given the importance of news to our health, safety and political process, making things up is the most serious kind of malpractice. Given the chaos of tight deadlines and everyone scrambling for the same sources during breaking news, it's easy to see how mistakes can be made. Those can be corrected in subsequent editions, posts or broadcasts. But deliberate fabrication does huge damage to media credibility and has a devastating effect on society. Mistrust of the media has contributed to the growing fractionalization of society. People feel vindicated in their biases because they claim they can't trust the news media to tell the truth.

Further undermining the media is their awkward pandering to millennials, which comes off like parents in matching argyle sweater vests trying to prove to their teenage kids that they're cool by working mentions of Snapchat into conversations. Many news outlets are routinely reporting what's trending on social media or displaying audience tweets or emails. Audience participation is as old as Letters to the Editor columns, but this new flurry of dispatches from the Internet is frequently unfocused gimmickry. Citizen journalists sometimes contribute valid reporting (such as on-scene photos of terrorism and natural disasters), but unfiltered amateur speculation is harmful to everybody (such as accusing the wrong person in the Boston Marathon attack). Following the presidential debates during 2015 and 2016, news outlets would tell us whom the pundits anointed as the winners and then tell us who "won" on social media based on Google searches of candidates' names. How is that scientific or even professional journalism? Social-media conjecture is not news. It does make the news outlet seem current, but it's faddish and damaging to journalistic integrity. The dirty secret of mainstream media's embrace of social media is that it's a lot cheaper to festoon a news show or home page with reader opinions than it is to send a trained reporter into the field to gather new facts.

WHAT HAVE THE NEWS MEDIA DONE FOR US LATELY?

Maybe the main reason for the public's growing discontent with the media is that even amid all the agreeable news and infotainment, the media still tell us some things we don't like to hear, information that's contrary to our beliefs and opinions. Journalists are seen as the purveyors of overcooked vegetables and bitter medicines that taste bad but that we must ingest because "They're good for you!" Basically, we want to kill the messenger for bringing us bad news, because otherwise we might have to do something about those in power who actually cause the bad news. The media have responded by adding much more friendly and fun news to the mix to take the edge off the hard stuff. Heartwarming stories of local heroism, especially if they involve puppies, kittens, children or cute seniors, are favorites.

Certainly things that are right with the world are as newsworthy as things that are going wrong. The paradox is that most people favor bad news to good news in their media-consuming preferences, according to researchers at McGill University in Quebec. While participants in the study told interviewers that they preferred good news and that, in general, the media focused too much on negative stories, during the testing phase the participants more often wanted stories with a negative tone. How to explain this disparity? Polling experts call this a social-desirability response bias—in other words, the respondent gives the answer that seems most respectable, especially to abstract questions. So in a way, the public's complaining about the press presenting so much dark news is a kind of self-loathing. The media often give us what we crave—and we're ashamed of our news cravings just as we're embarrassed about rubbernecking at the scene of an accident.

We need to remember that those dark stories often lead us to enlightenment. Lest we forget exactly what legitimate journalists do and why they are so important, here are some of the stories that recently won Pulitzer Prizes for Investigative Reporting:

▸ **2015:** Two winners: Eric Lipton, of the *New York Times*, "for reporting that showed how the influence of lobbyists can sway congressional leaders and state attorneys general, slanting justice toward the wealthy and connected," and the staff of the *Wall Street Journal*, "for 'Medicare Unmasked,' a pioneering project that gave Americans unprecedented access to previously confidential data on the motivations and practices of their health care providers."

▸ **2014:** Chris Hamby, of the Center for Public Integrity, "for his reports on how some lawyers and doctors rigged a system to deny benefits to coal miners stricken with black lung disease, resulting in remedial legislative efforts."

▸ **2013:** David Barstow and Alejandra Xanic von Bertrab, of the *New York Times*, "for their reports on how Wal-Mart used widespread bribery to dominate the market in Mexico, resulting in changes in company practices."

There are so many more articles like this in newspapers and magazines, as well as segments on television shows such as *60 Minutes*. Often these articles stir enough outrage to result in new laws and practices. While soldiers are the nation's defense against foreign enemies and police are the nation's defense against criminals, journalists are the nation's defense against the corruption hiding in the shadows all around us.

In the pilot episode of HBO's magnificent series *The Newsroom*, the famous news anchor Will McAvoy, who is sitting onstage at a university as part of a debate about news and politics, calmly responds to every question with a facile joke meant not to offend anyone or risk his ratings. But when he's pressed to respond to a student's question about why America is the greatest country in the world, he explodes with a rundown of facts that show how we aren't the greatest anymore. Then he explains why we used to be the greatest: "We stood up for what was right. We fought for moral reasons. We passed laws, struck down laws for *moral* reasons. We waged wars on poverty, not poor people. We sacrificed; we cared about our neighbors. We put our money where our mouths were, and we never beat our chest. We built great big things, made ungodly technological advances, explored the universe, cured diseases, and we cultivated the world's greatest artists and the world's greatest economy. We reached for the stars. Acted like men. We aspired to intelligence; we didn't belittle it; it didn't make us feel inferior. We didn't identify ourselves by who we voted for in our last election. And we didn't . . . we didn't scare so easy. We were able to be all these things, and to do all these things, because we were informed. By great men, men who were revered."

Though he fails to include the great women journalists, his point is that our greatness is directly related to our ability to be informed but, more important, to *want* to be informed. And that we stayed informed because we respected the journalists who brought us the news. Complaining about the relatively few missteps of most of the news media is not a reflection of their flaws as much as it is of the public's inertia when it comes to keeping informed.

HOW TO MAKE THE NEWS MEDIA BETTER

In *The Newsroom*, Will's passionate speech, which he later in a panic tries to blame on his medication, inspires his producer to assemble a group of dedicated journalists who make a quixotic pact to do the news as it was meant to be done: "Reclaiming journalism as an honorable profession. A nightly newscast that informs a debate worthy of a great nation. Civility, respect and a return to what's important; the death of bitchiness; the death of gossip and voyeurism . . . No demographic sweet spot; a place where we *all come together.*"

Yes, we can smirk cynically and make snarky comments about such naive idealism, but if ever there were something we should be intensely idealistic about, it's advocating for the principles of the First

Amendment. I'd rather stand with those crazy idealists who wrote the Constitution with little hope that such radical principles would be upheld, let alone inspire so much of the rest of the world to follow suit.

I have written for many news sources, including TIME, the *Washington Post*, *Esquire* and the *Los Angeles Times*. I've witnessed firsthand the financial pressure many of these publications are facing and the toll it has taken on their ability to gather news. I've also had my share of disagreements with editors about the content of my articles. However, what's so uplifting, even in these disagreements, even facing financial problems, is how everyone involved was dedicated to producing the best-written, most accurate articles possible.

Given the public's growing partisanship, the news media will have a hard time recapturing the public trust. In part, it would come from a population less fearful of differing points of view and more open to changing minds based on new information. Educating society in critical thinking may be a process that takes generations to achieve. Still, there are steps that can be taken to make the news media better.

1. Stop pandering.

The obsession with social media needs to be tempered. To be sure, social media has been a boon to journalism in some ways, especially by enlarging a story's audience. When I publish a column on Time.com, I benefit from the site's millions of Twitter followers hearing about it. And yes, sometimes it's fascinating to see what is spiking on Google, like when searches for "how to move to Canada" surged after Trump won seven primaries on Super Tuesday in 2016. But to treat rising and falling memes on Facebook or what is being searched for on Google as social science is misleading. It may be entertaining or chat-worthy, but in terms of accurately gauging the sentiment or intentions of the American people, it's no substitute for professional opinion polling, statistical research and just plain reporting. It's like forecasting the weather based on a swollen bunion.

The pandering includes the comments section that many news

websites include after each posted story. In theory, this is a good way to encourage public discourse on important issues raised in an article. But in practice, it's mostly nut jobs and trolls spewing nonsensical ranting. Many don't even read the entire article before launching their enraged opinions. Because most commenters don't have to use their names, they can say anything without having to take any responsibility. In the end, this doesn't further public discourse—it provides a community bouncy house for intellectual shut-ins, racists and cranks.

On April Fools' Day of 2014, National Public Radio's website published the headline "Why Doesn't America Read Anymore?" The "article" directly under the headline was the following:

> Congratulations, genuine readers, and happy April Fools' Day!
>
> We sometimes get the sense that some people are commenting on NPR stories that they haven't actually read. If you are reading this, please like this post and do not comment on it. Then let's see what people have to say about this "story."
>
> Best wishes and have an enjoyable day,
> Your friends at NPR

That was it. No article detailing the headline. Yet the comments section had numerous outraged readers who complained that the "article" was wrong:

> This article is horrible. Americans DO read, it's disrespectful to intelligent americans [sic] to state as fact that america [sic] no longer reads . . . America is a great and educated country, and one I am proud to live in.

Others commented on how such reactions made NPR's point. One commenter offered keen insight into the entire comments ideology:

> It is kind of funny, and fascinating (like a car crash) but I find myself more depressed as I read the comments. It's like every other comment thread—preconceived indignation, irrelevant Dem-Repub flame wars, and off topic information dumps. And worse, few of the people who just commented on the title ever figured out that it was a joke.
>
> I never thought I'd say it, but comment threads would be so much better if the commenters had a reliability ranking.

Reliability rankings would be too time-consuming and expensive for most media outlets. Instead, the news media should treat their comments sections as they would a Letters to the Editor section in a print newspaper, allowing only comments that offer an articulate and reasoned opinion and are written by a verifiable person willing to attach their name to their opinions. This would make the comments a valuable addition to the public conversation. The *New York Times*, for example, makes a concerted investment in curating its comments sections, offering "readers picks" and "NYT picks," which help sort the discerning from the dreck. But as it is now on many sites, the comment function is an open invitation to take a verbal dump on a news site, with the sites adding up the piles to prove how popular they are. Like a dog park.

2. Do not move the integrity line.

Back in the 1950s, 1960s and 1970s, the network news consisted of CBS, NBC and ABC. Their news divisions weren't expected to make a profit. News was a matter of prestige, citizenship and public-service requirements set by the Federal Communications

Commission. CBS's owner and chairman, William Paley, was over-heard in the early 1960s telling his news reporters not to worry about costs because "I have Jack Benny to make money."

That business model no longer applies. The amount of competition from other news sources has shrunk the audience size for any one source. Entertainment shows, also suffering from so many cable and online options, make less profit to subsidize news. Foreign news bureaus have been closed, layoffs are ongoing, and pooling of resources has become necessary for survival. Newspapers are doing even worse than TV news: ad revenues have shrunk to their 1950 level.

It's hard to blame the news media for trying anything to attract an audience, since their existence depends on numbers. Can any news outlet succeed in offering nonpartisan, enterprising journalism? While Fox News has been very successful in its model of providing partisan shows heavy on loud accusations and light on actual facts, there's no point in fighting over that audience, because they will not be wooed by reason. That's not what Fox's viewers want. The real battle is to appeal to an audience seeking intelligent, in-depth reporting. The hope is that future generations of Americans, who will be increasingly diverse, will be just as varied in their opinions and deep in their curiosity.

In many surveys during the past decade, Jon Stewart was chosen as the most trusted newscaster in America since Walter Cronkite, and Stewart's *The Daily Show* was selected as a top source for news, particularly among young viewers. Also in the top ranks of polls as a trusted source of news was Stephen Colbert of *The Colbert Report*. As both hosts made clear many times, theirs were comedy shows, not news shows, yet the stories they presented were effective, aside from the comedy, because they revealed a passion for social justice and civil reason. That torch has been picked up by John Oliver (*Last Week Tonight*), Larry Wilmore (*The Nightly Show*) and Samantha Bee (*Full Frontal*) and carried forth admirably. What was clear in those shows and in the new ones is a level of uncompromising integrity.

This is not a call for the news media to add comedy or to be more partisan, as all those shows are, in order to attract readers and viewers. It's a plea for real news shows to match the respect for the audience that the fake news shows display. Enough with the useless graphics, the forced 30-second "debates" between stock left and right representatives, and the interjection of stereotypical language like references to civil rights protesters as "rioters" or "thugs."

"AND THAT'S THE WAY IT IS"

When we talk about public trust in the media, maybe we're defining the issue in the wrong way. Perhaps the media are meant to be unsettling, just as other truth seekers can be. A 2015 Pew Research Center poll revealed a huge gap between scientists and the American public, with the public often in disagreement on scientific issues with the experts: in a survey, 88 percent of members of the American Association for the Advancement of Science said genetically modified foods are safe to eat, compared with 37 percent of American adults; 87 percent of the scientists said climate change is caused by human activity, while only 50 percent of the public agree; 98 percent state that humans evolved over time, versus 65 percent of the public. The public's trust in science is less than overwhelming—unless there's a serious medical or environmental problem. Then we suddenly have born-again faith: "Science will solve the problem." We tend to trust scientists, but we don't always like it when their opinions differ from our own traditional beliefs.

Same with the news media. The public follows the media but is frustrated with the news itself. It makes us feel helpless and marginalized. That feeling of helplessness and frustration typically occurs when the news media are doing their jobs well. Writing for Politico, Jack Shafer observed:

> It may seem counterintuitive but a strong case can be made that the public trusted the press *more* when it was *less* trustworthy . . . That the public might have

become less enamored of the press as it has grown more independent and combative only stands to reason. For one thing, the pushy, know-it-all, argumentative journalistic style required to dislodge information from governments and corporations isn't very likable. For another thing, the intelligent skepticism practiced by modern reporters, once released from the bottle, cannot be shoved back in. It only makes sense that the public, exposed to critical thinking by the press, should redirect that critical thinking back onto the press itself. The more people know, the less they trust.

Sure, the news media have their clowns and jesters, their liars and panderers, but the best way to ensure integrity is to ignore those shallow pretenders and embrace the discomfort that a good news story should bring.

Maybe it's a hopeful sign that *Spotlight*, a movie based on a true story of investigative journalism at the *Boston Globe* that uncovered widespread abuse of children by priests, won the 2016 Academy Award for Best Picture. Maybe it affirms not just the filmmakers' collective talent but also an appreciation for truth and for journalists seeking the truth, no matter how painful or uncomfortable it is. In the movie, *Globe* editor Marty Baron reminds his reporters, "Sometimes it's easy to forget that we spend most of our time stumbling around in the dark." The result of all that stumbling in the dark is an illumination of the path for the rest of us.

Or it should be.

8

—

Seniors
THE AGING OF AQUARIUS

"The privilege of a lifetime is to become who you truly are."
—CARL JUNG

SENIORS IN AMERICA ARE GENERALLY TREATED LIKE RUSTY
used cars with leaking oil, screeching brakes and "Good Lord,
what's that smell coming from the backseat?" We've turned them
into cartoon images that make them out to be some comic combination of doddering, cranky, forgetful, disapproving, anti-technology,
doily-loving marionettes who are shuffling off their mortal coils in
excruciating slow motion. Of all the biases in America today, this is
one of the most self-defeating, because being old is a role we all have to
play someday—if we're lucky—and it is a challenging role. The young
and middle-aged make it hard for themselves by embracing these
insulting stereotypes, because they are making the uncomfortable beds
that they will one day have to lie in. Seeing seniors as corny caricatures
is a bit like whistling past the graveyard, a comforting way to deny that
most of us this way will pass. Yet as they near the inevitable time when
they are eligible for senior discounts, they will learn that, as the French
author Jules Renard said, "It's not how old you are, it's how you are old."

Despite this harsh perception by the "pre-elderly," who react out

of fear of their own inevitable wrinkling cycle, I have found growing older to be enormously liberating and empowering. I especially
cherish my new superpower: saying no. Throughout my youth and
middle age, I often felt obligated to do things I didn't want to do in
order to further my career or fit in better socially or avoid conflict.
Now that I'm nearing 70, I just politely decline. Sometimes people
react to my no with surprise or anger, which is when I call on another
superpower of aging: the mighty, unstoppable Shrug of Indifference.

That doesn't mean I've stopped caring about the people I love or
the world in general. It's just that, given my limited time left on this
planet, I have to be more miserly in how I spend my last precious
years. I'm not sitting on my couch all day in my UCLA sweats with a
greasy TV remote molding to my grip, shouting at the screen, "Bring
back *Murder, She Wrote!*" I'm as active and socially committed as I've
ever been, maybe even more so. Two thirds of the year I'm flying
around the country to speak at schools, do book signings, discuss
social and political issues on talk shows or appear at education conventions promoting STEM programs. When I'm not traveling, I'm
writing books, articles and scripts. But everything I choose to do, I
do with passion and dedication because I'm doing what I want to,
not because I have to, need to or am obligated to. And that makes
everything more rewarding.

Having a longer-term perspective is another advantage of aging.
Tumultuous world events are less scary. When I was younger, every
disruption of normal international or domestic routine sent a chill of
panic through me. The headlines were scary: fluctuations in the stock
market, sending troops to fight abroad, rioting, protests, dictators testing nuclear weapons, AIDS, a president resigning. Everything seemed
like a *Dr. Strangelove* doomsday scenario of world annihilation.

Things haven't gotten any calmer, with more of the same plus
global warming, mass shootings, growing terrorist attacks, government shutdowns, droughts, epidemics like Ebola and honeybees
facing extinction. These events still concern me, and I want to contribute everything I can to alleviate suffering and secure a stable

future for the next generation. But because I've witnessed this same pattern of evil, abuse and natural disasters for so long, every breaking news story doesn't send my pulse thunking. I've come to accept that threats of world chaos eventually settle down into a remarkably predictable pattern. As the student named Rudge so eloquently says about the cycles of history in Alan Bennett's Tony-winning play *The History Boys*: "History is just one fucking thing after another." The moral: once you accept that human existence follows an elaborate quilt pattern, you live a more relaxed life.

While aging does bestow these delightful gifts, it also punishes us by stripping away some of our most fundamental and intimate pleasures. The body deteriorates into a series of chronic aches, diseases and physical challenges. We start to lose our loved ones in what seems like Obituary Russian Roulette to see whose funeral is next. We are marginalized by a society that ignores us unless we are wealthy and powerful. TV shows we like are canceled even if they have strong audience numbers because the viewers are "too old" and therefore not attractive to sponsors obsessed with the 18-to-34-year-old demographic. Movies are rarely made to address our interests and concerns. When they do portray older characters, they are often stereotypes that make fun of our infirmities, villainize us as grotesque grouches or infantilize us to be cooed over as if we were cute gray-haired toddlers. Major magazines are preoccupied with the young, featuring hard bodies, tech gadgets and whatever they think is trending, ignoring the urgent issues that affect our lives. When business and society write off people at age 35, they're writing off about five decades of every American's life.

This is a mistake, one that may be a vestige of the *Mad Men* era, when the young baby-boom generation was a bulging portion of the population and thus the plumpest target audience. Now those of us born between 1946 and 1964 are older, but it doesn't mean we're broke or housebound. We need our goods and services too. Although we're seen by the younger members of society as that aisle in Walmart that holds the randomly piled assortment of damaged goods reduced for quick sale, that attitude sorely underestimates the clout that American seniors could actually have if they managed not to accept the status quo as inevitable and began to work together to flex those aging but still powerful muscles.

The power in those muscles comes from what America understands best: the bottom line. In 2007, the University of Cincinnati created a consortium of students, faculty and corporations, including Procter & Gamble, with the goal of researching and developing products for consumers 50 and over. It concluded that "the world has never before seen such a powerful market," accounting for about $3 trillion a year in the U.S. alone. According to Nielsen, by 2017 nearly half the adult population in the U.S. will be 50 and older and will be responsible for 70 percent of the country's disposable income. This is a fact that advertisers ignore because they are blinded by the luminescent glow of our gray hair and shimmering bald heads. Only 15 percent of advertising dollars are spent on this age demographic, even though they buy half of the consumer packaged goods. But maybe American businesses will come around. As TIME reported about the 18-to-34 cohort in 2012: "Now that this age group is broke and facing huge student loans and a lackluster job market . . . the realization is setting in that perhaps it's not such a good idea to focus on a bunch of consumers with little disposable income and increasingly frugal habits."

Every day in America, 10,000 baby boomers turn 65. Right now that adds up to about 46.2 million people 65 and over. In two decades, there will be 75 million of us. By 2050, nearly 21 percent of the population will be 65 and older; more than 4 percent of the total population will be 85 and older. We're like the Jets street gang in *West Side Story*. A group of guys walking down the street snapping our fingers. Soon you've got a swarm of aging rockers with hearing aids claiming their turf.

Which brings us to the great paradox of aging. On one hand, several studies report that seniors are the happiest and most content age group. "The good news is that with age comes happiness," said

Yang Yang, a sociologist from the University of Chicago and the author of one such study. "Life gets better in one's perception as one ages." One reason for this blissful state is that about 75 percent of those between 57 and 85 participate each week in one or more social activities (visiting with neighbors, doing volunteer work, attending religious services). People in their 80s did these activities twice as often as those in their 50s. Furthermore, seniors have let go of the nattering demands of middle age, which studies conclude is the most stressful time in life. "Everyone's asking you to do things, and you have a lot to do," explained Cornell University sociologist Elaine Wethington. "You're less happy because you feel hassled." Then you discover the power of saying no, and your life seems to be better. On the other hand, that blissful golden age can also quickly deteriorate when facing the sudden loss of loved ones, the onset of severe physical ailments or unexpected financial problems. People 85 and older have the highest rate of suicide; the next highest rate is among middle-age people.

As the number of seniors grows, we will have an even greater impact on the economy and in the political arena. Because of that, America will have to learn better ways to perceive and understand the evolution of aging. And those who join the ranks of senior citizens will have to learn how to have their voices heard so they can guide the younger generations rather than have them, through ignorance and social conventions, passively imprison the elderly in geriatric gulags.

MIRROR, MIRROR ON THE WALL: THE MIND-BODY PROBLEM

I don't look in the mirror as much as I used to, since I'm always unpleasantly surprised by the stranger's face that stares back. In my mind, I expect to see the same face I had when I was in my 30s—bright and shining with expectation and worlds to conquer—not that sagging flesh that looks like a decaying Halloween pumpkin. The reason I continue to be surprised is that the face doesn't match what

I feel inside. In there, I still feel bright and shining with expectation and worlds to conquer. Even in the morning, when I'm dragging a little and the walk to the bathroom seems like a forced march across the Sahara with the French Foreign Legion, when I flip on the light switch, I expect to see a reflection that shows my excitement for the day, my curiosity about what I will learn, my drive to accomplish something good. But that's not the face I see.

This is a common experience of aging. I watched a sitcom when I was younger in which a woman said that when she was putting on a sweater that morning she was shocked to see her mother's hand emerge from the sleeve. And so the process continues, as each body part begins to resemble that of someone else, someone much older, until you feel like a robot that's had all its parts swapped out.

This is not the mind-body problem that philosophers ponder theoretically but the one seniors live with daily on a practical basis. In essence, the mind-body problem is the study of the relationship between the body, which is physical, and the mind (thoughts, beliefs, emotions), which is immaterial. The relationship could not be any clearer to those carrying the weight of 65-plus years on their back.

The hardest thing seniors must adjust to is the betrayal. When you're young, your body is like a best friend. You share adventures that you embark on only because you know you can trust your body to see you through. Sure, I'll climb that mountain. Yeah, I'll surf those giant waves. Dance all night long at a club? No problem. The youthful body is the conduit to physical and emotional pleasure, a metaphysical pimp. Then, as you age, your BFF falters. What used to provide exhilaration is now a source of exhaustion. You look at coliseum steps at the ballgame and remember how you used to bound up them two at a time. Now you get halfway up and wish you had a jetpack. As the Eagles sang in "After the Thrill Is Gone": "Time passes and you must move on / Half the distance takes you twice as long."

Worse than the gradual slowdown of the body is the aggressive attack on our health, both physical and mental. In 2010, personal health-care costs for those 65 and older averaged about $18,000, which is three times the cost for an average working-age adult and five times that for a child. Serious diseases nip eagerly at our heels like rabid badgers. There's no outrunning them. I've battled leukemia and heart disease, the latter resulting in quadruple bypass surgery. Although I'm healthy now, like every other senior I realize it's just a matter of time before the next badger sinks its razor teeth into another part of my body. This is not a battle that can be won. All we can do is postpone losing.

Then there is our darkest fear: the need for long-term care, which is a more realistic worry as we typically live well into our 80s. We may reach a time when our bodies give up on us altogether and those who knew us when we were vital and active, carrying our children on our shoulders and playing tennis with the neighbors, will see us hunched in a chair or bed. In 2007, about 12 million Americans required long-term-care services. By 2050, an estimated 27 million will need them. These are realities of aging that those lucky enough to make it that far will have to face. As Bette Davis famously said, "Getting old is not for sissies."

SENIORS: PUBLIC BURDEN OR SOCIAL ASSET?

Many of us have heard the folklore about how Eskimos would abandon their elderly on ice floes, letting them drift out to sea to freeze to death. Though instances of this actually happening were rare, the vivid imagery has stuck in our imagination as a metaphor of how societies view their seniors. They can isolate them through neglect, ridicule or oversight until they drift out of our awareness altogether.

Historically, senicide (the killing of the elderly through abandonment or murder) was a harsh reality. In some cultures, when resources such as food and water were critically scarce, the old and infirm were considered expendable. Sometimes villages would pack up and move during the night while the elderly were asleep. Sometimes the aged were encouraged (or even forced) to drink poison for the good of the community. As recently as 2010, in the state of Tamil Nadu in India, this practice was common enough that the government assigned officials to watch over seniors.

America still has an abundance of resources, but as the population continues to age, seniors will be putting a financial strain on those resources. Social Security provides 90 percent or more of the income for 22 percent of married and 47 percent of single recipients ages 65 and older. It is the largest federal program, spending $845 billion in 2014. By 2025 this amount will increase by 90 percent, to $1.6 trillion. Medicare spending was $618 billion in 2014 and is expected to rise 78 percent, to $1.1 trillion, by 2024. The cost of informal caregiving for seniors by friends and family is $522 billion a year. Despite all this money spent, more than 23 million Americans over 60 are living at or below the poverty level (defined as $11,880 for a single person). The situation is even worse for women and African Americans, who receive significantly less money in government benefits. In 2015, officials announced there would be no increase in Social Security payments for the following year because of a lack of consumer price inflation, despite the fact that one third of senior households have no money left over after meeting monthly expenses. Essentially, we are doing very little to alleviate the poverty of our elders even as the number of poor seniors continues to rise each day. They are trapped on an economic ice floe, drifting away. But out of sight doesn't mean out of mind, because whatever affects seniors has a domino effect on America's economy.

How can seniors be a burden if they are such a major source of consumer spending? While many seniors are wealthy, the number of poor seniors is growing, in part because of the rising costs of health-care expenses not covered by Medicare. We oldsters are not a cheap date, America. A 2012 report by the National Research Council titled *Aging and the Macroeconomy: Long-Term Implications of an Older Population* concluded that Americans will have to make major changes in their saving and spending habits and in how federal programs like Social Security and Medicare, which currently account for 43 percent of federal spending, are structured. According to one of the report's authors, Ronald Lee, a professor of demography and economics at the University of California, Berkeley, "We strongly believe that our nation needs to act sooner rather than later. The problem is not going to go away and it only gets tougher the longer we delay." The key problem is that Americans live longer (on average 78 years) while our birth rate is declining, which gives the country fewer workers to pay taxes in order to support more and more seniors.

Which prompts the question among younger people: Are the elderly worth the spiraling price?

That question is posed in W.D. Snodgrass's poem "A Flat One," in which a caregiver at a veterans hospital ponders the frustration of his job overseeing a comatose, bedridden war veteran:

> They'd say this was a worthwhile job
>> Unless they tried it. It is mad
>> To throw our good lives after bad;
>> Waste time, drugs, and our minds, while strong
>> Men starve. How many young men did we rob
>> To keep you hanging on?

In the last stanza, the caregiver answers his own question. At first, he decides that they kept the patient alive simply because it was their job. But then he realizes that there is a deeper motivation, beyond even gratitude for the veteran's service, something that goes to the core of our humanity.

> I can't think we did you much good.
>> Well, when you died, none of us wept.
>> You killed for us, and so we kept
>> You, because we need to earn our pay.
>> No. We'd still have to help you try. We would
>> Have killed for you today.

The value of seniors must go beyond the sentimental attachment we have to our own family, because that clearly hasn't worked out for millions of elderly living in poverty. Despite the best of intentions, many families can't support themselves and their elderly parents. Society at large has to pitch in as well. Yet the political clout of senior citizens is under attack. Voting laws requiring photo IDs, which primarily restrict minorities from voting, have the collateral damage of lessening the ability of seniors to vote. The Brennan Center for Justice estimates that while 11 percent of all eligible voters lack a photo ID, about 18 percent of those 65 and older have no photo ID, potentially eliminating some 6 million seniors from exercising their right to vote. While it is a simple matter for most people to just go down to the DMV and get a photo ID, for seniors the trip can be physically complicated and the expense prohibitive. So while we publicly proclaim how much we value our elder citizens, we seem to be doing everything we can to treat them as worthless.

Maybe we need to look at it practically. We may love our own grandparents, but what have seniors as a group done for us lately? One tangible value seniors offer society is the priceless commodity of wisdom from experience. Of course, growing old is not necessarily a Willy Wonka golden ticket to enlightenment. It doesn't automatically turn a person into Yoda or Mr. Miyagi, the guru from *The Karate Kid*. Failing eyesight doesn't translate into deeper insight. For some people, growing older doesn't enrich them; it just lowers their social inhibitions and they get nastier. Others grow old gracefully, with love and compassion and good cheer, but not necessarily with any more perception than they had when they were 20. Spouting tired clichés (or embroidering them on pillows) is not the same thing as perceptiveness. But there are many seniors who have distilled a lifetime of struggle into an elixir of wisdom that we can all benefit from.

I think of aging as the process of climbing a hill. When you are young, you are standing in a field of wheat as tall as your chin. You can see over the top of the wheat just enough to catch people's faces and see them moving about. That's all the information you have to understand the world. But as you age, you start climbing the hill before you. Each year, you're a little higher above the field and you see more people and where they're going and you understand the patterns of behavior. The higher you climb, the more landscape you see and the better you understand the bigger picture. From that elevated vantage you can recognize what's important and what's petty, what demands action and what requires patience. That knowledge is valuable to the generations still stuck in the wheat field or early in their climb up the hillside. We can show them the best path and point to the important sights. We can identify political patterns that seem to replicate the rise of tyrants. We can warn against entering into wars that have no real purpose. We can raise the alarm about institutional racism, sexism and homophobia. "Not another Nazi Germany!" "Not another Vietnam!" "Not another Jim Crow era!" A lot of young people don't know these lessons. This idea is echoed in William Butler Yeats's poem about aging "Sailing to Byzantium," published when he was 63. In the poem, the narrator longs to have his mind separated from his body, which he refers to as "a paltry thing, / A tattered coat upon a stick" and "a dying animal," so that he might have a golden body to sit "upon a golden bough to sing . . . Of what is past, or passing, or to come."

The problem with expressing this insight gained through age is the Cassandra phenomenon. In Greek mythology, Cassandra was a princess of Troy who was romantically pursued by the god Apollo. To win her over, he gave her the gift of being able to prophesy the future. But when she rejected his advances, he cursed her so that no one would believe her prophecies, even though they were true. She would have to live with the frustration and helplessness of foreseeing disaster after disaster for her people but not being able to warn them. It was Cassandra who told the Trojans to beware of accepting the wooden horse offered by the Greeks. They brought the Trojan horse into their city and were destroyed.

Most parents are aware of this phenomenon, because no matter how much they warn their children about certain inevitable events, the kids are determined to ignore the parents and act in direct contradiction. So it can be with society in general. Seniors with experience, knowledge and insight can advise because they recognize the same pattern repeating itself, only to be ignored by those in power eager to make their own mark.

Despite the Cassandra phenomenon, seniors express the culmination of their life experiences in other ways that inform and entertain and brighten their communities. Laura Ingalls Wilder published her first *Little House on the Prairie* book when she was 65. Harland Sanders was 62 when he first franchised Kentucky Fried Chicken. Anna Mary Robertson Moses, known as Grandma Moses, launched her painting career in her late 70s. (In 2006, one of her paintings fetched $1.2 million.) Momofuku Ando invented Cup Noodles at 61. Peter Roget published Roget's Thesaurus when he was 73. Ben Franklin, the only person to sign the Declaration of Independence, the Treaty of Paris and the U.S. Constitution, was 70 when he signed the Declaration. Nelson Mandela, after 27 years in prison for fighting apartheid in South Africa, became the country's first black president at age 75. At age 60, Mohandas Gandhi, carrying his own clothes, led the three-week, 240-mile Salt March to protest the British salt tax, sparking nationwide civil disobedience that led to India's independence. In 2000, 89-year-old Doris Haddock completed a 3,200-mile, 14-month walk from Pasadena, Calif., to Washington, D.C., to push for campaign finance reform. At 64, Diana Nyad became the first person to swim from Cuba to Florida without a shark cage—a feat she had failed at four times before, even when she was 28. "The truth is," she said, "I am a better athlete in my mid-60s than I was, even as a world champion, in my mid-20s."

These seniors faced many of the physical, mental and social challenges that age pummels us with, but they fought back, they endured, they inspired.

So cancel the Uber ice-floe app. The villagers can unpack and tiptoe back to bed. Granny and Gramps can sleep peacefully tonight. Although there are real economic struggles ahead, the country has millions of reasons to value the enormous contributions of its oldest generations, even when there is a price.

THE SEVENTH-INNING STRETCH: HOW TO FIX THE SENIOR SITUATION

Popular perception may be that seniors are in life's winding-down period, but that's not how most of us seniors see it. We're just taking the seventh-inning stretch as we prepare to make the most out of the last two innings (or, with luck, overtime!). We're like lottery winners with millions' worth of experience, figuring out how best to spread the riches. In the Yeats poem mentioned earlier, "Sailing to Byzantium," the narrator declares that this "is no country for old men." But it should be, it can be and it will be if we, young and old alike, agree on a plan that benefits all of us. Three ways we must change in order to make that happen:

1. Shore up Social Security.

Social Security, the lifeline to 91 percent of seniors, is in serious jeopardy. Collecting that check at the start of the month has been an American entitlement since 1935. By the time we hit 60, visions of gold watches, retirement parties, sentimental speeches and more time with the grandchildren begin to dance in our head. The first country to institute social insurance for seniors was Germany, which established its system in 1889, 46 years before the U.S. At first, Germany set the retirement age at 70, but in 1916, the country lowered it to 65. When America started its own system, officials debated whether to make the retirement age 65 or 70. (Half the country's state pensions started at 65, the other half at 70.) After conducting several studies, the federal government decided that 65 was sustainable with relatively small tax payments.

That was then. In 1935 there were 7.8 million Americans 65 and older (about 6 percent of the population). Today there are 46.2 million age 65 and older (about 14 percent). In 1900, the average American who reached 65 had about 12 more years to live; in 2000, a 65-year-old had 18 more years. In 1950, 46 percent of men 65 and older worked; in 2003, that figure was below 20 percent. Today, men and women are retiring five or six years earlier than they did in the

1970s—but living considerably longer. What all these figures tell us is that we're paying a lot more, the amount will continue to increase, and the system is no longer fiscally sustainable. It is estimated that Social Security's trust-fund reserves will be gone by 2037. Until 2010, payroll deductions were greater than the payout, with surpluses helping to reduce our federal deficit, but by 2014, Social Security had a $73 billion deficit.

One way to close this gap is to raise the age at which one can begin collecting Social Security. Currently, the full retirement age is 66 for people born between 1943 and 1954; it then rises on a gradual scale to 67 for those born in 1960 or later. (Seniors are able to claim early benefits as soon as age 62 but at a greatly reduced amount, and they receive larger payments for the rest of their lives if they wait until age 70 to start collecting.) Some politicians, largely Republicans hoping to incur favor with fiscal conservatives, have proposed raising the retirement age to between 68 and 70. One problem with this proposal is that it punishes blue-collar and non-college-educated workers. A 2014 study reports that those workers are 55 percent more likely than higher-income workers to file for early retirement, often because of the physical effects their work has had on their health and their inability to sustain intense physical activity. Members of this group also have a shorter life expectancy than college-educated white-collar workers, so postponing their retirement can be even worse on their health and the quality of their remaining years.

Another social force that pushes seniors into early retirement is age discrimination in the workplace. Despite legislation against it, studies indicate that some employers follow a pattern of pushing out older workers through layoffs and job eliminations. It starts when the employees are in their 50s and earning their highest salaries; it occurs again when they are nearing retirement age and ready to collect pensions. "There is this sense that it is legitimate to discriminate against older people in a way that it is not legitimate to discriminate on the basis of race and gender," said Vincent Roscigno, a sociology professor at Ohio State University, who has studied the issue.

Raising the retirement age would result in smaller payouts for retirees. According to *The Atlantic*, those who retire at age 67 today would see their benefits reduced by 20 percent if the Social Security threshold were raised to 70. These hardships might be worthwhile if they promised to make a huge impact on the deficit, but some experts calculate that raising the retirement age to 68 would reduce Social Security's deficit by only 12 percent over the next 75 years. Clearly, more will have to be done. One solution is to remove the cap on Social Security payroll deductions. Currently, high-income taxpayers get a huge break, since as of 2015, income is taxed for Social Security only up to $118,500, a cap that rises very gradually. By eliminating this limit, Social Security could reduce its deficit by 70 percent in 75 years.

2. Raise our voices.

Seniors sometimes feel they are under siege—and we have good reason. Politicians want to restrict our ability to vote. Employers want to dump us because our paychecks reflect our experience. Some families want to warehouse us in substandard long-term-care facilities. Internet and telephone con artists are trying to scam us out of our money. The media demean us with stereotypical caricatures. It's enough to give us gray hair—or grayer hair. We cannot afford to just wring our hands and depend on the kindness of strangers. We have to bring about change on our own.

Political change occurs through the strength of numbers, and, with more than 46 million of us, seniors certainly have that. Plus, there are millions of other pre-elderly in their 40s and 50s who realize they'll soon be pulling into the Seniorville station. When they arrive, they'd like some assurances that they won't have to struggle to make ends meet and won't be marginalized by the rest of society. We need to actively enlist their help.

The best way for seniors to build political clout is to keep a close watch on the issues that will affect them. Laws are often debated and passed affecting seniors' pensions, voting rights and health care without the subjects of these legal changes ever being aware. If you're a senior, or soon to become one, try to become a political junkie for your cause. Setting a "senior citizens" Google Alert will generate automatic emails with a list of relevant news items. Know your advocates too: AARP, the Alliance for Retired Americans, Justice in Aging and many other groups. (For a fuller list, go to the U.S. Department of Health and Human Services' Administration for Community Living at acl.gov.)

We don't necessarily have to be standing on the steps of Congress waving signs: I'M OLD, I'M BOLD, AND I WON'T BE LEFT OUT IN THE COLD. But politicians do respond to blocs of voters making demands. And the larger the bloc, the greater the response.

3. Bury the stereotypes.

It has been said, "The secret of change is to focus all of your energy not on fighting the old but on building the new." That's especially apt when considering the condescending way seniors are portrayed in pop culture. There's not much we can do about the insulting stereotypes of seniors in books, TV shows and movies that are already in the social ether. But we definitely have to do something to influence new, more accurate images that reflect the broad spectrum of aging.

The problem is that non-seniors see older people as one of a few cartoonish types: the grumpy coot who growls at everything, the kindly cookie baker who's always saying "dear," the smiling codger in the flannel shirt who dispenses wisdom like Pez candies, or the crazy, colorful oddball who dresses and acts like a teenager. These images have desexualized and deprived older people of their humanity, like neutering a pet. The young often view seniors with fear and trepidation, as if they are alien invaders. Seniors look and act nothing like us, say young people. Seniors complain and warn and lecture. But that's part of the job. They show youth what's coming so they can prepare for it.

M. Night Shyamalan's 2015 horror film *The Visit* embodies society's worst nightmares about the ravages of aging by making the elderly couple the monsters. Shyamalan creates wonderfully nuanced and complex children with witty and realistic dialogue that would be a triumph in any genre, but the elderly couple the kids go to visit are gross exaggerations of seniors, with each symptom of aging presented as yet another horrific excuse to induce terror. Dementia, incontinence and other ailments of age are used to frighten and disgust. Despite Shyamalan's usual twist ending, the image of a rampaging oldster grinding a soiled adult diaper into a child's face adds to the public's collective unconscious portrait gallery of What It Is to Be Old. When women, blacks, Latinos, LGBTs or other minorities are portrayed with demeaning stereotypes, there's a rightful outcry. When seniors are portrayed as such . . . crickets.

Stereotypes aren't funny or cute. They are toxic. They influence how people are treated. Other minorities have experienced this threat. Predominant images of tap-dancing, fried-chicken-eating black men and women prompted white society to see them as childlike people in need of white guidance. Portraying women as giggling girls who talk only about shoe shopping and defer all the big decisions to men left a legacy that justified paying them less and treating them as lesser. The stereotype that reduces all Asians to one supernationality of bowing, Confucius-quoting math geniuses allows society to ignore them as individuals.

Constantly portraying seniors in these limiting caricatures can become a self-fulfilling prophecy. As we age, seniors can slip into the stereotypical roles because that's what society expects of them. This is what "acting your age" looks like, society tells them, and so that's how they act. Treat people as though they are useless, fragile, insignificant and invisible, and they tend to wither into those roles.

Compare the portrayal of seniors in *The Visit* with that in the cult classic *Harold and Maude*, in which 80-year-old Maude teaches suicidal 20-year-old Harold the joys of life and sex. Or the delightful characters in *The Best Exotic Marigold Hotel*, which features seniors on a path of self-discovery as they reconcile their past with their desires for the future. There are other films that portray seniors realistically without romanticizing them, but there aren't that many. And those that do aren't generally seen by younger audiences; they're shown in small specialty theaters in metropolitan areas. Blockbuster films that dominate most theaters rarely portray an elder at all, and if they do, it's usually a simplistic stereotype. Television shows like *Grace and Frankie*, *Parenthood* and *Transparent* have done an admirable job of portraying older generations with a delicate balance of humor and dignity, but gray hair is generally absent in significant roles in most TV shows.

In a thoroughly insightful article in 2015 in *The New Yorker*, "What Old Age Is Really Like," the social anthropologist and acclaimed novelist Ceridwen Dovey discusses her own challenges of being in her mid-30s while trying to accurately portray the elderly in her novel:

> In other words, I modeled my characters on the two dominant cultural constructions of old age: the doddering, depressed pensioner and the ageless-in-spirit, quirky oddball. After reading the first draft, an editor I respect said to me, "But what else are they, other than old?" I was mortified, and began to ask myself some soul-searching questions that I should have answered long before I'd written the opening word.
>
> The first was: Why did I so blithely assume that I had the right to imagine my way into old age—and that I could do it well—when I would approach with extreme caution the task of imagining my way into the interior world of a character of a different gender, race, or class? Had I assumed that anybody elderly who might happen to read the book would simply be grateful that someone much younger was interested in his or her experience, and forgive my stereotyping?

"What are they other than old?" is the question every writer, director and producer should be asking every time they feature a senior character. And when they forget to ask, we should be right there reminding them by publicly announcing our displeasure, individually through social media and collectively through organized campaigns. The public have been bombarded daily for so many years with negative images of seniors that this is their default opinion. This negative opinion permits them to marginalize seniors as pesky obligations when they bother to see them at all. Changing these images to reflect a wider variety of who we really are will eventually erode the stereotypes and make society more aware of our value.

IN CONCLUSION, DEATH

Contrary to Captain Kirk's famous prologue, death, not space, is the final frontier. To those of us over 65, death is no longer that faraway theoretical concept like time travel. It's knock, knock, knockin' on our haven's door while we're scrambling to make the most of our time before finally answering its insistent pounding.

Death is like an arranged marriage with someone you've never met but about whom you've heard unpleasant rumors. Coming to grips with this inevitable meeting is a challenge to one's character. It forces us to assess our lives and judge whether we have lived worthy ones, as if we're writing some macabre Yelp review.

Throughout history, most serious literature has addressed this death judgment process by awarding the protagonists of stories either a "good death" or a "bad death," depending on their life choices. Because death is the non-negotiable outcome of every life, the best we can hope for is a good death, which means we die happy and content with the knowledge that we lived a life that was true to our values and that we've left the world better in some way. A bad death is dying with the knowledge that we have lived selfishly, alienated from the affection of others, having had no positive impact. In *Gladiator*, *Man on Fire* and *Braveheart*, each protagonist dies a violent death, yet each dies happily, knowing that he died fulfilling his ethics of putting the welfare of others before himself. The bad death is often portrayed in tragedies such as *Othello*, *King Lear* and *Citizen Kane*, in which the protagonists have seen themselves as godlike, acting only in self-interest, which leads them to misperceive the world and thereby lose everything, including their lives. Their deaths are marked by a sudden realization followed by profound regret. They die alone and unmourned. Like New Coke.

So in the end, the best that we can hope for on this plane of existence is that our good life has led to a good death, surrounded by loved ones who cherish us, and that we live on in the positive impact we've had on their lives. The good news is that it's never too late to become that person. On our slow shuffle to answering that knocking at the door, there's so much we can accomplish.

The proximity of death is a rousing wake-up call to live more fully, more compassionately, more humbly. But it is also a challenge for us to live more significantly. While environmentalists encourage us to live well by leaving less of a footprint on the earth, death encourages us to leave a bigger imprint on the hearts and minds of our family, friends and community. Psychoanalyst Carl Jung clarified the evolutionary role of seniors when he said, "A human being would certainly not grow to be 70 or 80 years old if this longevity had no meaning for the species to which he belongs. The afternoon of human life must also have a significance of its own and cannot be merely a pitiful appendage to life's morning."

9

Dear Generation Z
UNSOLICITED ADVICE FOR AMERICA'S YOUTH

"There's talk on the street, it sounds so familiar
Great expectations, everybody's watching you."
—THE EAGLES, "NEW KID IN TOWN"

Dear Generation Z,

You are *sooooo* screwed.

Saddled with huge college debt. Living at home. Competing for fewer well-paying jobs. Inheriting a national debt of $19 trillion.

Having no faith in the American dream.

And yet . . .

Everyone will soon be talking about how you are the hope of the future, the next generation after the celebrated millennials. All those upbeat commencement speeches from valedictorians and famous alums are how we older generations slyly empty our social-responsibility backpacks and jam the toxic contents into yours. We never got around to fixing systemic racism, so here ya go, grads. Oh, and broad-spectrum sexism: still a lot of work to be done there. We'll just shove it right next to the crumbling infrastructure of bridges and highways. And we never quite figured out how to Viagra-ize the limp economy, so we'll just squeeze it between Wall Street excess and global warming. LGBT rights, Middle East tensions, suicidal terrorists, almost weekly mass murders in the U.S. No room? No problem. We'll just duct-tape them to the top of your backpack.

Good luck, kids! Your future's so bright, you'll have to wear shades.

The first step, dear Generation Z, is to ignore the hype about your being the hope of the future. Yes, you're technically the future, but that's a default setting, not a spiritual calling. Taking on the responsibility of trying to fix everything that's wrong with the world leads to either hipster cynicism about how everything is too corrupt to fix or depression at achieving only incremental gains. There are things you can do—and should do—but we'll get to them later.

For now, the good news is that, though the setting is different, this hope-of-the-future narrative is the same one that every generation has faced. It's like *High Noon* becomes *Outland*, *The Taming of the Shrew* becomes *10 Things I Hate About You*, and *Pride and Prejudice* becomes *Pride and Prejudice and Zombies*. Same basic plot, just updated for a new audience. In real life, it's the "go out and change the world" recruitment speech; the only thing that changes is the music cranked up in our earbuds that we use to drown out the speech.

Every generation has an antiestablishment soundtrack of pop-culture heroes to articulate its particular fears and frustrations. Their job is similar to how author Gabriel García Márquez (*Love in the Time of Cholera*) describes the role of the philosopher: as a necessary adversary to authority figures. When the next generation sees us being seduced by political delusions or cultural lies, they need to sound the alarm to wake us up, whether it's the 19th-century gospel with the line "I ain't gonna study war no more" or Phil Ochs in the 1960s singing, "Since I left my parents, I've forgotten how to bow" or today's Imagine Dragons' plaintive "I'm waking up . . . This is it, the apocalypse . . . Welcome to the new age . . . I'm radioactive."

As long as I can remember, generational voices have emerged to complain about the sins of the past generation and the legacy of corrupt ideas, values and culture force-fed them to produce socially acceptable foie gras of the soul. In literature, J.D. Salinger's *The Catcher in the Rye* kicked off the postwar analysis of America's low-calorie values in a generational relay race that included Jack Kerouac's *On the Road* (1957), Philip Roth's *Goodbye, Columbus* (1959), Erica Jong's *Fear of Flying* (1973), Marilyn French's *The Women's Room* (1977), Bret Easton Ellis's *Less Than Zero* (1985), Tama Janowitz's *Slaves of New York* (1986), Douglas Coupland's *Generation X: Tales for an Accelerated Culture* (1991), David Foster Wallace's *Infinite Jest* (1996), David Wong's *John Dies at the End* (2007) and so on. Today's cultural sirens may be YouTubers and Web writers like Adam Conover, whose crossover TV show, *Adam Ruins Everything*, reveals some uncomfortable truths behind the facades of daily life.

The problem each generational "hero" faces is figuring out the difference between the generic angst everyone suffers just by growing up and the specific issues that are unique to that generation and no other before it. In *West Side Story*, Doc, the amiable old guy who runs the snack store where the Jets street gang hangs out, makes the mistake of trying to offer advice by starting with these deadly words: "Why, when I was your age—." He's immediately cut off by an angry teen named Action: "When *you* was my age? When my old man was my age. When my brother was my age. You was never my age, none of ya! And the sooner you creeps get hip to that, the sooner you'll dig us!"

He's right. We creeps (i.e., everyone older who is judging them) never were the age of the next generation. Oh, we were their chronological age, but we never lived *in their Age*. We shared the same struggles that most endure through the early stages of maturation—body image, family, popularity, sex, school, the future—but we weren't in the same setting, with the same influences or the same culture. We've all grown up with war, but each of our wars has been different in origin and nature, so its influence on the youth growing up with it has been different.

Previous generations didn't grow up hooked into a vast international social-media system or possessed of the ability to retrieve all human knowledge instantaneously. We couldn't post our every move to a thousand "friends" and await their judgment of whether the hive deemed it "like"-worthy.

It's still unclear how much of that is good and how much is bad. On the good side, sports-bar bets are easily settled by Google. On the bad side, the ability to constantly be plugged in to an endless stream of texts, tweets, Facebook updates, Instagram and Snapchat photos, and the dozens of other distracting nudges, pokes and attention-sucks is mightily distracting. All these random stimuli can keep people from assessing information, thinking about it, putting it in context and coming up with original thoughts that aren't vacuum-packed and microwave-ready. Of course, there will always be those creative individuals who can break from the herd instinct and keep their focus, but how many otherwise innovative minds are put to sleep by the numbing lull of LOL?

Maybe they stay plugged in so much to avoid the equally endless stream of numbing advice from previous generations (like this letter), usually delivered with a furrowed brow and somber voice. In *Spider-Man*, Uncle Ben Parker lays that serious guilt trip on his nephew Peter when he says, "With great power comes great responsibility." Sure, that makes sense *for people with great power*! What a relief, then, that the rest of us without great power—since we can't crawl up buildings or punch through brick walls—don't have to take on that great responsibility. Right?

Not so fast, Generation Z.

On Aug. 8, 1945—two days after the bombing of Hiroshima— French philosopher Albert Camus published an essay warning future generations about the choices they needed to make: "Faced with the terrifying prospects that are opening up before humanity, we see even more clearly than before that peace is the only fight worth engaging in. This isn't a plea any more, but an order that has to rise up from peoples to governments, the order to choose once and for all between hell and reason." Actually, he sounds a lot like

Uncle Ben, in telling us that we have a great responsibility in the face of the unprecedented power to destroy the world. And that responsibility is to use reason, logic and critical thinking in making decisions and not be slaves to the prejudices, traditions and fuzzy logic wrapped in false sentimentality and selective patriotism. He's telling us to choose between a hellish world dominated by the ego-centric mistakes of past generations and a sane world dominated by reasonable thinking.

"Great power" isn't just about the magnitude of power one wields but also about the power each decision we make has in defining who we are. We are crafting our character one choice at a time. In that way, everything we do is a great responsibility, because it's a template for who we want to be and how we want others to act. Power isn't measured by how much weight you can lift but by how much weight you are willing to bear to be the person you want to be. Chalk one up for Uncle Ben.

Yeah, you've been screwed over the same way every new generation is screwed over when handed the reins of the future of the American dream. Perhaps this is where we get the myth of Phaethon ("the shining one"), son of the sun god Apollo, who insisted on driving the chariot of the sun across the sky, only to lose control and perish. Too much power, too little training. It's not surprising that anti-anxiety medication consumption has nearly doubled in the past 20 years.

The problem isn't in the chariot driver—it's in the sun. We have practically deified the American dream, making it something it was never meant to be and therefore a disappointing ideal, when most can't reach it. The American dream should not be a one-size-fits-all concept. It should be a fluid notion that embodies the principles of the U.S. Constitution in a practical philosophy. But those practical-ities seem to change with each generation. For the vast majority of baby boomers, the dream priorities were financial independence and home ownership.

Somewhere along the line, financial independence somehow got interpreted as fabulous wealth. People had the Gold Rush mentality of instant fortune followed by a lifetime of leisure. Dire Straits' 1985 satiric song "Money for Nothing" captured this entitled zeitgeist perfectly: "That ain't workin', that's the way to do it. Money for nothin' and your chicks for free." Today, that concept is illustrated by the Kim Kardashian phenomenon: fame and fortune heaped upon someone who offers no particular talent except good luck in existing at the sweet spot in the advent of social media, reality TV and smartphone advertising. She has more than 43 million followers on Twitter, but her insights are the foam peanuts of pop culture. Money for nothing, indeed.

The financial independence so important to the baby boomers has been tarnished by the reality of the Great Recession (2007–09), from which the world is still in the process of recovering. Upward mobility is on a downward slide. Studies in 2013 concluded that the U.S. (along with the U.K. and Spain) shows the least economic mobility of the 13 wealthy, democratic countries in the Organization for Economic Co-operation and Development. Based on this definition, one can see why millennials are so disillusioned with the American dream.

Nearly half of our hope for the future has no hope for the future.

But maybe their disillusionment isn't a rejection of the American dream as much as a rejection of the way the previous generations defined it. A CNBC commentator countered the millennial rejection by stating, "[The American dream is] so strong that I believe more self-made millionaires will emerge in the next 10 years than ever before." Clearly, he missed the point of exactly what is being snubbed. A recent Harvard University survey found that 51 percent of that same age group—18-to-29-year-olds—do not support capitalism. That doesn't mean they don't want to make a good living, but they want the economy to focus less on the accumulation of personal wealth and more on the fair distribution of the opportunity to seek wealth.

The phrase "American dream" was first made popular by the historian James Truslow Adams in his 1931 book *The Epic of America*:

But there has been also the *American dream*, that dream of a land in which life should be better and richer and fuller for every man, with opportunity for each according to his ability or achievement. It is a difficult dream for the European upper classes to interpret adequately, and too many of us ourselves have grown weary and mistrustful of it. It is not a dream of motor cars and high wages merely, but a dream of social order in which each man and each woman shall be able to attain to the fullest stature of which they are innately capable, and be recognized by others for what they are, regardless of the fortuitous circumstances of birth or position.

Note that this definition deliberately rebuffs the notion of wealth as a measure of success in achieving the American dream; instead it honors a life that is "better and richer and fuller" ("richer" referring not to wealth but to an innately rewarding life).

So here's the advice I promised earlier. Each generation must customize the American dream to fit its own circumstances and the realities of the surrounding world. Instead of promoting a generic dream, we need to encourage the members of Generation Z and beyond to prioritize their own values. Polls indicate that millennials see travel as a major part of the American dream (38 percent), as well as self-employment (26 percent, versus the boomers' 16 percent). They also see close friends as part of their family (11 percent, versus boomers' 3 percent).

The one part of the American dream that cannot be changed or compromised is our commitment to make the opportunity for a life that is "better and richer and fuller" available to everyone. Much of this book has been an indictment of those who preach the gospel of the American dream while secretly doing everything they can to pervert it. Like velvet-rope bouncers at an exclusive club, they aim to extend the best of the country to the few they select while denying it to those they deem unworthy. They wish to maintain strict social classes and restrict the mobility of those who seek to rise out of their economic class assigned by accident of birth.

This is where preachy Uncle Ben's "great responsibility" shtick comes in. Because while I applaud your courage and intelligence in redefining the American dream, it's important that along with travel, self-employment and friends, your commitment to promoting the values of the U.S. Constitution be included, particularly the parts that condemn racism, sexism, homophobia and the exploitation of the poor.

That is an American dream worth dreaming.

Sincerely,

Kareem Abdul-Jabbar

INDEX

ACKNOWLEDGMENTS

I want to thank my writing mentors, those teachers and editors who helped me by challenging me and encouraging my ability to write. The very first of these people is my dad. His love of reading was very much a primary part of the legacy and imprint he left on my life. The summer of 1964 was a special episode in my life and my path to being an author. The Haryou-Act journalism workshop that I participated in gave me a sense of community and shared experience with Harlem. Learning about the Harlem Renaissance and the brilliant black writers of that era inspired me and has kept me motivated ever since.

I would also like to voice my appreciation for my co-author, Raymond Obstfeld. His skills and discipline make my job so easy. Audy Contreras and Janice Contreras have the responsibility of running our office and arranging my busy schedule. Without these dedicated, hardworking folks lending their support and expertise, I'd be lost! Last, but certainly not least, I want to thank our editor, Steve Koepp, who worked nonstop to make this project a huge success. And a special "Thanks!" to my manager, Deborah Morales, for her visionary guidance that enabled my writing career to bear such awesome results. Thank you, one and all.

KAJ

ABOUT THE AUTHORS

KAREEM ABDUL-JABBAR is the NBA's all-time leading scorer and a Basketball Hall of Fame inductee. Since retiring, he has been an activist and in-demand speaker, a basketball coach and the author of nine books for adults and three for children, many of them *New York Times* best sellers, including *What Color Is My World?*, which won the NAACP Image Award for Best Children's Book. Abdul-Jabbar is also an essayist for such publications as TIME, the *Washington Post* and *The Hollywood Reporter*, writing on a wide range of subjects, including race, politics, aging and pop culture. In 2012, he was selected as a U.S. Cultural Ambassador. He lives in Southern California.

RAYMOND OBSTFELD is the author of more than 50 books of fiction, nonfiction and poetry, as well as a dozen screenplays. He has co-authored five books with Kareem Abdul-Jabbar and has been nominated for an Edgar Award from the Mystery Writers of America. He teaches literature and creative writing at Orange Coast College in California.